GORDON JACK

PUTTING FAMILIES FIRST

PREVENTION AND CHILD CARE

Also by Bob Holman

Trading in Children
Poverty: Explanations of Social Deprivation
Kids at the Door
Resourceful Friends

PUTTING FAMILIES FIRST

Prevention and Child Care
A study of prevention by statutory and voluntary agencies

BOB HOLMAN

MACMILLAN
EDUCATION

First published 1988

Published by
MACMILLAN EDUCATION LTD
Houndmills, Basingstoke, Hampshire RG21 2XS
and London
Companies and representatives
throughout the world

Printed in Hong Kong

British Library Cataloguing in Publication Data
Holman, Bob
Putting families first: prevention and
child care: a study of prevention by
statutory and voluntary agencies.
1. Child welfare — Great Britain
I. Title
362.7'32'0941   HV751.A6
ISBN 0–333–43793–4 (hardcover)
ISBN 0–333–43794–2 (paperback)

To the memory of Donald Bowie
deputy director and director of the Church of England
Children's Society 1964 to 1982.

Contents

Preface

I have spent my working life as a child-care officer with a local authority, as an academic, and as a member of a community project belonging to a voluntary society. In all these occupations preventing children from being unnecessarily removed from their natural parents and preventing them from having to endure social disadvantages within their families have been major concerns of my life. I am therefore grateful that my former employers, the Children's Society, allowed me the time and facilities to make a study of prevention in child care. Its director, Ian Sparks, gave me much encouragement both to start and complete the task.

My thanks are due to a number of colleagues and friends who took the time and effort to read and make suggestions about parts of the book. In particular, I make mention of Winifred Stone, Mary Joynson, Jane Rowe, Robin Chapman, Jo Tunnard and Jo Campling. The study entailed visiting and staying at over twenty voluntary and statutory projects and centres and within them interviewing many staff, volunteers and local residents. I am grateful to them all for their patience and kindness. I am especially indebted to Audrey Browne, who typed much of this book and who, for nearly a decade, put up with my idiosyncrasies. Lastly, as ever, my thanks go to Annette, Ruth and David for their continuing interest and support.

In writing this study I received great help from three child-care studies, which I read in draft forms. They have now been published and I take this opportunity to list them: J. Packman with J. Randall and N. Jacques, *Who Needs Care?*, Blackwell, 1986; M. Fisher, P. Marsh, D. Phillips with E. Sainsbury, *In and out of Care*, Batsford, 1986; and S. Millham, R. Bullock, K. Hosie and M. Haak, *Lost In Care*, Gower, 1986.

Also, since the chapters were completed, the government has published a white paper, *The Law on Child Care and Family Services* (HMSO, 1987) in which it accepts that the state should be ready to help parents to bring up their children and to lessen the risk of family breakdown. It then proposes legislation based on some of the recommendations of the *Review of Child Care Law* (HMSO, 1985). If enacted, the legislation would facilitate prevention in child care, though the government does not give a date by which it will make resources available to local authorities to implement such new responsibilities.

This book is published in conjunction with the Children's Society, which is a firm advocate of prevention. However, I wish to make it clear that the views expressed in the book and any errors made are attributable to the author. My hope is that this volume will stimulate more extensive and more effective practice of prevention in child care.

Glasgow   BOB HOLMAN

1. The Victorian Legacy

Prevention, defined in the dictionary as 'to deal with something before it is expressed', is now a concept in much use. Governments wish to prevent a host of eventualities, ranging from road accidents to nuclear war. The term is now so widely employed within the health services that preventative medicine has become another speciality. Within the social services prevention can refer to preventing the mentally disordered from entering institutions or preventing the elderly from having to leave their own homes. This book has a much more limited focus. It is concerned with prevention in child care, with the prevention of the kinds of problems that are likely to bring families to the attention of the courts and the personal social services. In particular it gives attention to preventing the difficulties and circumstances which can lead to children having to leave the care of their natural parents, although, as will be seen, over time the meaning and objectives of prevention have expanded beyond this brief.

My own interest in prevention has continued throughout my working life. I was employed as a child-care officer with a local authority children's department, when, in 1963, government legislation for the first time placed a duty upon local authorities to undertake preventative work. Subsequently, as an academic, I studied the reasons why children had to be admitted into public care. Then, for 10 years, I was employed by a voluntary agency to run a community project, one of whose aims was to prevent the reception of children into public care. My employer, the Children's Society, was equally concerned about prevention and gave me the time and resources to make this study. Its objectives are to narrate the development of prevention in child care in both the statutory and voluntary sectors and, in particular, to identify the part the voluntary child-care bodies can play. The book will trace the influences on prevention from Victorian times to the present. It will then describe the present contributions of today's statutory social services and draw upon some original study to analyse the

1

preventative work of voluntary projects. Lastly, an attempt will be made to state the case for prevention and to outline a preventative strategy. But the story must start in the era in which many child-care agencies were established – the nineteenth century.

Nineteenth-century Conditions

In her narrative *Children in Care* Jean Heywood explains how the state, the church and voluntary bodies, along with relatives, friends and neighbours, have always accepted some responsibility for children who were neglected, cruelly treated or homeless.[1] The need for such intervention reached a peak in the nineteenth century. The rapid increase in population meant more mouths to feed. Simultaneously the drift from rural to urban settings led to families finding themselves in need at the very time when they had distanced themselves from relatives and friends. Moreover the overcrowded slum conditions produced illnesses that not only made some adults unable to work but in many cases caused their early deaths, so leaving their children as orphans. True, the production of raw materials, the escalation of manufacturing in-dustries and expanding trade markets abroad led to higher stan-dards of living for many. But for others mechanisation, trade depressions and movements in the location of industries resulted in, at best, a low income and, at worst, unemployment – and unemployment meant no money for the rent and no food or clothes for the children. The consequent suffering of masses of Victorian people has been well documented. Two accounts are particularly impressive because they concern people who experi-enced poverty themselves. William Booth knew unemployment before he became the founder of the Salvation Army. Thus his *In Darkest England and the Way Out* has a passion and empathy which comes over with more power and urgency than even the well collected statistics of his namesake, Charles Booth, in his *Life and Labour of the People in London*.[2, 3] Just as interesting but now almost unknown is an earlier book by A. L. Calman, which draws upon the diaries of John Ashworth of Rochdale. As a child, Ashworth knew abject poverty, went barefoot, and often returned to a home where his beloved mother had no food. Eventually he prospered and opened a Chapel for the Destitute. He recorded the illnesses, the suffering, the homelessness and the despair of the poor. Typical of his diary, are two days in 1866.

> Monday, Oct 22 . . . trustees gave me £5 for my poor people; was called this morning to pray with a dying child in the Gank – a bag of shavings, a bed of rags. A boy in his shirt, three drunken women, a child in brain fever; all in one room, with a small window; a dreadful sight.

> Tuesday, Oct 23. I do not feel at all well; fagged and weary . . . Never had so many able-bodied poor men seeking relief. Lord give me patience; may I not say one sharp word.[4]

Many entries like these reveal how frequently Ashworth was summoned to the dying whose passing then left children with no support, how sometimes the poor would retreat into a drunkenness and violence which ended in cruelty towards children, and how sordid and brutal were the daily experiences of many youngsters. The voices and pens of men like Ashworth eventually led to widespread efforts to help children.

The Poor Law's Care of Children

During the active years of Victorian reformers like Booth and Ashworth the Poor Law was the state mechanism for coping with the destitute. Oddly enough, the system – whose origins date back at least to the Elizabethan Relief Act of 1601 – could be said to possess a preventative element in the years immediately preceding the Victorian era. In some parts of the country it was the practice to dispense 'out-relief' to pauper families, the effect of which was to allow them to stay together in their own homes. This approach soon felt the cold blast of criticism of the Poor Law Commissioners. They reasoned that the handing out of money encouraged people to laze instead of work and, moreover, was a heavy burden on public funds. The Poor Law Amendment Act of 1834 thus established a new regime which stipulated that the able-bodied would receive their keep only on condition of entering the workhouse. Within these institutions conditions were made as severe as possible, including the separation of husbands and wives, the loss of voting powers (if they had the vote) and the compulsory undertaking of irksome tasks. The objective was to deter applications and to push people into seeking employment. After 1834 the number of workhouse inmates rose rapidly, from 78,000 in 1838 to 306,000 in 1848.[5] The subsequent administration of the Poor Law has become identified with cruelty and suffering. Certainly some people starved rather than cross the workhouse doors. The fear of the workhouse was to haunt working-class people into the 1940s. Yet it is fair to add that some officials did seek ways of mitigating the system and, in particular, wanted to shelter children from its worst effects. A move to give schooling to the children of workhouse inmates was instituted, on the grounds that they should be equipped to find themselves employment when they came to adulthood. Most workhouses were too small to afford schools of sufficient quality and so Poor Law Unions began to combine into districts to form large schools which had the advantages of economy of scale. By the mid-century several schools held over 1,000 pupils. Yet the very size needed to produce economic savings did not lead to the desired educational advantages. By the late 1870s the Local Government Board (which after 1871 controlled the Poor Law) acknowledged that the herding together of thousands of children actually harmed their development.

The idea of cottage homes, already being used by voluntary agencies, began to take root. In some unions children were thus grouped together into cottages which held about ten inmates and thus approximated more to family life. Yet this system also had its drawbacks, for the cottages were made up into what became self-contained villages, with their own schools and values, which were quite isolated from the outside world, to which, at some stage, the children would have to return. The next logical step was the development of a method of care which not only reared the youngsters within ordinary communities but which was also cheap – boarding-out. Drawing upon experience in Scotland, where the practice was well established, the Poor Law pursued boarding-out or fostering in the last 30 years of the nineteenth century by appointing local committees and full-time inspectors. Despite some objections that the children were exploited as servants, cruelly treated and inadequately supervised, the numbers expanded so that in 1908 some 8,659 pauper children were boarded-out. Even so, it is worth noting that 27,698 remained in cottage

homes, district schools and scattered homes, 21,498 in the workhouses and workhouse infirmaries, and 11,225 in other institutions.[6]
The Poor Law administrators had thus shown some flexibility in
trying different methods of looking after children in their care.
Significantly one approach never won official approval. Although,
in some parts of the country, out-relief was appearing again
towards the end of the century, no countenance was given to the
thought that destitute parents were the best people to look after
their own offspring.

The Voluntary Contribution – 'The Saving of the Children'

The limitations of the poor-law system did not go unnoticed. Dr
Barnardo perceived two major failings inherent in the state system. One was that it depended on people approaching it while
simultaneously being devised to deter them from making application. The outcome, not surprisingly, was hundreds of destitute
children who tried to survive on the streets. The other failing
concerned the standard of care offered to those who did take
shelter within the workhouse portals. The philanthropic doctor
thus wrote:

> The pauper child was stamped with the brand of his pauperism
> in huge barrack workhouses, where all the inmates lost their
> rights and individuality, and became machine-turned figures,
> helpless and nearly predestined to ruin in the face of the new
> conditions of outside life when they left the workhouse walls
> behind them.[7]

The second half of the nineteenth century then witnessed a host of
voluntary child-care agencies which were stirred not only to provide for those children outside the Workhouse but also to develop more humane forms of care as an alternative to it. Along
with Barnardo were others who also ranked as national figures.
The Rev. Thomas Bowman Stephenson was an outstanding example. In 1869, as a young Methodist minister in Lambeth, he
wrote: 'I soon saw little children in a condition which made my
heart bleed. There they were, ragged, shoeless, filthy, their faces
pinched with hunger . . . and I began to feel that now my time had

come'.[8] Of course Stephenson could have directed them to the workhouse, but, as he wrote tactfully at a later date, 'Not but that I think our workhouses are a credit to England . . . but they must be so managed that we should not send any children there if we could help it. The associations connected with them, and the enormous scale upon which they are conducted, give little hope for the children'.[9] The outcome of Stephenson's drive was the National Children's Home and Orphanage. In the same period Edward Rudolf was founding the Waifs and Strays Society (later called the Church of England Children's Society), and Cardinal Vaughan was instrumental in integrating various Roman Catholic charities into the Crusade of Rescue.

The numbers of children received were astonishing. In 1882 the Waifs and Strays was coping with 34 children. By 1902 it was 3,071.[10] In the year of Barnardo's death in 1905, his society maintained 11,277 children.[11] In addition to these nationally known organisations, hundreds of lesser known homes were also opened. A remarkable one was George Muller's Homes in Bristol, where the founder never asked anyone for a penny but relied upon God to provide.[12] Interestingly, John Ashworth visited the Home in 1866 and records that he addressed 1,150 orphans.[13] An example of a much smaller initiative was in Fulham, where the now almost forgotten Sydney Black recognised that the poor did not want to find 'their refuge, most hated and most feared, in the workhouse'. He thus established a small home for fatherless boys where they would wear no 'distinctive garb' or anything that 'would stamp the distressed with the badge of his misfortune'.[14]

The pioneering founders were frequently motivated with a concern for the spiritual welfare of the young outcasts. But that was not all. By and large they also wanted to present them with a positive experience of family life and with a trade or skill to take into adulthood. In an effort to distance themselves from the barrack-like image of the workhouse and district schools, some societies started small cottage homes. Others were prepared to mix rather than separate boys and girls. The voluntaries were also prepared to look after children for up to 3 years after they would have been discharged from the state institutions. Not least, during the last part of the century, the voluntary societies also expanded the numbers they placed in foster homes.

The various agencies differed in the emphasis they gave to the different methods of care. But there was one broad similarity in their approach – they regarded themselves as rescuing and removing children from bad environments. As Barnardo put it, 'If the children of the slums can be removed from their surroundings early enough, and can be kept sufficiently long under training, heredity counts for little, environment counts for everything'.[15] Or more precisely, 'I am set primarily for the saving of the children'.[16] At the start of his first children's home, Stephenson distributed a pamphlet which boldly declared: 'Statement and appeal on behalf of the children's home, the object of which is to rescue children who, through the death or vice or extreme poverty of their parents, are in danger of falling into criminal ways'.[17] The National Society for the Prevention of Cruelty to Children was unusual in that it had much more contact with children in their own homes than did most other agencies. But even in its work the stress was on removal or the threat of removal. Significantly, legislation in 1889 gave powers to the police to take away children from parents suspected of neglecting or cruelly treating them and powers to the courts to continue the separations.

The concept of 'rescue' and 'fresh start' reached its logical conclusion in the practice of emigration. As early as 1830 a home in West Ham was teaching a trade to destitute children and then despatching them to the colonies.[18] Barnardo's first homeless boy, Jim Jarvis, became his first emigrant. Between 1867 and 1906 Barnardo's sent 18,645 youngsters abroad.[19] By the end of the century all the large child-care societies were doing the same, with the majority going to Canada and others to Australia, New Zealand and South Africa, where most of the boys were destined to be farm labourers and the girls domestic servants. Despite evidence of the unhappiness of many of the emigrants, the practice continued well into the twentieth century and only petered out after the Second World War.

Given the appalling social conditions of urban Britain, a 'rescue the perishing' banner may have been the only possible war chant. But the voluntaries tended to emphasise not just a saving from bad material conditions but also from bad parents. The result was to build in a punitive attitude towards what were regarded as irresponsible parents. Thus one of the aims of the Crusade of Rescue was 'to rescue the children of dissolute and degenerate parents'. Benjamin Waugh of the NSPCC declared: 'What is wanted is not the ever-open door of Institutions for the wretched children, but ever-open doors of prisons for those who make them wretched'.[20] Dr Barnardo, who recounts with passion and love his tales of meeting ragged children, would change his tone when mentioning the parents and add a comment such as 'His mother was a woman of the poorest sort . . . a drunken and immoral creature who cared little or nothing for her unfortunate son'.[21] Stephenson was a man whose heart was full of love for the children in his homes. He related closely to them, enjoyed games with them and they welcomed his visits. Yet he did not extend the same spirit towards their parents. He spoke of 'the children of vice: children who may be orphans or who may not: but if they are not orphans, are more to be pitied than if they were. The parent of that child is not fit to be trusted with him'.[22] It emerges that many of the children taken into the charitable institutions were not orphans. Many possessed parents, but in the eyes of the voluntary societies that was a hindrance. They were better off without parents.

No Place for Prevention

The Poor Law and the voluntary systems of child care are often held up as contrasts. Certainly the latter were formed partly as a response to the limitations of the former. Yet it is not sufficiently acknowledged that in their attitudes towards preventing children having to leave their own homes, and towards encouraging rehabilitation between children and parents, the two systems reinforced each other with few dissenting voices. They thus established a pattern of child care that was to dominate welfare practice.

Firstly, both state and voluntary agencies combined to establish the principle that *needy children were best brought up outside the influence of their parents*. The justification of this practice had several strands:

1. Within the poor-law system, the separation of children from parents served as both a deterrence and a punishment. The reasoning was that adults would be reluctant to apply for state help if they realised they would lose contact with their offspring. The argument was correct and Victorian accounts – both fictional and real – paint harrowing scenes of the agonising choice between starvation and separation. Then once inside the

workhouse, the deliberate break-up of families was perceived as a part of the punishment which made life inside the institution less attractive than life outside.

2. Another element, often found within the philanthropic societies, was that rescue and separation were justified simply because parents could not cope. In some cases the children had no parents and were living rough. In others, the parents – or parent – were so ill, physically handicapped or destitute that there was no prospect of them ever looking after their families in a satisfactory manner. In such instances any contact between parents and children was regarded as pointless.

3. Both state and voluntary societies agreed that parents who could not look after their own were an evil influence on the children. They were frequently painted as drunken, immoral and lazy, so that the best interests of the child entailed a complete removal from the taint of the mothers and fathers. Thus district schools and children's homes were well placed in that they were usually located far away from the children's own neighbourhood. Within the Poor Law it became deliberate policy to seek boarding-out outside the children's locality. Significantly, when the Local Government Board appointed the redoubtable Miss Mason as their inspector in 1885, her job was to inspect children fostered in Unions other than that of their origin. The drive to keep children away from the pernicious values of the parents was seen most clearly in the great numbers who were shipped abroad to make a fresh start.

4. Any continuing contact with parents was seen as unsettling to the children and threatening to the substitute parents. Dr Barnardo's foster parents had to sign an undertaking that they would 'permit no visit from relatives or friends of the child without the director's authorisation'. He also forbade any correspondence between foster parents and natural parents. Any letters from a child to a parent had to go via the central office and any letters received from relatives had to be sent to the director 'before allowing the same to be opened'.[23]

Miss Mason agreed. She stated: 'Only really permanent children can be boarded-out. Neither (boarding-out) Committees nor foster parents would be willing to receive children liable to be removed at any time'.[24]

Thus, for both the voluntary societies and the Poor Law,

Heywood concludes: 'Boarding-out was therefore regarded as making a complete break with the natural family and it is clear that parental contact was regarded as something which would have interfered with the success of the arrangement'.[25]

As the century progressed, the practice of separating parents and children showed no signs of abating. It might have been considered that the gradual amelioration of social conditions would have led to the conclusion that, with some support, vulnerable parents could be helped to cope. It might have been thought that the obvious decrease in the number of completely parentless children would have prompted a re-think. Far from it. In fact, the greater interest displayed by some parents led both systems of child care to seek stronger measures to exclude them. Edward Rudolf, when receiving children into his homes, drew up a contract to be signed by the parent(s) which forbade them to remove their children on pain of having to repay the Waifs and Strays Society the sum of 4 shillings for every week the children had been resident there. Barnardo had a number of heated exchanges with parents but the matter only achieved publicity when a Roman Catholic charity objected to the decisions he made, such as sending children abroad, without the full consent of Roman Catholic parents. He discovered that voluntary societies had no legal rights over the children and no powers to control what he deemed as damaging parental interference. A public campaign led to the Custody of Children Act 1891 which gave the societies some authority to rescue children while curtailing some of the rights of neglectful parents.

Simultaneously some Poor Law officials were objecting to the continuing influence of parents and some resented the fact that on leaving their institutions or foster homes at the age of 16 the children returned to families, which undid all the good that had been achieved. Thus section one of the Poor Law Act of 1889 gave the Poor Law guardians power to resolve to assume full parental rights over certain children, who were maintained by them until the children were 16 if male and 18 if female. Parents were given the right to appeal to a magistrates' court. In 1899 legislation extended the guardians' powers to pass resolutions for deserted children, for orphans, for those whose parents were unfit by reason of mental deficiency or of 'vicious habits or mode of life', for those whose parents were under sentence of penal servitude or had been imprisoned for offences against their children, and for those whose parents were permanently bedridden or disabled and who were the inmates of a workhouse and who consented to the resolution.

Secondly, both the poor-law system and the voluntary societies must take some responsibility for *linking stigma with the receipt of help*. Stigma means a sense of social disgrace for a certain act or condition. The Poor Law deliberately cultivated this sense of shame for anyone who entered its doors. Further, the uniform mode of dress enforced upon inmates made their debased state clear to all. As mentioned already, some social reformers reacted strongly against 'the badge of shame' and deliberately cultivated homes where the children did not wear uniforms and cropped heads which would identify them as different from others. In fact, later biographies by adults who were brought up in voluntary homes shows that a sense of stigma persisted even into the next century.[26, 27] However, the point made here is that the voluntary societies, while wanting to protect their children from a sense of shame, certainly made their parents feel disgraced. With visits not encouraged and letters sometimes unanswered, it is not surprising that parents sometimes felt as though they had committed a crime. The result was to structure into child-welfare practice not only a physical gap between parents and children – in the sense that the latter would be placed many miles away – but also a psychological or emotional gap in that parents felt too ashamed or too powerless to make demands on the agency which had taken over their children.

Thirdly, *the rehabilitation of children to their parents never became a policy* with the Poor Law or the child-care societies. True, the workhouse was ready to discharge any children and any parents – that saved money. But the poor-law system actually militated against such reunions. For instance, any persons entering a workhouse were expected to have sold all their belongings; and if they lacked kitchen utensils, furniture, bedding, etc., there was very little prospect of them making a home to which their children could return. Further, as their children were usually reared away from them, the links between the family members grew weaker. The voluntary societies would hand children back if parents were persistent in their demands, but, apart from the fact that poverty-stricken or sick adults were rarely in a position to make demands, the societies rarely encouraged reunions. Indeed, as was shown, they made contact between the two parties very difficult. Thus in

Barnardo's Table of Ten Years Disposals 1897–1906 there are columns for children emigrating, for finding 'situations' (i.e. employment) and for dying, but none for rehabilitation with parents.[28]

Fourthly, a reading of Victorian child-care narratives reveals *the class-related nature of the child-care system*. The children taken by the Poor Law and the voluntary societies were predominantly the children of the poor, that is the lowest social class in a society dominated by class distinctions. The class attitudes towards the children were shown both in contemporary feelings that the children should feel very grateful for being rescued and also in the almost universal acceptance that on leaving care they should take their place as servants, i.e. as persons inferior to those who had rescued them. More pertinent for this study, the parents were regarded as members of a class judged to be full of vices. As Barnardo put it, 'parents are my chief difficulty everywhere; so are relatives generally . . . because I take from a very low class'.[29] It followed that the predominantly middle-class enthusiasts and officials in the child-welfare agencies felt justified in removing children from a class which was seen as a threat to the values, morals and standards of higher social classes.

Fifthly, any *ideas of prevention were very limited*. Of course Victorian Britain possessed many individuals and many charities which did help the destitute in their own homes. Thus John Ashworth's diary for 5 May 1869 records: 'Prevented a poor family being "sold up"'.[30] Barnardo's was active in supplying clothes, boots and meals to the 'deserving poor'.[31] Charities which concentrated on the physical health of children began to emerge, with the Children's Fresh Air Mission in 1883 and the Children's Country Holiday Fund in 1884. Indeed, so numerous were the charitable societies that the Charity Organisation Society was formed to co-ordinate giving and to stop indiscriminate relief. However, these efforts were rarely seen as a means of enabling parents to retain the care of their children but rather as an immediate, and usually one-off, step to relieve suffering.

To be fair, the occasional voice pleading for a more enlightened policy was heard. Thus with the Poor Law again countenancing out-relief, Edward Rudolf wrote:

There will be an election of guardians shortly throughout England and Wales. It will be well to vote only for candidates who

will support a wise and judicious system of out-relief. In a large
number of cases an overburdened widow is able, with assistance
from the rates, to keep her home and family together, which is
far preferable to her becoming an indoor pauper, and her
children being sent to the workhouse school.[32]

But such a voice tended to be overshadowed by those who stuck to
the hard line that out-relief was harmful to individual recipients
and to the pockets of ratepayers. Indeed, Middleton's study of
Poor Law practice at the end of the century discovered that 'there
was no wish to change the system' except for wanting to reduce the
out-relief that did occur.[33]

It can be concluded that prevention, in terms of wanting to assist
parents avoid the break-up of their families or in terms of wanting
to rehabilitate children once a family had been split, hardly existed.
Yet one concept of prevention was articulated and practised. For
instance, as early as 1846 Mary Carpenter had become involved
with a Ragged School in Bristol which then developed into a
reformatory for delinquents. She argued that the enlightened
institutional life of the reformatory was a means of converting
young delinquents from a life of crime and so stopping the almost
inevitable drift to an adult life in and out of prison.[34] She thus
defined the effect as preventative. Similarly, the Poor Law officials, who advocated the formation of district schools, saw residential education as an opportunity not only to remove the
children from their harmful parents but to fit them with the skills
and attitudes which would prevent them becoming as feckless as
their parents. Similar trains of thought were used to justify the
residential life of the voluntary institutions, with their emphasis on
inculcating children with the right religious beliefs and the motives
to enter adulthood as hardworking domestic servants, farm
labourers or members of the armed forces. They would thus avoid
the fate of the parents. The word 'prevention' was quite frequently
used in this connection. Thus at the opening of a larger home for
Sydney Black's Orphanage, the leading nonconformist minister,
Dr John Clifford, proclaimed:

We are not simply here to provide a shelter for these children,
but we are supplying them with training and education. We are
preventing them from drifting into the masses of the unemployed.

Let Fulham take note of that. We are preventing them from becoming a burden on the rates. Let Fulham Guardians and Councillors take note of that.[35]

Thus the objective of prevention was not to forestall the separation of children from mothers and fathers, it was to stop them becoming like their mothers and fathers. Prevention existed but it was *prevention without the parents*. Prevention in the sense of enabling parents to keep their children just did not exist as a policy in Victorian times. Its absence was due not so much to the fact that it was not possible but rather to the belief that it was not desirable. Successful child care was expressed in many public speeches – especially by Dr Barnardo – as having the ingredients of providing a faith to live by in the context of a loving residential or foster environment with the parents permanently excluded.[36] One of the abiding results of the work of state and voluntary child-care bodies in the nineteenth century was, as Jean Heywood concludes, that a 'pattern was set . . . by which the neglectful home and the substitute home became exclusive of each other'.[37]

The Legacy

The close of the Victorian era was followed by years of rapid economic and social change. Perhaps most significant was the gathering strength of working-class movements as expressed in trade unions and the Labour Party. They articulated their opposition to the rigid class distinctions and to the operation of the Poor Law as a mechanism which led to distress and suffering for pauper families. Further, state welfare services – services which had the potential to enable more parents to cope with their children – were being established. School attendance had been compulsory since 1880, while the Education (Provisions of Meals) Act of 1906 and the Education (Administrative Provisions) Act of the following year gave local authorities the powers to provide a basic school meal and to detect ill-health. The lot of some struggling parents was thus eased by the existence of what amounted to a day-care system plus food. Health and unemployment insurance schemes were added in 1911 and the improvements were such that Jean

Heywood claims that they 'could not fail to reduce the amount of sickness and neglect and consequent poverty'.[38]

These improvements should not be exaggerated. Poverty and unemployment were still rife. Louie Stride in her *Memoirs of a Street Urchin* gives an account of a child's life in this pre-war period in the slums of Bath. She pays tribute to school meals and to a kindly teacher who presented her with a dress. But there were no school meals in the holidays and at weekends and frequently her lone mother had no money at all after she had paid the rent with the proceeds of her cleaning job. Then mother sometimes resorted to part-time prostitution and Louie 'grew up scavenging food where I could, in the gutter pretty often, surprising what one can find edible'.[39] Louie's lot improved when her mother married a soldier and so did the lot of many others, for the coming of the First World War led to a demand not only for manpower in the armed forces but also in industry. Thus political, social and economic circumstances appeared to be creating the possibilities of new policies for deprived children. To cap it all, the time seemed opportune for the national voluntary societies to move in new directions. The master pioneers were passing away. Muller died in 1898, Barnardo was discovered dead at his desk in 1905, while the self-effacing Edward Rudolf outlasted them all and retired in 1919. New regimes took over.

Yet despite all the favourable circumstances, despite all the signs that new child-care policies would be forthcoming, the initial three decades of the twentieth century witnessed child-welfare practices as a modified image of the old. The powerful, continuing legacy of the Victorian era can be illustrated by looking at the experiences of children who fell within the full-time care of the Poor Law. They were the children of the state.

Children of the State, 1900-39

During these years the Poor Law always seemed on the verge of being replaced yet somehow always survived. The Minority Report of the Royal Commission on the Poor Laws in 1909 argued that the reputation of the Poor Law was so bad that the whole apparatus should be abolished and its functions taken over by the local authorities. The report had no immediate effect but the following years did indeed see the abolition of the Boards of Guardians and the increasing intervention of local government. Yet instead of the Poor Law being replaced by local authorities, it was incorporated into them. Thus the Poor Law Act of 1930 placed its administration with county and county borough councils under the general direction of the Minister of Health. One result was the retention of stigma. Deeply implanted into British society was the notion that to turn to the public authorities for financial help was an admission of personal failure. The great socialist leader George Lansbury waged a life-long battle against its cruelties and in 1934 was still looking for the time when 'we shall not be cursed by the penal poor law, and nobody, not even the worst among us, will be left to starve'.[40] Another result was that the Poor Law authorities continued to set the tone for the care of the children of these families.

The children looked after by the Poor Law – or Public Assistance as it was later renamed – were placed in the following ways: in the workhouses, in large institutions, in smaller children's homes, or in foster homes. The type of care was thus similar to that of the Victorian period. In 1913 it had been officially decided that children aged 3–16 years should not be maintained in workhouses for more than 6 weeks. Initially the decree resulted in the Poor Law authorities having to make more use of voluntary homes, so that in 1914 the latter were caring for 15,500 Poor Law children.[41] However, the stipulation was difficult to enforce and in 1946 the Curtis Committee was to report finding several thousand in workhouses in conditions which provoked grave concern.[42] The larger institutions, which sometimes catered for hundreds of children, included the barrack schools, which emphasised drill and routine and whose semi-military regimes began to lose favour after the First World War, along with grouped cottage homes and large single homes. Smaller homes, sometimes called family group homes or scattered homes, began to find more favour as the adverse effects of large institutions on children began to be perceived. But whatever the form of care, and whatever the quality of the staff – and there were staff who cared about the children – the primary objective of the Poor Law was not to maximise the well-being of each individual child. The main aims were to deter applicants, to save money and, in words repeated in the Poor Law Act of 1930 'to set to work or put out as apprentices all children whose parents are not . . . able to keep and maintain their children' (Section 15(1)).

It followed that the only conception of prevention within the major state institution responsible for deprived children continued to be prevention without the parents. The training covered by institutions and the character-building instilled by foster parents were intended to develop young adults who would not be a burden on the rates as their parents had been. Unfortunately the outcome was often the reverse.

The fixed class ideas of both lay people and public officials associated with the system took it for granted that the children of the state should be prepared only for lowly occupations – the same occupations as had prevailed in the previous century, such as domestic service, agricultural labour, and the armed services. In addition, the Poor Law institutions would sometimes be used as recruiting grounds for such unpopular and dangerous occupations as mining and deep-sea fishing. The fishing industry had a notoriously high death roll, so the Poor Law Chief Inspector's words had a certain irony when he declared: 'The fishing trade is a most valuable means of disposing of a certain type of boy'.[43] Yet what the authorities never seemed to appreciate was that they were directing youngsters into the very occupations that were likely to send them back to the workhouse. In proportion, the former occupations most usually given by persons admitted to the workhouse were labourers, fishermen, farm workers and seamen. Amongst women, domestic servant was the leading occupation noted.[44] Later, in the 1930s, when some Poor Law children passed entrance examinations to grammar schools, they were frequently not allowed to take advantage of the offer because further education would have to be paid for out of the public purse. The paradoxical result was that a system which kept children apart from their parents, in order to prevent them becoming like their parents, often ended up by forcing them to adopt the same life-styles as their parents. Far from being preventative, the system led to the break-up of more families.

The lack of any substantial change in the Poor Law's attitude to the natural parents can be illustrated in other ways. Once parents and children were placed in their respective institutions, the authorities saw no need to and no benefit from facilitating contact.

Providing the establishments were within walking distance, a line
of parents would be taken on a visit at monthly intervals – even
weekly in some progressive areas. Sometimes not even this was
tolerated, and a mother, desperate to see her children, would
resort to discharging herself from the workhouse, claiming back
her family, and then spending a few happy hours with them before
humbly applying for readmittance. The administrative work caused
annoyed the officials, so it took a bold woman to follow this
course. Such a woman was the mother of Charlie Chaplin, as he
tells in his moving account of their days in the Lambeth workhouse.[45]
In another autobiography Lucy Sinclair reveals that the pattern of
visiting, with parents being taken for a brief period to the child's
institution but never allowed to take them out, continued into the
1930s.[46] In foster homes, too, letters between children and parents
were censored and visits seen as an unsettling imposition. In short,
the Victorian belief in removing children from the evil influence of
their parents retained its power. Thus Nigel Middleton, in his
excellent survey of this period, cites the statement of a social
worker that 'there is the necessity for a complete break, for a new
start in life away from old surroundings. This can only be partially
successful if the child is being constantly reminded of home by
letters from parents'.[47]

Similarly the possibility of preventing children from entering
institutions by supporting them in their own homes received short
shrift. To the Poor Law officials this smacked of out-relief. In the
years immediately preceding the First World War some Boards of
Guardians were under pressure to extend out-relief to widows.
However, even here, the amounts allocated for each child were
below what even a poor labourer was earning. The effect could be
long-term harm to the family's health as well as to their unity.
Thus Poor Law policy continued its rigid course. After the war the
introduction of widows' pensions and the extension of means-
tested unemployment pay did bolster the chances of families
avoiding the workhouse. But once inside its doors, there was still
no encouragement to rehabilitate children and parents into the
community. As Middleton concludes, they were 'largely receiving
the treatment of the nineteenth century Poor Law'.[48] Thus the
state welfare organisation, which had the primary responsibility
for families, had failed to give a lead towards the practice or
philosophy of prevention. Indeed, the unchanging nature of the

Poor Law was such that any progress towards prevention now depended on its demise.

Explanations

Why did policies and practices to prevent children having to be removed from their families fail to surface in this period? It is impossible to give definite answers about something which did *not* occur but some probable factors can be identified.

Firstly, *the economic slump* of the 1920s and 1930s was accompanied by a poverty and destitution almost as bad as that of Victorian Britain. True, for those who remained in jobs, the standard of living improved somewhat. But throughout the period the number of unemployed never fell below a million while, for a number of years, one in five of the workforce was out of work. The distress and sufferings of the workless and their families have been vividly portrayed by the journalist Hugh Redwood, who accompanied Salvation Army officers on their visits. He described how in the slums the 'darkness, depression and despair . . . the dirt, the noise, the dampness and staleness, the lack of sanitation and the complete absence of privacy are fused in a nightmare offensive to every sense'.[49] The government response to the slump was to cut public expenditure. One result was to supply ammunition for advocates of the retention of a harsh Poor Law as the best means of keeping down costs; another was that newer welfare services became tainted with the Poor Law spirit. Thus unemployment pay, which had its origins in respected National Insurance schemes, became subjected to a bitterly resented 'genuinely seeking work' clause, a means-test, and in 1931 to a 10 per cent reduction.[50] Poverty again became a destructive force which could split families asunder. Then, if the parents did hand their children over to an institution or did enter the workhouse themselves, they found that the inadequate welfare services offered little hope of them ever reaching the point where they could all be reunited again. Thus the economic depression served to hold back any practices aimed at preventing family break-ups or of rehabilitating the separated ones.

Secondly, *the working class movements did not gain prolonged political power*. Even with the extension of the franchise to almost all adults, the Labour Party held power for only two brief periods and had little direct effect on social policies. Interestingly, unemployed workers on the Hunger Marches of the 1930s would sometimes show their hostility towards the Poor Law. At one workhouse they protested over the wire netting which separated families and where 'little tots pressed their lips to the wire in awkward kisses for their father stooped low on the other side'.[51] But their protests were to no avail. The poorest remained those without power and without recognition, and so reforms to enable their families to live together in decent conditions were not forthcoming.

Thirdly, *the plight of deprived children stirred little national concern.* The children's champions of the Victorian age, the Charles Dickenses, the Lord Shaftesburys, the Dr Barnardos, did not exist in the first three decades of this century. The cause for concern certainly existed. Standards in some children's homes were low, with the children being regimented and institutionalised. Muddle, overlap and delay in the administration of children's services began to appear as the responsibility for deprived children became spread over Public Assistance Departments, Education Departments, the Home Office, the Ministry of Pensions and voluntary societies. If these apparently obvious defects led to no government investigations, to no crusade by children's champions, then it is no surprise that the newer concept of prevention was not taken up as a national child care issue.

Fourthly, *the child-care voluntary societies ceased to be such a powerful influence in society.* During the previous century they had frequently set an example to the state: they had set out to run better services for deprived children than did the Poor Law; and their promotion of cottage homes, of vocational training, of boarding-out, set directions which the statutory authorities felt some obligation to follow. But in the first third of the present century they were neither making pungent criticisms of the state services nor moving on to set an example in the practice of prevention.

The Voluntary Contribution, Interwar Years

The part of the voluntary child-care societies during this period is worth considering in more detail. The interwar years certainly witnessed no slackening of voluntary involvement. Indeed, the distress of the economic depression brought forth an impressive response from a wide range of agencies. An article by Self looks back at what happened in Bethnal Green and observes the busy lives of church missions, five residential settlements, housing associations, evening institutes, youth clubs and so on.[52] The commitment of some churches was particularly noteworthy. When visiting a penniless old woman in Tottenham in the 1930s, the Rev. Walter Hall was met with the plea, 'don't let them take me to the Union'. The cry activated a movement which set up the Methodist Homes for the Aged.[53] In Poplar the activities of the Rev. William Lax culminated in him becoming mayor of the borough.[54] The energy of these newer, broader based, organisations tended to overshadow the older child-care agencies. Even so, like the latter, they concentrated on relieving immediate distress rather than on practices of prevention.

The by now traditional child-care voluntary societies still undertook extensive and valuable work. Indeed, Wrong points out that they were running over 1,000 residential homes and maintaining as many children as the public authorities.[55] But the atmosphere and outlooks of the homes had changed little from the previous century. A good example is found in the evocative autobiography of Dorothy Haynes. She speaks thankfully of the years she resided at Aberlour Orphanage from 1929 to 1933, and pays tribute to some devoted staff and particularly to the leadership of the superintendent, Dean Wolfe. Yet she had to endure a regimented, even Spartan, regime in large stone buildings which housed 500 children. The same staff forbade children spending holidays with parents on the grounds that it would have unsettled them; and, just as in Victorian times, no consideration seems to have been given to the possibility of supporting Dorothy's capable father in order that he should retain the care of his children.[56]

New steps were not entirely absent. The child-care societies began to undertake adoptions. Greater interest was expressed in the needs of delinquent children. Small grants were awarded to deserving unmarried mothers. But the general directions remained the same as in the previous 50 years – children were removed, they stayed long term and had little contact with their relatives. During the early 1930s the Waifs and Strays Society awarded small cash payments as a contribution towards the expenses of mothers struggling to maintain their children at home but, as John Stroud points out in his history of that Society, its financial difficulties meant that 'various new ventures and improvements had to be postponed indefinitely'.[57] Consolidation rather than enterprise became the keyword and with it the Society seemed to lose its self-confidence. The same could be said of the other national societies. They lost their position of leadership and made much less impact on the philosophy of how to treat deprived youngsters. The decline of the voluntary agencies – not in numbers but in leadership and influence – was particularly inopportune for three reasons. Firstly, the kind of children being accepted by the agencies were now neglected and delinquent youngsters, not just homeless ones. The gradual growth of local authority engagement in child care made it likely that the state also would largely concern itself with children who came from unsatisfactory rather than destitute homes. The voluntaries thus missed the opportunity to develop specialised social-work services, rather than just removal services, for them.

Secondly, in regard to delinquents, the voluntary societies appeared to want to do the same as the emerging state bodies. The Children and Young Persons Act of 1933, with its defining the grounds under which children could be protected by the courts, its emphasis on the 'welfare of the child', and its establishment of 'approved schools', was considered a social landmark. Yet the Act contained no provisions for preventing delinquency and spoke of 'removing him (the delinquent) from undesirable surroundings' rather than about improving the surroundings. The voluntary societies, instead of going beyond the Act, responded by moving with the state by also running similar kinds of approved schools. An interesting illustration of this point is found in the life of Katherine Scott, who, despite an early death, did much to extend church social work and probation work in Scotland. As the state was recognising the contribution of probation, the Church of Scotland appointed Katherine Scott as a court officer in Edinburgh. Gifted and enlightened as she was, her probation work was defined as 'Prevention and Rescue'. She used a probation order to prevent a girl committing more offences. But rarely, if ever, did she talk of prevention in terms of enabling parents to help their children. In short, it was still prevention without the parents, with the voluntary agency supplementing the practice of the statutory bodies rather than leading it into different approaches to child deprivation.[58]

Thirdly, the national child-care voluntaries were slow to seize upon any preventative suggestions which were surfacing. For instance, the National Council for the Unmarried Mother and her Child was formed in 1918 and one of its main aims was that 'of keeping mother and child together'. A few years later the Save the Children Fund, in declaring that 'the child has a right to the best that can be given it', was implying that the treatment of deprived children was second class.[59] Yet the suggestion that the voluntary societies adopt policies which aimed to treat them like other children, i.e. that they should stay with their own families, met no concerted response. On the contrary, the increasing state support services were seen as harmful. As Miss Wrong, in speaking for the voluntary bodies, put it: 'In providing nursery schools, in feeding school children free, in prosecuting parents for cruelty and neglect, and in housing illegitimate children, are you not destroying or damaging the institution of the family?'[60] Thus the child-care agencies served to decrease rather than increase the provision of preventative services both by themselves and by the state. Like the Poor Law, they brought into the twentieth century a Victorian legacy which laboured to perpetuate Victorian child-care practices and reacted against newer concepts.

Signs of New Directions?

It should not be thought that the interwar years saw no developments favourable to the promotion of prevention. Already mention has been made of the fledgling state-support services which were of help to hard pressed families. Amongst these, following the First World War, the grants made by the Ministry of Pensions were noteworthy in that they carried no stigma, were not means-tested, and were sometimes set at a level which allowed mothers to cope financially with their children. Again, after 1923, a minority of local authorities decided to let their education departments be responsible for boarding-out and children's homes. Thereafter, a small number of educationalists and psychologists, who appreciated the influence of home life on children's social progress, began to be interested in deprived children. Not least, within the Home Office, a few inspectors 'were beginning to wonder whether the elaborate administrative machinery (of the approved schools) was too heavily weighted on the side of institutional and substitute family care and too little emphasis put on the preventive social services'.[61] They argued, and the staff in some schools agreed, that if links between offenders and their parents were maintained while the former were in custody, then the chances of rehabilitating them into their own families would be enhanced. Although not widely accepted, the idea that the involvement and strengthening of natural parents was a means of preventing family break-downs was being discussed.

Interesting as the ideas were, the reality of practice was much the same. A graphic example of what did happen to families in the late 1930s is found in the autobiography of Tom O'Neill. Raised in Newport, he endured slum life at its worst. His father served in two world wars but was mainly unemployed in the intervening years. Relapsing into booze, his bad temper made life a misery for his wife as she sought to care for a large family. Tom was eventually sent to an approved school and his brothers to a children's home. He recounts his pain when he received few visits from his parents. But there were reasons for their absence. Convicted of neglect and unable to pay a fine, they had been sent to prison. Thereafter, their lack of money and the long distance to the institutions proved obstacles to visiting their children. The local authority in whose care the children had been placed had no policy of encouraging parental contact. Moreover the low level of unemployment pay and of other state-support services, in combination with the parents' unstable life-style, meant that it took years before they secured a home to which the children could have returned. Tom never saw one brother again – Dennis was killed by his foster parents 6 years later. It took Tom 30 years to trace another sibling. No wonder he wrote that, unknown to him, the prison sentence signified 'the final break-up of the family . . . We were never to be together again'.[62] Their experiences were not untypical, and Macleod concludes of this time: 'Attempts to rehabilitate children in families after a period of separation were, therefore, rare and regarded as likely to be unsuccessful'.[63]

Grounds for Change

Large-scale efforts to meet the needs of deprived children began to flourish in the nineteenth century. The major organisations which provided the services during the Victorian era were the state's Poor Law and the voluntary societies' child-care agencies. Although the two systems of child welfare differed in many ways, and were critical of each other, this chapter has attempted to show that neither believed in or practised policies which attempted to keep children in their own homes or to return them to their natural parents. Events at the start of the twentieth century did suggest the possibility of new child-care directions. However, the economic slump, the failure of state support systems to develop fully, and the continuing lack of political power for working-class people all served to undermine these hopes. Perhaps even more important, the Poor Law and the voluntary societies maintained rather than altered their outlooks. Both systems continued to be characterised by the removal and rescue of children, by an emphasis on permanent care away from the influence of parents and by attitudes which inhibited parental involvement by making them feel ashamed of their inability to cope. Thus, despite the emergence of some ideas and movements which did see the advantages of prevention, the Victorian grip was maintained on child-care practice in the first three decades of the twentieth century.

An assumption underlying this book is that welfare services should attempt to support families, so that children do not have to leave them. Thus, in regard to the period at the end of the 1930s, it is appropriate to draw upon the preceding history to ascertain what changes were necessary if preventative objectives were to become a part of the children's services. Five steps can be identified.

Firstly, the Poor Law would have to be removed. Concluding his study of the Poor Law, Nigel Middleton stated: 'Whatever faults were inherent in the Poor Law, and there were many, the consequential destruction of the family must rank as probably the most damaging; not only did it strike at the very unit of society, but the resulting damage to individual personalities was often irreparable'.[64] Even though the functions of the Poor Law were gradually taken over by local authorities and the boards of guardians abolished, the spirit remained the same. The insistence on blame, on deterrence and on keeping aid at the lowest possible level made its outlook incompatible with practices of prevention, which entailed providing parents with sufficient resources to enable them to cope adequately with their children. The Poor Law had been set up to deal with the threat of pauperism but had also become the major state agency responsible for deprived children. In so doing, it carried over its mechanism of condemning people for being poor to condemning parents for failing to look after their children. It followed that any improvement would necessitate not just abolishing the Poor Law but ensuring that in future any service for deprived children would be kept separate from mechanisms which dealt with the poor. Further, as the Poor Law was particularly feared by and detested by lower income groups, its abolition would turn on the prospects of working-class people gaining effective political power.

Secondly, social conditions would have to be alleviated and state social-support services improved. The removal of slums, homelessness and squalor was necessary in order to cancel out the motive of rescuing children from unbearable environments. The provision of a basic income, decent housing and access to health care would ensure that parents at least had the essential equipment with which to look after their own families.

Thirdly, welfare services, both state and voluntary, would have to be available without the imposition of the 'badge of shame'. Vulnerable parents would only make use of resources if they considered that their acceptance did not cast them in the role of spongers or failures.

Fourthly, the value of children remaining with their parents, no matter how lowly the class of the latter, would have to be recognised by society. The nineteenth and twentieth centuries had witnessed profound changes in the valuation of children. The introduction of compulsory education signified that working-class children were not regarded just as units of labour. The gradual improvement of the methods of care of deprived children, for which the voluntary societies must take much credit, indicated that even they deserved humane environments. Slowly, in the twentieth century, the battle was being fought to acknowledge that deprived children were of such value that they too should have access to secondary education and some choices in the careers they pursued. But the final recognition was that value be placed upon both them and their parents. Only then would prevention without the parents be replaced by policies which aimed at prevention with their parents.

Fifthly, the achievement of these changes would need to be stimulated by a public concern for deprived children. The nineteenth century had had no shortage of well known figures willing to devote their whole lives to championing the causes of children. By the beginning of the 1940s the scene was once again set for child-care issues to be placed before the British public.

The prospect of the above five changes must have seemed slight in 1939, following a century of entrenched child-care attitudes. But there followed the Second World War, which caused the mass evacuation of British children and profound shifts in political power and social outlooks. The subsequent years were then to see new policies and new statutory provisions for deprived children. It is to these years that this study must now turn.

2. The Children's Departments and Prevention

In the later 1930s responsibility for deprived children was fragmented between a number of government and local-authority departments – none of whom saw it as their prime responsibility – and voluntary bodies. The Poor Law still wielded an influence over the treatment of children. Preventative work hardly existed. In 1948 legislation created children's departments as the local-authority organisations with the sole function of looking after children deprived of a normal home life. In the same year the Poor Law was wiped from the statute book. In 1963 further legislation placed both powers and duties upon the children's departments to undertake prevention. This chapter will be concerned to render an account of how these changes occurred and how prevention was implemented by the children's departments.

The Impact of the Second World War

The Second World War had a decisive influence on the course of social welfare. The sufferings were borne by civilians as well as soldiers to the extent that it was called 'the people's war'. As the government's official historian, Professor Titmuss, put it, 'the war created an unprecedented sense of social solidarity among the British people, which made them willing to accept a great increase of egalitarian policies and collective state action'.[1] The coalition government, sensing the need to build a better Britain, appointed William Beveridge to chair a committee to inquire into social insurance. As his wife, Janet, records, he saw it as 'a heaven-sent opportunity . . . to bring to a head at last in a single comprehensive scheme the principles of his work on social security which had been developing and maturing in his continuous preoccupation with the problems over a period of nearly forty years'.[2] Published in 1942 as the *Report on Social Insurance and Allied Services*, it contained a detailed plan to attack the five giants of 'Want, Disease, Ignorance, Squalor and Idleness'.[3] He envisaged a comprehensive health service, full employment and family allowances. Given this foundation, he then proposed a social insurance scheme which, in return for weekly contributions, would give financial protection against sickness, unemployment, widowhood and old age. Its emphasis on universalism, that is on benefits which applied to all people without recourse to a means-test, stood in happy contrast to the Poor Law. As Thane states, 'It expressed the desire for a more socially just, more materially equal, more democratic society, in short everything that pre-war society had not been'.[4]

The report divided the war-time coalition government. It had agreed on the Education Act of 1944, which ensured free secondary schooling for all, and on the Family Allowances Act of 1945, but the Conservative leader, Churchill, was wary both about the costs and implications of the Beveridge proposals. By contrast the Labour Party's identification with them no doubt contributed to their landslide victory in the election of July 1945. The door to social reform had been opened.

The war also witnessed significant developments concerning deprived children. Over 3 million children were evacuated. The social historian Arthur Marwick concluded that this mass movement of mainly working-class children 'brought to middle and upper-class households a consciousness for the first time of the deplorable conditions endemic in the rookeries and warrens which still existed in Britain's greatest industrial cities, and so, among the articulate few, aroused a new sense of social concern'.[5] Among those few was the Women's Group on Public Welfare, which catalogued the bad health and housing of many evacuees and put forward a radical plea for reforms to ensure tolerable living standards for all children.[6] Simultaneously some psychologists were identifying the traumas forced upon children who were separated from their parents.[7] Certainly their deductions were not widely circulated but they contained seeds which were later to grow into arguments for state action to prevent the break-up of families.

Meanwhile government officials were postulating that at the end of hostilities the existing systems of child care would be unable to cope with the numbers of children orphaned or made homeless by the war. Professor Parker points out that, as early as 1943, government departments were anticipating the break-up of the Poor Law and making suggestions about new systems of child care to replace it.[8]

Not least, the war was instrumental in drawing the attention of a number of influential women to the needs of children. One such was Lady Allen of Hurtwood. In her *Memoirs of an Uneducated Lady* she explains how her early interest in nursery education moved her to concern for the standards of day nurseries which were set up for the children of mothers required by the war effort.[9] With others, she began to campaign for better services for children.

Thus, by the end of the war, the social and political climate was very different to that prevailing in 1939. For the first time a Labour government with a large majority and a clear mandate for social reform had been elected. Wholesale evacuation had led to a general public concern about the needs of working-class children and to a small but growing interest in preventing the separation of children from even disadvantaged parents. Not least, within government a few officials were alerted to the need to restructure the shape of children's services, while outside a number of articulate public figures were prepared to campaign on behalf of deprived children.

The Curtis and Clyde Reports

Unknown to Lady Allen, a boy named Dennis O'Neill was being murderously treated in a foster home. Both the forceful campaigning of Lady Allen and the awful death of the boy were to contribute to inquiries which shaped the children's services for the next two decades.

During the war years Marjory Allen stumbled across the plight of some children in residential institutions. With government officials ignoring her complaints, she wrote her famous letter to the *Times* of 15 July 1944. She claimed that thousands of children were 'being brought up under repressive conditions that are generations out of date' and she concluded: 'The social upheaval caused by the war has not only increased this army of unhappy children, but presents the opportunity for transforming their conditions'. The response was overwhelming. Letters from officials, welfare staff and children even rivalled those being written about the war. Marjory Allen had sparked off a concern for children the like of which had not been witnessed for a century. The Home Secretary, Herbert Morrison, was impressed with Lady Allen – in her autobiography she reveals that he proposed to her – but not by her arguments. However, under pressure from many MPs, he agreed to establish a committee.

By early 1945 Morrison had still not named the committee. At this point occurred the O'Neill tragedy. The O'Neill brothers were in the care of the Education Department of Newport County Borough Council, which fostered Dennis and Terence on a lonely farm in Shropshire. Here, on 9 January 1945, Dennis died from the beatings of the foster father and the neglect of the foster mother, both of whom were subsequently imprisoned. The case received national headlines and had a threefold impact on child-care events. Firstly, it reinforced the public call for reform. Secondly, it appeared to prompt the Home Secretary into naming, on 8 March 1945, the persons for the promised committees. One for England and Wales was to be chaired by Myra Curtis and one for Scotland by James Clyde. Thus the O'Neill death did not, as is sometimes claimed, lead to the initiation of the Curtis and Clyde Reports but it did hasten them. Thirdly, Sir Walter Monckton was appointed to examine the tragedy. His findings, published in May 1945, attributed blame to the inadequate supervision of the foster home by Newport Council and, to a lesser extent, by Shropshire County Council. In turn these faults were related to the use of staff unqualified in child-care matters and to a break-down in communication between two very different kinds of welfare organisation within each authority. Thus the Monckton Report supported Lady Allen's plea for a more comprehensive and unified system of public care. But Monckton did not make a case for prevention or rehabilitation. He dismissed criticisms that Dennis's parents did not have sufficient access to him.[10] Like Lady Allen, he assumed that official intervention should occur only *after* children were removed from their parents. Dennis's brother, Tom, sadly pointed out that when he was with his parents, Dennis was dirty but 'he was fairly well nourished and he was alive'.[11] However, Tom was writing years later. In 1945 the time for prevention had not quite come.

The Clyde and Curtis Committees reported in 1946 on their
brief, which was 'To enquire into existing methods of providing for
children who, from loss of parents or from any other cause whatsoever, are deprived of a normal home life with their parents or
relatives; and to consider what further measures should be taken
to ensure that these children are brought up under conditions best
calculated to compensate them for the lack of parental care'.

They
had received the views of statutory and voluntary agencies, visited
children's homes, and listened to child-care experts, but, they do
not seem to have sought the views of any parents whose children
were in care. The Clyde Committee reported first and argued
strongly for a new emphasis on fostering, because 'By this means
the child should get the nearest approximation to family life'.[12]
Failing that, children's homes should be small enough to approxi-
mate to family units and should be run by trained staff. Given the
bewildering number of agencies having some but not full responsibility for deprived children, it urged that each local authority
should place the responsibility upon a children's care committee.

The Clyde Report is silent on prevention. It could have interpreted the words in its brief concerning children 'deprived of a
normal home life with their parents' to embrace those experiencing an unsatisfactory life while still with their parents. But it
contained not a single word on how to improve home conditions so
as to enable children to stay there and not one recommendation
concerning rehabilitating children back to their parents. Despite
its stress on the value of the family, it did not really argue for the
value of families of deprived children. As the committee said, the
question was 'How then is the family to be recreated for a child?'[13]
The question was not yet 'How can the family be preserved?'

The Curtis Report, four times as long as its Scottish counterpart,
extended its coverage to include delinquent children, so that it
enumerated 124,000 children within its scope. It made a detailed
investigation of residential establishments, including workhouses,
where it found many children who lacked personal love and
attention. Although well meaning, staff failed to grasp the significance of a child's home background, so that in public homes 'The
possibility that some children might have relatives, who with
encouragement might take an interest, seemed an idea which had
never been really considered'.[14] While recognising that adoption
was suitable for young children with no family ties, the committee

considered fostering as the most suitable placement for most children in care. However, it observed that the lack of drive to find foster parents and, indeed, the lack of direction in child care sprang from administrative confusion about responsibility. At local authority level the public assistance, education and health committees might all be dealing with deprived children, and all might be locked in overlapping communication with the government departments of Health, Education, Pensions and the Home Office.

The Curtis Report ends with sixty-two recommendations, which follow from its masterly analysis. For the purpose of this study the most relevant are the following. Firstly, the public care of deprived children should be the responsibility of one central government department and one local authority committee, the latter to be called the Children's Committee, with a chief executive, the Children's Officer. Secondly, the order of preference for the methods of caring for deprived children should be adoption, boarding-out, and residential care. Recommendations were also made as to how to improve each type of care. Thirdly, training should be introduced for staff of all kinds. Fourthly, the voluntary organisations should continue to play a full part in caring for deprived children, although subject to closer statutory inspection.

The importance of the Curtis committee is summed up by its own claim to be 'the first enquiry in this country directed specifically to the care of children deprived of a normal home life'.[15] No report before or since has so movingly shown how deprived children require and deserve the maximum rather than the minimum which society can give them. The arguments presented by Curtis made an unanswerable case for establishing one local-authority committee whose single purpose was to look after the interest of children who lacked a normal home life. For all its logic and compelling arguments, however, the committee failed to pursue its findings in one area. The committee acknowledged 'the extreme seriousness of taking a child away from even an indifferent home'.[16] It applauded residential staff who encouraged contact between children and their natural parents. Yet it held back from advocating policies to stop children having to leave their natural parents and from recommending practices and powers by which the new committees could return children to their families.

The Children Act 1948

Following the reports, the government acted swiftly. The Children Act of 1948, passed with all-partly support, applied to England and Wales and with some adaptations to Scotland. It stipulated that all local authorities were to create children's committees and through these they were given a duty under section 1 to receive into their care children under the age of 17 whose parents or guardians were unable to provide for them and whose welfare required the intervention of the local authority.[17, 18] In addition, the committees took over responsibility for children committed to local authorities by the courts, for protecting private foster children and for supervising certain adoption placements. The Home Office was later announced as the central government department responsible for deprived children.

The message that children required individual attention found expression in Part II of the Act. Accepting that fostering entailed personal care, it decreed that every local authority had a duty to board-out children in its care, and where this was 'not practicable or desirable for the time being' to maintain them in residential homes.[19] Amongst many other provisions, the Act established an Advisory Council on Child Care to advise the Secretary of State on how to discharge his or her child-care duties.[20]

The Children Act wins little attention in histories of the welfare state. Fraser awards it just one mention and Thane just two paragraphs.[21, 22] Yet it marked a turning point for services to deprived children. The confusions and inefficiencies associated with responsibilities fragmented between many different departments were abolished. Further, it marked the end of the influence of the Poor Law over children. The National Assistance Act became law on the same day as the Children Act and opened with the memorable words, 'The existing poor law shall cease to have effect'.[23] Adults needed no longer to fear the workhouse, while the introduction of the Children Act wiped from the statute books the sombre sounding duties of 'setting children to work' and 'putting them out as apprentices'. In this way the Act is at one with other social legislation of the period in fulfilling the strivings of many working-class people to abolish an institution which had threatened their families.

Next the Act more than any other piece of previous legislation, emphasised the value of a deprived child. Far from being treated as a burden on the rates who deserved just the minimum of help, the Act contained the noble and humane statement that in respect of such a child the local authorities had a duty 'to exercise their powers . . . so as to further his best interests, and to afford him opportunity for the proper development of his character and abilities'.[24]

Not least, the Children Act had implications for the voluntary child-care societies. Lady Allen had been critical of some voluntaries and, in an era of great enthusiasm for state services, some critics even questioned whether there should be any place for them. These doubts were put to rest by Part IV of the Act, which allowed local authorities to make grants to them. Simultaneously, it also ensured higher standards by empowering the Secretary of State to make regulations for their conduct of residential care and boarding-out.[25]

Roy Parker, while praising the enactment, notes that 'in several respects it failed to promote important changes, for example it did not deal with the question of prevention'.[26] The criticism is justified, for, in keeping with the reports which preceded it, the Act concentrated on the mechanisms of how to admit children into public care and on the methods of dealing with them after they had left their families. Indeed, in one important respect the Act weakened the rights of natural parents, against the advice of the Curtis Committee, which had been worried at the ease with which parents could be deprived of their parental rights simply by the resolution of a local-authority committee without an initial application to a court of law.[27] Despite this objection, the Children Act under Section 2 did give local authorities, providing certain conditions were fulfilled, just such a power to assume parental rights by a committee resolution, with the proviso that parents could subsequently appeal to a court.[28] Thus, although the new Act enshrined a new humane approach towards the treatment of deprived children, it did little to improve the rights and powers of their parents and thus little to promote the practice of preventing children having to be received into public care.

Despite these comments, the Children Act of 1948 was not altogether without significance for the development of prevention. In regard to children received into their care under section 1, local authorities were instructed 'where it appears to them consistent with the welfare of the child so to do, (to) endeavour to secure that the care of the child is taken over either (a) by a parent or guardian of his, or (b) by a relative or friend of his'.[29] True, the Act said nothing about resources to facilitate this policy, but at least the concept of rehabilitation was on the statute book. Accordingly one of the strongest Victorian ideas – that once removed from their parents, children were best kept away from them – was challenged.

Not least, the very creation of children's departments contained the seeds from which the tree of prevention could grow. When no one department had the responsibility for deprived children, then it was difficult even to think of attaching a brief for preventing children coming into care on to one of them. Now such a department and such a possibility existed. Moreover, the new departments gave rise to two new and enthusiastic occupations – the children's officers and their subordinates, the child-care officers. They soon formed themselves into the Association of Children's Officers and the Association of Child Care Officers. Simultaneously the Advisory Council for Child Care was supporting the development of training and numbers of qualified child-care officers soon became an important source for articulating views on policies for child care. In time both the associations were to press for their departments to be given powers to undertake prevention.

Other Reforms

The Children Act was but one of a number of social enactments of the 1940s. The new Labour government initiated a sweep of legislation which transformed the welfare map of Britain. The National Health Service Act of 1946, the National Insurance Act of 1946 and the National Assistance Act of 1948 were accompanied by a massive housing drive and rising employment. These reforms may seem to have little connection with prevention. Certainly Beveridge's biographer makes no mention of his interest in the subject. Yet there is a link, for Beveridge himself declared: 'The first principle should be that we should regard it as a primary aim of social policy to ensure every child against want, against going hungry, cold, ill-clad and ill-housed . . . a second principle that we should do that in such a way as to preserve parental responsibility as completely as possible'.[30] Thus the social objective was to enable parents to cope with their children. Their increasing attainment of decent health, housing and income, then, had two important implications for prevention. Firstly, the reduction of extreme poverty weakened the drive of those who wanted to 'rescue' children from evil environments to which they should never return. Secondly, the existence of employment, of a dry home, of improving health, did provide the physical basis on which to build family life. Given this basis, prevention in terms of trying to stop more children leaving their own homes became more of a realistic option. The case for prevention could now be made.

The Case for Prevention

Following the Children Act, most local authorities quickly formed their children's committees and children's departments. In his semi-autobiographical novel, John Stroud describes both the 'tremendous crusading atmosphere about the new service' and also the dedicated and overworked children's officer who 'looked as though she had spent the last two months on some maniac task, such as trying to get a swarm of flies into a tea chest'.[31] The hard work was initially directed at coping with a bombardment of applications for reception into care. Thereafter, the crusaders were concerned to pursue the objectives of the Children Act, namely to board-out more children, to humanise residential care and to rehabilitate children. The proportion fostered rose from 35 per cent in 1949 to 44 per cent in 1954.[32] Many large institutions were replaced by small group homes. Rehabilitation is harder to assess. Two-thirds of all children admitted into care were soon discharged, but the figure is associated with an unanticipated impact of short-term work, i.e. of those admitted because of mothers' temporary illness or confinement.[33] A substantial number also stayed in care, with 19 per cent still being there after 2 years and 11 per cent after 5 years.[34] The serious reasons for admittance – desertion, mental disorder, homelessness or adverse home conditions – often proved too much for the hard pressed officers.

For all the successes, the practices of the children's departments came under a scrutiny which was to bolster the case for prevention.

Much of the debate was about costs. Numbers in care in England and Wales multiplied from 55,255 in 1949 to 63,309 in 1953. The increase was partly due to the upward trend in the birthrate following the war, but it still proved expensive. A Parliamentary select committee drew attention to the high costs of residential care and reminded local authorities that fostering was cheaper.[35] Unfortunately, it was also becoming evident that fosterings often broke down. The findings of Trasler's seminal study, which were being circulated in the mid-1950s, estimated that up to two-fifths of long-term placements were unsuccessful.[36] It followed that while admissions to residential establishments were questioned in terms of cash, fosterings were in terms of multiplicity of break-downs, which harmed children. No wonder the select committee went on to suggest that domestic disasters should be 'dealt with and remedied before the actual break-up of the home occurs'.[37]

The theory that children's psychological health was harmed by separating them from parents was being popularised by John Bowlby's review of child-deprivation studies and published in 1952 as *Maternal Care and Mental Health*.[38] He emphasised that a child's normal development required 'a warm, intimate and continuous relationship with his mother (or permanent mother substitute)'. 'Separation', he wrote, could have 'adverse effects on the children (a) during the period of separation, (b) during the period immediately after restoration to maternal care, and (c) permanently'.[39] Bowlby argued that adoption or fosterings were more likely to create child/mother relationships than institutional settings. However, he conceded that fosterings were liable to breakdowns, while adoptions needed to start in a child's first 2 months to facilitate success. It followed that a better approach was to stop separations in the first place, and Bowlby welcomed the new children's departments by stating: 'A child care service should be first and foremost a service giving skilled help to parents, including problem parents, to enable them to provide a stable and happy family life for their children'.[40] By skilled help Bowlby meant social workers with a psychiatric training. He thus wanted childcare officers to carry out prevention based on his psychological theories.

Arguments for prevention based on costs and psychological theories lent strength to children's officers who were claiming it to be an essential part of good child-care practice. The officer for

Hertfordshire wrote: 'Children's Officers soon found that attempting to wipe the slate clean and rebuild a child's life was rarely satisfactory and that substitute home care, however kindly, was but a pale shadow of the real thing'.[41] The conclusion that good child care entailed working with families before they split up was also reached in London. Area 5 of the LCC Children's Department had experienced a steep rise in the numbers received into care. The administrative system was still based on pre-1948 days, so that applications from parents were decided by a clerk. In a case study Donnison and Chapman have documented how the reception procedure was then taken from the clerk and placed with social work staff, so that they were in contact from the start, and how, in addition, two 'intensive caseworkers' were appointed in 1955 to forestall admissions to care.[42] Thus the conviction gained ground that a child's own family was, in most cases, the best place for him to be and also that the child-care officers were the persons best equipped to attain this objective. Significantly the Association of Children's Officers in 1952 added to its list of objectives the aim 'to encourage and assist in the preservation of the family'.

If early child-care intervention could prevent admissions to care, then could it not also prevent other problems? The Oxfordshire Children's Officer, Barbara Kahan, reasoned it could help the estimated 300,000 children 'growing up in circumstances likely to produce delinquency, mental illness or . . . emotional deprivation'.[43] The Home Office had some sympathy, for in a section on 'Children Neglected In Their Own Homes' in its *Seventh Report* it indicated that local authorities could follow the example of some voluntary bodies by dealing with families before serious problems manifested themselves.[44]

The prevention lobby was also backed by academic research. In 1954 David Donnison concluded from a study in Salford and Manchester that many admissions to care could have been avoided by earlier use of child-care officers.[45] Some MPs lent their weight and Somerville Hastings, who had been a member of the Curtis Committee, suggested a programme for prevention;[46] and to these powerful voices from the outside of social work were added those of the practitioners. To be sure, some sounded a note of caution. The Children's Officer for Cornwall warned of 'the danger of forgetting the possible magnitude of his (the child's) suffering when he is left where he is'.[47] But these were minority voices, for the Associations of Children's Officers and Child Care Officers had become advocates of prevention. The pressure for prevention did not go unnoticed by government. In 1950 a joint circular from the Ministries of Education and Health and the Home Office urged local authorities to form co-ordinating committees which could make plans for families liable to neglect children.[48] Soon after, the Children and Young Persons (Amendment) Act of 1952 placed on children's departments a duty to investigate any information suggesting that a child was in need of care and protection whether or not the apparent neglect was 'wilful'. The central- and local-government tide appeared to be moving in favour of prevention and Packman records 'by the mid 1950s, most children's departments were actively engaged in preventing the admission of children to care'.[49] In England and Wales the numbers in care declined to 61,580 by 1959, though, as the departments themselves pointed out, this figure gave no indication of success in preventing the neglect of some youngsters in their own homes whether or not they were at risk of admission to care.[50]

However, the apparent successes were made in the face of certain snags. The Younghusband *Working Party on Social Workers* commented in 1959 that the co-ordinating committees failed both to obtain early notification of vulnerable families and to stop the overlap of visits by several social workers to the same family.[51] Further, although local authorities had a duty *to investigate* complaints about neglect, doubts were expressed as to whether they were legally entitled *to make expenditure* on families to lessen neglect or avoid reception into care. Thus objections were made about children's departments which helped pay the rent of families about to be evicted in order to keep the families together. When the LCC wanted to appoint its intensive caseworkers in 1954, the Director of Establishments advised that their preventative functions were outside the scope of the 1948 Children Act.[52] After a battle the appointments were made, reflecting the extension of preventative practice, which itself became another pressure to clarify the law.

Meanwhile, yet another aspect of prevention was being drawn into the open arms of the children's departments – the prevention of delinquency. After the Children Act 1948 it was sometimes assumed that deprived children came under the children's departments while delinquents were the concern of the Probation Service. In practice such a distinction was blurred. Some children who were received into the care of the children's departments happened to be delinquent as well as deprived. At time courts would deal with offending youngsters by committing them to the local authority under a Fit Person Order, which was then discharged through the children's department. It followed that when public concern focused on the prevention of delinquency, the elected members of children's committees and the staff of children's departments already felt that they had both knowledge and experience of the subject.

The concern about juvenile delinquency occurred with its sharp increase in the post-war years and with the failure of custodial methods to change criminal behaviour.[53] As attention focused on its prevention, so members of children's departments began to claim a stake not just on their experience in meeting young offenders but also on the contention that delinquency, like deprivation, had its causal roots in family life, on which they were becoming the specialists.[54] Packman recounts how the Oxfordshire Children's Department led the way by encouraging the police to refer 'at risk' children to it and by persuading courts to commit delinquents to the local authority rather than to approved schools. In 1960 the Home Office inspectors commended their success in keeping delinquents out of institutions.[55]

Thus during the 1950s much social attention was taken up with the discussion of how to prevent neglect and reception into public care and also how to prevent and treat juvenile delinquency. The various strands were brought together in 1956, when the Home Office appointed a departmental inquiry under the chairmanship of Viscount Ingleby. Its brief (which applied only to England and Wales) was (a) to inquire into the workings of the law relating to the courts, to juveniles brought before them, to approved schools, and the prevention of cruelty to juveniles, and (b) to ascertain whether local authorities should be given new powers and duties to prevent the suffering of children through neglect in their own homes. It reported in 1960.

The Legislation of 1963 and 1969

The Ingleby Report contained none of the far-reaching proposals which had characterised the Curtis Report. There was no comprehensive plan for reforming juvenile justice and no clear strategy for combating delinquency. It was difficult to see the connections between its 125 diverse recommendations. Consequently, it provoked a cool reception. An editorial in *Child Care* complained 'there is no flood of illumination thrown upon our troubled way'.[56] Thus, whereas in Scotland there was a movement towards the abolition of juvenile courts, Ingleby wanted to retain them while advocating that they 'should move further away from the conception of juvenile justice'.[57] Peter Boss criticised its 'naivety of thinking'.[58] For instance, it put forward the idea of family advice centres without discussing what they were.[59]

Yet, for all the criticism, Ingleby was not without importance. For a start, it was the first government report to give prominence to prevention. It stated: 'In the past the main problem has been seen as the proper *treatment* of juvenile delinquents . . . less thought has been given to the more difficult problem of *prevention*'[60] (my italics). The report then proceeded to propose legislation which would make it quite clear that local authorities could undertake preventative work, could spend money on families for this purpose and should regard families as the main focus of their outreach.[61]

Further, the report did make proposals to back its belief that offences were symptoms of family problems which should be treated by the courts in the context of the family. It wanted the age of criminal responsibility raised to 12, so that young children should not be prosecuted but rather brought to court 'in need of protection or discipline'.[62] For those aged 12 to 14 it recommended that courts think in terms of supervision rather than probation orders.[63]

Finally, although it did not pursue the matter, the report recognised that effective prevention of delinquency and deprivation might require the restructuring of the personal social services. It thus became the first official body to call for a 'study by the government and the local interests concerned of the reorganisation of the various services concerned with the family'.[64]

The Ingleby Report, unlike Curtis and Clyde, never won a place in the child-care hall of fame. Yet within a decade a number of its recommendations were implemented into legislation which proved to be of significance to prevention. Section 1 of the Children and Young Persons Act of 1963 declared:

It shall be the duty of every local authority to make available such advice, guidance and assistance as may promote the welfare of children by diminishing the need to receive children into or keep them in care . . . or to bring children before a juvenile court; and any provisions made by a local authority under this subsection may, if the local authority thinks fit, include provision for giving assistance in kind, or in exceptional circumstances, in cash.[65]

The doubts were over. The campaign had succeeded and the child-care staff had the legislation they wanted. Its impact was to extend the range of their work greatly. As MacLeod put it, 'For the first time social workers had a duty to help any family whose children were not in the care of the local authority';[66] and as one children's officer, Sylvia Watson, observed,

Overnight the children's service – from being a curative and rescuing service – became, in addition, a service with the almost limitless aim of promoting the welfare of children by helping the family as a whole as well as a service charged with the task of attempting to combat incipient juvenile delinquency without recourse to the juvenile court.[67]

The 1963 Act by no means served as a final word. On the contrary, the decade was marked by a number of government and political party reports which debated not only the part of prevention but also the causes and treatment of delinquency. In Scotland the outcome was the Social Work (Scotland) Act of 1968, which reorganised the social services and replaced juvenile courts by children's panels for children who admitted their offence. In England and Wales a less radical line was pursued by the Children and Young Persons Act of 1969. The age of criminal responsibility was to be raised to 10. For offenders aged between 10 and 14 it was the intention to replace criminal prosecution by care proceedings. An offence in itself was not to be grounds for such proceedings; it also had to be shown 'That he is in need of care or control which he in unlikely to receive unless the court makes an order under this section'.[68] For offenders in the age group 14 to 17 years prosecution for the offence was to remain an option but should not be brought if adequate arrangements could be made elsewhere.[69]

The above steps were designed to prevent children being drawn into the penal network and to direct them towards local-authority and voluntary social-work help. What was to be done with those who did appear before the courts? As mentioned, some would receive care orders. Again, both offenders and non-offenders could be placed on a supervision order under which the local authority or a probation officer could direct supervised persons where to live and what activities to participate in. The intention was that generally the persons could be supervised in their own homes.[70] A new form of treatment, 'intermediate treatment', was to be developed. As Packman put it, this treatment would offer 'something between the potentially long-term removal from home of a "care order" and straightforward supervision in the home'.[71] Further, the powers of courts to send offenders to attendance centres, detention centres and borstals were modified. Lastly, as the approved schools were to be absorbed into the local-authority system of residential establishments, magistrates could no longer make approved school orders. To remove a child they would have to make a care order to the local authority, but it then decided the living arrangements for the youngster.

The new Act was an attempt to merge the means of dealing with deprived and delinquent youngsters, to reduce the role of criminal proceedings and to place both the prevention and treatment of offenders firmly in the hands of the local authorities, where the duties were mainly discharged by the children's departments. Yet, after all, the Act was never fully implemented, for the Labour government, which had initiated it, lost power. The new Conservative administration retained many of its provisions but decided against raising the age of criminal responsibility, against placing restrictions on the prosecution of offenders in the 14 to 17 age group and against limiting the powers of magistrates to send offenders to attendance centres, detention centres and borstals.

The 1969 Act has been widely criticised both for being 'too soft' and 'half-baked'.[72] Its scope – not all of which can be covered here – was focused on delinquency. Yet it did contain two important implications for prevention. Firstly, it confirmed the intention of the 1963 Act in making prevention a role of the local authorities. Whereas the earlier legislation placed a clear duty on the local authorities, the 1969 Act encouraged its performance by providing the procedures for keeping some children out of the courts and by creating a wider range of treatment options within their own homes. Secondly, the Act widened the scope of the children's departments (as the agents of the local authorities) by conferring upon them new functions in relation to young offenders. The once small departments were growing into what was being called a family service.

Prevention Undertaken, 1963–71

The children's departments were not slow to pursue their new duties. The number of child-care officers in England and Wales multiplied from 1,549 in 1963 to 3,591 in 1969. Moreover, within a year of the 1963 Act, nearly twenty departments took over from housing departments the responsibility for homeless families in order to provide accommodation swiftly and so avert receptions into care.

The expanding service practised prevention by using the three social work methods. The main one was casework, which Timms defined as 'work on cases guided by certain principles, and the use of knowledge and human relation skills with the object of fulfilling the function of a particular agency'.[73] Casework operated through an individual relationship and, in regard to parents, Timms suggested it could be used to enable them to co-operate with authority, to deal with their own immaturities and to raise their standards of child care.[74]

Group work, as Brown explains, is characterised by members influencing each other.[75] It was never as popular as casework but, by 1968, Davies was listing examples of 'unwed mothers, or angry adolescents or adoptive or foster parents' brought together into groups by social workers in order to improve their patterns of behaviour.[76]

Early experiments in community work received encouragement from the suggestion in the Ingleby Report about family advice centres. A few children's departments did establish them in areas of high social need, and a study of Leissner, Herdman and Davies identified their accessibility and other virtues as expressions of 'the growing awareness of the need for preventive approaches'.[77] They did not become widespread but they served as forerunners of a means of prevention to become popular two decades later.

Whatever the method used, there is no doubt that prevention became a prominent part of child-care social work. What were the outcomes? Firstly, the departments did expand their clientele to include, as Watson points out, teenagers showing problems of sexual misbehaviour, drug-taking, delinquency and truancy.[78] The numbers of families offered advice and assistance rose from 54,458 in 1967 to 78,460 in 1969. Secondly, the numbers of youngsters brought before the courts did show a decline. Of course, as Packman explains, the reduction was not just due to child-care officers but also reflected a greater use of cautions by the police.[79] But the number of teenagers being sent to detention centres and borstals actually showed an increase. The explanation mooted was that some magistrates, disliking having to commit younger children via the local authorities, were making more frequent use of their other custodial powers. Thirdly, the number of children received into public care dropped from 53,381 in 1967 to 50,938 in 1968 but the number *remaining* in care remained constant at around 69,000. Thus the children's departments responded to the new legislation by adapting social-work methodology to prevention and by holding down the numbers received into care or brought before the courts. On the other hand they found it difficult to rehabilitate children once settled in care, and they were realising that combating delinquency amongst older teenagers might require more than the resources of their lone departments.

Apart from the question of whether or not prevention achieved its objectives, its incorporation into the child-care service did highlight other issues of importance to the development of social work. For a start it drew the children's departments into far more contact with other statutory bodies. Child-care officers found themselves helping vulnerable families to avert eviction threats from housing departments, aiding others to obtain their dues from the National Assistance Board, and liaising with the police over offenders and with teachers over poor school attenders. At policy level the children's officers had to negotiate with welfare departments to obtain temporary accommodation for families and with health departments over the criteria for getting children into day nurseries. At both field and chief officer level the negotiations were sometimes sweet, sometimes sour. In all cases they again demonstrated that prevention depended upon more than just the enthusiasm of one service.

Next the permission given to children's departments to spend money on preventative work brought into focus the question of what part material relief should play in social work. No sooner had the child-care officers received the power than some of their number perceived disadvantages. Some wondered if officials of the National Assistance Board would be more reluctant to help families in need in the expectation that the children's department would always come to their rescue. Those whose casework was informed by psychoanalytic theory 'feared that the new power' . . . would inhibit a person from seeking a solution to his life problems through discussion and self-examination.[80] By contrast some critics accused child-care officers of using the bait of financial aid to coerce clients into playing the casework/therapy game. Handler cited officers refusing 'to restore electricity during the summer months until the family co-operated . . . or permitted evictions so that the family, in their words, would "see the reality of their situation"'.[81] However, most child-care officers probably regarded the giving of material aid as a useful if limited tool in helping to keep children out of care and out of the courts. Certainly this was the finding of a study by Heywood and Allen. Aid was considered useful by officers using cash to avoid an eviction or to provide a cooker for a family under stress,[82] but limited in that little money was spent under section 1 of the 1963 Act, so that in 1969–70 the highest spending department used only £8,000.[83] Thus the use of material aid became a means of averting immediate crises but not one of long-term support to poor families.

No matter how small the expenditure, the new duties, powers and roles conveyed by the two Acts did change the exposure of the work of the children's departments. By bringing neglected and delinquent children and their families into their orbit, the children's departments not only increased their clientele by many thousands but also brought themselves much more under public scrutiny – and that scrutiny could be critical. Sylvia Watson points out that 'Rescuing children from poverty, degradation and suffering is regarded as a noble activity'. But work to keep unpopular families together and the risk of leaving at home a child who is then injured by his parents opens the worker to criticism 'for failing to protect the child'.[84] Again, the powers delegated to officers to determine the place of residence for children on care orders led to press criticisms of 'softness' in allowing offenders to return home. As far as the children's departments were concerned, the honeymoon was over.

The Voluntary Societies

So far this chapter has been dominated by the preventative role of the local authorities. What of the voluntary societies? There are scores of voluntary child-care societies but the emphasis in this publication is on the ones that dominated the voluntary scene. During the 1940s about half the voluntary children's homes were run by just four large agencies. These and three other bodies had formed the National Council of Associated Children's Homes, which, through its journal *Child Care*, revealed a cautiously welcoming and defensive reaction to the Curtis and Clyde Reports and the Children Act 1948. They feared for their future if the state took over child care and, in particular, if residential care went out of favour, for, in 1947, the voluntaries were caring for 40,100 children in their children's homes, almost as many as the 40,600 in public institutions.[85]

Given these fears, the years immediately following 1948 witnessed the voluntaries stressing both the continuing value of residential care and their expertise in running it. Some opened reception centres so as to assess the needs of new admissions more quickly while more attention was paid to training of staff. Interestingly, when Myra Curtis wrote an article for *Child Care*, she spoke only about the voluntary agencies' residential expertise and made no mention of adoption, fostering or prevention.[86]

But the old pattern could not last. With children's departments placing more children in foster homes or in their own establishments and making less use of the voluntaries, the population in voluntary homes in England and Wales dropped to 21,918 by 1954.[87] If their momentum was to continue, the voluntaries needed other outlets. In 1952 the Church of England Children's Society (formerly the Waifs and Strays Society) reviewed its objectives and decided that it would strive to enable children to stay in their own homes provided 'home conditions are reasonably satisfactory', to develop adoption, expand fostering and continue residential care.[88] In fact, apart from some grants to unmarried mothers, it did little about the first objective. Nonetheless the review did mark a turning point, for it did expand its fostering and adoption work. Other voluntaries did likewise. As they began to appoint more child-care or welfare officers, so adoption became a speciality, and by the mid-1960s they were responsible for about 40 per cent of all adoptions. Slowly their proportion of children in foster homes also increased, although it never reached that of the children's departments.

In line with the Curtis recommendations the voluntaries endeavoured to replace their large residential institutions by smaller, family units. In addition, they perceived their role in providing specialised residential care. Most children's departments had under 500 children in their care and so were unlikely to cater themselves for those small numbers of diabetic, epileptic, physically and mentally handicapped children wanting residential establishments geared to their needs. The voluntaries began to fill the gap and, in turn, were warmly commended by the Home Office for so doing.[89]

Thus the large voluntary bodies followed the local-authority practice of humanising their children's homes, lagged behind them in fostering, set an example in adoption and found a role in providing specialised residential care. Did they also take up the children's departments' enthusiasm for prevention? Voices within and without urged them to do so. In 1948 an editorial in *Child Care* pointed out that the new Act failed to set up preventative services and urged its members to grasp the opportunity.[90] With some doubts about the legitimacy of local-authority expenditure upon prevention in the 1950s, the Home Office called upon the voluntaries to experiment in 'preventing the breakdown of family life'.[91] Certainly some modest attempts did follow. The principal of the National Children's Home called upon his staff to accept that the aim of rehabilitating children back to parents was a fact of life.[92] Most of the voluntaries revamped their small grant schemes. For example, during the 1950s Barnardo's was prepared to award 10 shillings and 6 pence a week to enable single mothers to retain care of their child and later the scheme was extended to 'sound families . . . where the wage-earner had been incapacitated by illness or accident'.[93] Following the legislation of 1963 giving local authorities permission to spend on prevention, Barnardo's reorganised their grants into a Family Assistance Scheme which made a condition that they would not pay families already in contact with the children's department nor be used as a supplement to National Assistance. Clearly the intention was to reduce rather than increase the numbers receiving grants.[94] In addition, some of the child-care agencies established a few hostels and flatlets for unsupported mothers and their children.

The ventures into prevention were small and scattered. By 1956 the National Children's Home had appointed just one officer, whose limited caseload would allow some scope for preventative work.[95] No senior staff were set aside with a brief for prevention. In her history of social work Eileen Younghusband observes the small changes in Barnardo's and concludes:

> but the emphasis was on long-term care for children apart from their families in residential homes all over the country. It was a long hard struggle for Barnardo's to abandon the image of the ever-open door for any child in need, to concentrate on specialist services, and to try to keep children in their own families.[96]

Her words applied equally to all the other major child-care voluntaries.

Three reasons explain the voluntaries' lack of commitment to prevention in this period. Firstly, their members were not united in believing the case for prevention. The National Council of Associated Children's Homes gave a cool reception to the 1963 Act and questioned the wisdom of returning children to 'their original inadequate homes'.[97] Secondly, even those agencies which did favour prevention soon perceived that their resources were locked up elsewhere. They were still running many residential institutions – made more costly by better staff ratios – and were also recruiting more field-workers to undertake fostering and adoption work. It followed that they found it difficult to spare staff and money for an assault on prevention. Thirdly, the voluntaries were handicapped by comparison with local authorities. Children's departments did have some access to the wider council services of home-helps, housing and day nurseries, which could be used to forestall receptions into care. The voluntary bodies had much less call on such facilities. Not least, children's departments after 1963 had a right to call upon their local authorities to increase cash resources for prevention. The voluntary societies feared that a public which gave generously to support children's homes would be less inclined to dip into their pockets to keep children with neglectful parents or to stop delinquents from being sent away. The voluntary bodies, therefore, far from pioneering prevention in the two decades following the Children Act 1948, tended to lag behind the example of the children's departments.

The Meaning of Prevention

The era of the children's departments witnessed the first legislation specifically concerned with prevention in child care. The seminal Children Act of 1948 concentrated on the treatment of children after removal from home but it also stipulated that certain children should be rehabilitated with their families. The Children and Young Persons (Amendment) Act of 1952 implied that officers could help children within their own homes if they were considered to be in danger. The Children and Young Persons Act of 1963 placed a clear preventative duty upon local authorities. Thus more preventative legislation was enacted in these 15 years than in the previous 150, and these statutes, now largely incorporated into more recent Acts, still remain the basis of preventative work in Britain.

Margaret Cole points out that a major social advance occurred when the state accepted responsibility to *support* the victims of unemployment, but that a more important step was when it accepted responsibility to *prevent* unemployment.[98] Similarly, whereas the 1948 legislation signified the state accepting a humane obligation towards the victims of deprived childhoods, the succeeding enactments enshrined a commitment to prevent those deprivations reaching the point where children had to be taken from their parents. Of course both the legislation and subsequent child-care practice had shortcomings. But if compared with the philosophy, which still prevailed up to the Second World War, that such children should be rescued and kept away from 'evil' parents, then it can be realised what advances were made during the lifetime of the children's departments.

The review of the legislation and child-care practice now allows some discussion of the meaning of prevention by the close of this period. It can be summarised under the headings of the agents, the scope and objectives, the subjects and the tactics of prevention. If prevention emerged as an important social service activity, it was the children's departments which became the main *agents*. True they were not the sole agents. Health, welfare and education departments were frequently represented at co-ordinating committees, and Family Service Units, the NSPCC and other voluntary societies were also at hand. Nonetheless the preventative mantle mainly rested upon the shoulders of the child-care officers, so that a Home Office Survey was to find that, on average, each officer was spending a quarter of her or his time on preventative work.[99]

As the years passed, the preventative agents found the *scope* and objectives of their work were widening. Initially they concentrated on children so deprived of a 'normal home life' that intervention was necessary to avoid immediate reception into care. Next came children who were suspected of being physically neglected in their own homes. The objective here was to lessen suffering whether or not they were on the brink of a family break-up. As Packman put it, 'Prevention thus came to be a two-pronged concept; prevention of admission to care; and prevention of neglect and cruelty in the family'.[100] Lastly, the scope widened to embrace delinquent or near-delinquent children.

The *subjects or targets* of preventative action were obviously the above-mentioned children. But the children were often influenced via their parents. In many cases the child-care officers concentrated on improving the parents' treatment of their children or on alleviating the parents' debts or housing conditions, so that the benefit would be felt by their offspring. Then social work writers began to argue that parents and children could not be viewed as separate subjects and that the focus was therefore the family. As the Ingleby Committee put it, 'It is the situation and the relationships within the family which seems to be responsible for many children being in trouble'.[101] Further it was beginning to be acknowledged that the families could only be helped effectively if welfare practices and policies were changed: for instance, if housing departments would accept that the granting of a house for the purpose of rehabilitating children should weigh heavily in their priorities when allocating accommodation. The targets thus widened from the children to families and then to the nature of the social services.

Even when the subjects and objects of prevention were established, there still remained the question of *tactics*, i.e. the best manner of achieving prevention. During the 1950s child-care officers appeared to assume that prevention was best achieved by casework which influenced children or parents to improve their behaviour or conditions to the point where the children were no longer considered 'at risk'. Although this approach held sway for the lifetime of the children's departments, two other tactics were also identified. One entailed finding an alternative to the 'at risk' home without actually removing the child. The best example concerned the use of day-nursery placements, which provided safe care while also relieving the strain on harrassed parents. At times short-term receptions into care were also used to relieve mothers at the point of break-down. The other tactic can be termed 'postponement', such as efforts to reduce the number of court appearances, perhaps by prevailing upon the police to administer cautions, to stop the escalation of a youth's criminal career. This particular approach was to be much developed in later years.

Prevention Established

At the close of Chapter 1 it was suggested that the long-held opposition to preventative practices would only be overcome when the Poor Law was destroyed, when social conditions were improved, when welfare services became more acceptable to working-class people, when greater public concern for children existed, and when the value of children remaining even with poor parents was widely recognised. During the 1940s and 50s progress was made. The Second World War hastened the processes by raising the expectations of what could and should be achieved in society. The election of a Labour government led to the final destruction of the Poor Law and the creation of extensive social services. The evacuation experiences seemed to open some middle-class eyes to the needs of deprived children and so prepared the way for public campaigners like Lady Allen. The combination of a reforming government, reforming lobbyists and heightened public concern resulted in the creation of children's departments in 1948. Soon after, public representatives and officials began to be influenced by arguments which stressed the advantages of keeping children with natural parents. The next step was the establishment of preventative services.

The outcome was that, within two decades of the creation of a statutory service solely for deprived children, local authorities also received legislative duties to pursue prevention. These authorities, sometimes in conjunction with voluntary bodies, then extended the range of youngsters coming within the preventative net, enlarged the targets of preventative policies to embrace families and agencies as well as children, worked out tactics for meeting their objectives and sought to apply the various social-work methods to prevention. Considering that the concept of prevention took so long to be established, the progress made in such a short time was remarkable.

Oddly enough the very establishment of preventative practice was to raise issues which were again to question the nature of child-care social work. Consideration was being given to the organisational implications of the growth of prevention. Some voices were arguing that effective prevention needed more resources and powers than those possessed by the children's departments. The next chapter will discuss the escalation and outcome of this debate.

3. Problems for Prevention

The dawn of the 1970s promised much for social workers in general and those who advocated prevention in particular. Moves were afoot to reorganise the local-authority social services into a family service with the expectation that more effective prevention would follow. Yet by the end of the decade some disillusionment was evident and the very value of prevention was under fire. In short, prevention met problems.

Reorganisation and Prevention

The call for reform

During the 1960s political party publications, government reports and outside bodies were making a case for changing the structure of the local-authority social services.[1] In reviewing the many sources Phoebe Hall identifies the main factors which fuelled the fires of the campaign. First there was growth. Work amongst deprived children, the elderly and the handicapped had outgrown the small administrative units set up as children's or welfare departments. Second came co-ordination. Families in need were often served by two or three departments which sometimes failed to liaise properly. Third, there were social work methods. Some social workers were arguing that their basic skill was family case-work and this required an administrative structure which covered families rather than just children.[2] Prevention played a part in all these developments. It had contributed to the growth of children's departments, it had figured largely in the debate about how to co-ordinate services for 'at risk' families, and its practitioners had expounded the case that prevention entailed casework with the whole family.

The calls were heeded and in December 1965 the government set up a committee under the chairmanship of Sir Frederic Seebohm with the brief to review the local-authority personal social services and to 'consider what changes are desirable to ensure an effective family service'. It reported in 1968, the same year in which the Social Work (Scotland) Act legislated for new services north of the border.

The Seebohm Report

The *Report of the Committee on Local Authority and Allied Personal Social Services* is usually considered a landmark in the development of the social services. Its main theme was to justify reorganisation and to specify its form. To this end it recommended the amalgamation into one social services department of the local-authority services provided by the children's and welfare departments, along with the educational welfare, child guidance, home-help, mental health, day nurseries and certain housing welfare services. Within the new department it was reckoned that 'a family or individual in need of social care should, as far as possible, be served by a single social worker'.[3]

The scope of the Seebohm Report cannot be detailed here, but it is worth noting that it devoted a chapter to prevention in which it argued that 'An effective family service must be concerned with the prevention of social distress'.[4] Another chapter discussed community, which meant 'both the physical location and the common identity of a group of people'.[5] The committee wanted services to be accessible to communities and it wanted communities to participate in the running of services.[6] Years later these ideas were to resurface and to have some bearing on the promotion of prevention. Not least, it was the concepts of prevention and community which stimulated some of the visionary aspects of the report. It regretted that families reached the points of dependence, disintegration and despair and urged: 'It is crucial, therefore, that this vicious circle is broken by a forceful and widespread commitment to prevention'.[7] It also called for a service 'directed to the well-being of the whole of the community and not only of social casualties and seeing the community it serves as the basis of its authority, resources and effectiveness'.[8]

The report received a warm welcome from the press and an enthusiastic one from most of the social-work associations.[9] Yet legislation did not follow. The newly formed Department of Health and Social Security (DHSS), which would be the central government department responsible for the new service, was headed by Richard Crossman, who described Seebohm as 'a contemptible report' and devoted his interests to pensions and health.[10] But the Labour cabinet did contain supporters and eventually a bill was published in 1970. In contrast to the bulky report the bill contained just a few paragraphs, which reorganised services on the proposed lines. The enactment followed with the Local Authority Social Services Act 1970, coming into operation on 1 April 1971.

High hopes and hopes dashed

Social workers, many of whom were now united as the British Association of Social Workers, anticipated a larger and more effective service. Initially hopes seemed likely to be realised. From 1969 to 1979 expenditure on the personal social services rose from £171 million to £1,641 million on revenue and from £28 million to £68 million on capital. In their first 5 years SSDs multiplied their staff by 47 per cent.[11] Yet, within a few years of the high expectations, the Social Services Departments (SSDs) were subject to severe criticisms. Advocates of prevention were disappointed. A working party headed by Professor Roy Parker acknowledged that many long-term separations between children and parents were not being avoided.[12] More pointedly, Jane Tunstill, a leading academic and BASW member, stated that after 1973 SSDs were 'paying inadequate attention to the prevention of children being received into care or, once they are in care, being rehabilitated with their own family'.[13] To be sure, the criticisms did not only appertain to prevention. The press was to trumpet even stronger complaints that social workers were no longer protecting children from abuse by their parents. Other voices accused them of losing the skill to place children with good quality substitute parents. The unifying factor was that the outcome of the Seebohm reorganisation was a dilution of the quality of children's services.

Reasons for decline

A working party, set up by the National Children's Bureau to examine the criticisms, reported that although they were exaggerated – partly because too rosy a view of the work of the Children's

Departments was circulating – they did have some justification.[14] What were the reasons for the decline?

The first was the impact of the family social worker. The extent to which all social workers went generic has been overstated but there is no doubt that, as many extended their range to include the elderly, the mentally disordered and other client groupings, so they were less able to develop child-care skills.

The second was to do with staff changes. The expanding departments recruited new social workers, seconded others for training and promoted many to managerial posts. Thus in 1973, for instance, social-work posts experienced a 20 per cent turnover.[15] Not surprisingly clients suffered from changing workers and a lack of continuity. Preventative work seemed particularly to lose out, for it often depended on the mutual trust between client and social workers developed over a long period.

The third reason was pressure of work. Not only were former specialist social workers taking on social-work tasks to which they were not accustomed, but their departments were attracting more clients of all kinds. Thus in 1973–4 nearly 450,000 children were referred to English SSDs as against a comparable 150,000 to the children's departments in 1965–6.[16] Of course the reorganised departments had more resources, but demand was outstripping supply and the Barclay Report later had to state of this era that 'it must be recognised that the social services' contribution is seriously underfinanced'.[17] The intense pressures and shortage of resources had an unfortunate spin-off for prevention. Departments felt obliged to give priority to existing clients, so that children already in care rated above those who might possibly come into care. Thus the National Children's Bureau working party calculated that of local authorities expenditure on children and families, only 1 per cent was being allocated to preventative and supporting services.[18]

Fourth came the size and complexity of the new departments. The 377 children's and welfare departments of England and Wales had in 1971 become 174 social services departments. But in 1974 further local government changes made them into just 116 SSDs. The outcome was the establishment of large-scale bureaucracies with complicated managerial systems. In the short term, far from improving communication with other agencies, the vast increase in numbers and layers of staff seemed actually to hinder it. Yet improved co-operation as a means of more effective prevention had been one of the arguments in favour of reorganisation. So the much awaited reorganisation was eventually succeeded by a fall in the standards of child-care practices. Was the Seebohm report to blame? Whatever the nature of the reforms recommended by the report, some disruption through staff turnover and adaption to new roles was inevitable. Seebohm could hardly be blamed for that. Further, much of what the report had recommended about delegation, community participation and resource provision had been ignored by government. But whatever the reasons, preventative practice did not advance as anticipated. The spread of the scope of prevention in the 1960s to include delinquents and neglected children had been one of the grounds for arguing for a wider, family service. Ironically that family service often became staffed by generic social workers who lacked both the time and skills to promote prevention with these clients. The argument that child-care officers needed to communicate more effectively with other social agencies in order to prevent receptions into care had been taken as a justification for a larger, all-embracing service. Unfortunately the outcome was a bureaucracy which experienced even greater difficulties of communication. Perhaps saddest of all was a decline in the sense of purpose which had characterised some children's departments. As Phoebe Hall concluded, 'The many problems faced by social services departments have clearly affected the morale of the professionals working within them. One frequently expressed concern is that the service now seems to be almost totally crisis-orientated with very little chance for preventive work'.[19] Some of the vision was lost. Prevention had its problems.

Parenting and Prevention

The establishment of SSDs coincided with the election of a Conservative government. Its Secretary for Social Services, Sir Keith Joseph, soon delivered a major speech which offered an explanation of why 'deprivation and problems of maladjustment so conspicuously persist'.[20] Entitled the cycle of deprivation, he postulated a core of parents whose inadequate child-rearing practices spawned offspring unable to take advantage of education, ill equipped with work skills, lacking morality and unable to form stable relationships. As adults they became 'in their turn the parents of the next generation of children who are deprived emotionally and intellectually' and who become the next batch of abused children, delinquents and those received into public care.[21] In eloquent words Sir Keith then argued that if means could be found 'to break the cycle then we shall be doing preventative work in the most fundamental sense. Surely here be treasure if we can together discover it'.[22] As for the means, the government then provided more resources for birth control to limit the growth of such families, for social-work intervention to improve parental behaviour, for play groups and day-care experiences to stimulate the development of young children and for improved educational services to prepare children for adulthood.

Impact on practice

Sir Keith was by no means the first person to proclaim the cycle of deprivation.[23] The importance of his speech rested not in original-ity but in the open adherence of a government minister to a particular explanation of social problems. Nor was there anything new in the preventative means he advocated. The difference was that, as the social services minister, he was pointing the way in which social workers should practise. As Jordan explains, hitherto social workers had tended to work on the basis of using casework 'to re-establish the deviant member within his family and neigh-bourhood by means of his relationship with his client'. [24] By contrast, the new explanation stressed social rather than individual pathology, on a self-perpetuating culture of faulty child-rearing methods rather than on isolated families falling out of step with mainstream life. The strategy for prevention was thus different. The cycle would only disappear if the inadequate species as a whole bore fewer children, applied new child practices and accepted new values.

Some social workers took on Sir Keith's thesis, and 'to break into the cycle' became a 'part of the vocabulary of many social workers during the seventies'.[25] Why then did it cause problems for others? For a start, they doubted its validity. Jordan demon-strated that the kind of problems Sir Keith wanted to prevent were not confined to a core of families.[26] Research threw severe doubts as to whether, in general, problem behaviour was automatically transmitted from one generation to the next.[27] Other commentators accepted that many social problems were disproportionately experienced by one social grouping, namely, low income families, but showed that they had very similar values and aspirations as the rest of society and that their different behaviour resulted as a reaction to unfavourable environments.[28]

Further, the same social workers reckoned that the cycle of deprivation theory and practices were harmful to the very people they were intended to help. The new approach cast social workers in a more controlling, almost policing, position. The families, as Jordan explained, were regarded as 'a group whose behaviour was characterised by a lack of adequate self-discipline and control . . . and whose financial, personal and emotional affairs thus needed to be managed for them by the wisdom of appointed authority'.[29] The managing aspects did not fit easily into the style of social workers who relied on the warmth of their relationships and who believed that clients would reject authoritarian approaches and so lessen rather than enhance the chances of effective prevention.

In addition, the social workers feared that the plan to concentrate on a sub-culture of problem families – the 800 or so inadequates which one SSD director informed Sir Keith accounted for nearly all the social problems in his city – would earn their departments such reputations that people would be reluctant to come in for fear of being stigmatised as one of the species.[30] The worry was that even parents requiring a straightforward preventative service like day care would be inhibited by the prospect of being drawn into a cycle of deprivation package. If life in the new departments was not hard enough, some social workers thus found themselves having to contest the preventative implications springing from Sir Keith's programme.

Poverty and Prevention

The departure of Sir Keith from office in the mid-1970s lessened the impact of the cycle of deprivation thesis on SSDs. Yet one continuing spin-off from the controversy was that the focus on explanations also highlighted the question of why children were admitted into public care. At the risk of over-simplification, it can be said that three views were in vogue. One kind highlighted individual limitations. Thus the psychoanalytic tradition theorised that unsatisfactory psychological relationships in childhood could result in some individuals developing the kind of personalities which later could not cope with children. Next came explanations emphasising the impact of inadequate child-socialisation experiences, which led to children whose values and behaviour was such that eventually they had to be removed from home. Obviously the cycle of deprivation fitted into this category. Another analysis identified a lack of access to essential facilities. Packman pointed out that affluent parents could buy means of coping – for example, sending their children to boarding school while less privileged families might have to ask the local authority to intervene.[31] Similar kinds of explanation were made about delinquency and the recourse to custody. The blame was attributed to genetic endowment,[32] family malfunctioning,[33] poor parenting, to the lack of opportunities for working-class children,[34] and so on. What is noticeable is that neither the accounts of why children entered care or custody gave priority to the effects of poverty on behaviour. It was acknowledged that low-income families had less access to facilities and opportunities, but poverty itself was not isolated as a major causal factor. Then, during the 1970s, the effects of poverty on families began to be felt. The outcome was more difficulties for social workers.

The rediscovery of poverty

Writing of post-war Britain, Forrester states, 'It was widely felt . . . that Britain had become a markedly more equal society, most of Beveridge's giants had been slain'.[35] Beyond doubt the post-war reforms did improve the quality of life for many people. But poverty had not disappeared, as a number of social scientists were to show.[36] Their work culminated in Peter Townsend's exhaustive, and exhausting, *Poverty in the United Kingdom*, published in 1979.[37] From this and the other studies[38] the following deductions were drawn. Firstly, poverty required a relative rather than a subsistence definition, i.e. to be poor is not just about lack of food but concerns the extent of social differences between various sections of society. Townsend focuses on ' "relative deprivation" ' by which I mean the absence or inadequacy of those diets, amenities, standards, services and activities which are common or customary in society . . . If they lack or are denied resources to obtain access to these conditions of life and so fulfil membership of society, they are in poverty'.[39]

Secondly, far from disappearing, poverty or social deprivation was actually increasing in the 1970s. If the Supplementary Benefit scale rates (which had replaced National Assistance) are taken as an income sufficient to enable people to participate properly in community life, then those whose income is *below* this amount are the poor. Accordingly in the United Kingdom the numbers in poverty had risen to 2 million by 1975.[40] However, empirical studies established that the scale rates allowed a very restricted life-style and many commentators accepted that poverty consisted of an income (less housing costs) less than 20 per cent above the scale rates. Certainly the DHSS began to publish annual figures of people in this category, showing that by 1975 the number had risen to 8,880,000.[41] Similarly other deprivations continued to breed. In March 1966 the number of homeless persons, i.e. those living in local authority temporary accommodation, was 13,031. By 1971 it was 28,879. Even where deprivations were not actually increasing, it became clear that the educational, employment and health advantages of some sections of the population were lagging behind those of more fortunate sections. In short, differences were widening.[42]

Thirdly, the studies identified an explanation of poverty. Attention was directed at the manner in which inflation bore more heavily on the poor: on the taxation allowances and private-welfare schemes which gave yet more advantage to the privileged; and on the numerical growth of pensioners, one-parent families and the unemployed, i.e. of population groupings particularly liable to financial hardship. In the face of such factors the view gained ground that poverty could not be blamed merely on the individual deficiencies of the poor nor on the below-standard child-rearing practices of the inadequate families. In short, a structural explanation emerged, in which poverty was regarded by some politicians and academics as the product of the state. I have elaborated on the structural explanation elsewhere[43] and here it suffices to say that it is by no means new and is most powerfully and eloquently expressed in the writings of the Christian socialist Richard Tawney.[44]

The focus on poverty prompted social workers to explore the connection between it and receptions into public care. Families who were separated from their children were most likely to dwell in locations of social deprivation[45] and to be drawn from the categories with lowest incomes. Obviously, poverty is not the only factor associated with separations, and poverty does not inevitably lead to children being neglected or removed. But, as Thorpe put it, research.leads 'to the lamentable conclusion that poverty and deprivation are still closely associated with reception and committal to care'.[46] The association exists because social deprivations restrict access to facilities, deny basic amenities, and adversely affect behaviour. During the 1970s many families under stress, particularly lone parents, found they could not obtain access to day-nursery places, which had a priority waiting list of over 12,000. Lacking the cash to find good day care, some had to part with their children to public care or to private foster parents.[47] Other families could not afford decent housing conditions. In 1979 over 6,000 children were received into care because of 'homelessness' or 'unsatisfactory home conditions'.[48] Putting together studies made in this period, Tunnard thus identifies the 'clear link between inadequate accommodation, family poverty and admission to care'.[49]

Probably the connection most often turns on the cumulative effect of poverty on behaviour, as illustrated by the research of Wilson and Herbert. They established that although poverty-stricken parents did supply inadequate diets and unhelpful socialisation experiences, they did also share the values and aspirations of a more affluent control group. It was their deprived conditions which forced them into adopting practices of which they themselves did not approve, such as sending children on the streets to relieve the stresses of overcrowding. Their different behaviour arose from the depriving pressures, and the penalty they paid was that their children faced lower standards of care, were more likely to commit delinquent acts and were more vulnerable to reception into care.[50]

Poverty and preventative social work

The increase in poverty meant more demands on SSDs. Some people came because social deprivations were threatening the unity of their families. Others came, or were sent by social-security officials, simply because they lacked money. Expenditure under section 1 of the 1963 Act shot up to £4.3 million by 1976–7, yet, as Fuller and Stevenson pointed out, 'It is highly debatable whether or not payments of the kind described can be seen as preventing reception into care'.[51] Some social workers thus felt confused, helpless and de-skilled. They felt confused because it became difficult to distinguish between a poor family whose children were at risk and a desperate family whose hardship made them appear at risk. They felt helpless because SSDs lacked the powers and resources to provide income maintenance. Moreover, if the roots of poverty resided in the structures of society, what could social workers do about that? They felt de-skilled in that the old child-care skills of compassion and support which had sometimes held families together during moments of crisis seemed less applicable to parents who just wanted cash for the gas bill.

Preventative social work did continue. But in the new climate there were unfortunate repercussions for both social workers and clients. Under increased demands, social workers became rationers as they spread their time between those who wanted their case-work skills for help with personal problems and those whose difficulties were confined to straightforward financial need. With the latter another form of rationing had to occur, for the social workers had to say 'yes' to some, and 'no' to others. Looking back at this period, the Barclay Report stated that social workers had come to be seen 'more as withholders of resources, than as distributors . . . this has had a damaging effect on the image and morale of social workers'.[52] Moreover, clients who asked for money disliked the questions about their family lives; as Jordan explained, the parent resents 'having herself assessed as to her ability to bring up children'.[53] Clients also felt anger if their requests were turned down while others received money. Thus not only did the morale of social workers fall, but also their standing in the eyes of consumers.

A social-work response

No doubt most social workers would have sided with Jordan's plea for a 'personal social service department which had no connection with poor relief',[54] but they could not just ignore desperate, low-income callers. As of old, they could offer small, one-off payments which could sometimes get families through a financial crisis. Gradually other tactics were pursued. Within their departments some statutory social workers made a case for the kind of resource, particularly day care, which was of immediate help to poor families facing child-care problems. Like-minded colleagues attempted to make welfare-rights expertise an accepted part of social-work practice, so as to help clients – whether at risk of coming into care or not – receive their full dues from social security. Such workers were sometimes accused of 'humanising' poverty by persuading the poor to accept the intolerable. The criticism was ill founded because they were also pressing for wider reforms.[55] Sometimes through BASW, occasionally in league with such consumer groups as Claimants' Unions, they bore, as Brown and Madge record, 'eloquent witness to the meaning of deprivation . . . for the families who experience it'.[56] Although the number of social workers so engaged was not large, they did play a part in establishing that the problem of poverty could not be blamed on its victims and that the cure could not just be left to social workers.

The re-emergence of widespread social deprivation did succeed in concentrating social-workers' minds on the connection between poverty and family break-ups and did provoke some into developing a preventative strategy which embraced a structural concept of poverty. But the effect on prevention was adverse. More families were shattered by poverty, social work began to lose some public credibility and many social workers were weighed down by increasing and complicated pressures. As far as prevention was concerned, poverty meant problems.

Permanency and Prevention

Reorganisation of the social services and the impact of poverty engendered work pressures which made it more difficult for social workers to undertake prevention. Next occurred events which, by placing a renewed emphasis on removing children permanently from their natural parents, served to undermine any emphasis on prevention.

The Colwell tragedy

Maria Colwell had been in the care of East Sussex SSD, which did not oppose her mother's application to a court for a revocation of the care order. Once home, in January 1973, the 7-year-old suffered a horrific death at the hands of her stepfather. A government inquiry criticised the SSD for not opposing the revocation and for not properly monitoring the return, as well as highlighting a lack of liaison between welfare officials. In a minority report Olive Stevenson dissociated herself from blaming individuals and attempted to look at the social forces which provoked such tragedies.[57]

The case fascinated the mass media, though a contemporary incident of a man killing his 5-year-old adoptive son rated hardly a mention. Whatever the reasons, the press furiously accused social workers of worshipping 'the blood tie' and so insisting on returning children to unsuitable relatives.[58] A psychiatrist, John Howells, in an emotionally titled book, *Remember Maria*, asked, 'What makes us, supposedly lovers of children, stand exclusively on the side of parents?'[59] Curiously these writers ignored the fact that Maria's killer was not a blood relative. But such complications were ignored as reporters then blamed social workers for ignoring the extent to which children were being battered by their parents throughout the country. The implication was that unless social workers gave less attention to prevention and more to removal, then the number of Maria Colwells would escalate.

In the same year, 1973, two respected social work authors, Jane Rowe and Lydia Lambert, published *Children Who Wait*. From a sample of children in care they estimated that about 6,000 children were being allowed 'to drift' without decisions being made for their permanent futures. They conceded that a substantial minority could be rehabilitated with their parents, but, in a study conducted for the Association of British Adoption and Fostering Agencies, attention was largely centred on the desirability of placing them with substitute parents. The book became ammunition for a growing pro-adoption lobby. In November 1973 a leader in the *Guardian* cited it in claiming that 2,000 children in care should be adopted. By June 1975 it had upped the figure to 6,000.[60] In reality the authors had carefully stated that their numbers applied to children who might be fostered *or* adopted. Even these were based on projections and the actual number thought to need adoption was just thirty-five.[61] Such niceties were ignored as the campaign to facilitate the cutting of ties between natural parents and their children gathered momentum.

The permanency movement

The Colwell case and the Rowe and Lambert book appeared to show that children were in danger from inadequate parents and that many could be placed with substitute parents. The final link was the popularising of the doctrine that removal from such natural parents should be for keeps.

The main communicators of the permanency belief were Goldstein, Freud and Solnit, whose *Beyond the Best Interests of the Child* was also published in 1973. Drawing upon psycho-analytic theory, they asserted that children could not relate satisfactorily to two sets of parental figures – natural and substitute. They needed permanence. They were even critical of fostering, because it contained the possibility of rehabilitation. They argued that, once removed, children who could not be quickly returned to satisfactory parents should be legally and permanently put with adopters.[62] Goldstein and his colleagues' second volume, *Before the Best Interests of the Child*, made overt their political position. They opposed state expenditure on families because it weakened their readiness to stand on their own feet. If families, including poor ones, could not cope by their own efforts, then consideration should be given to placing their children with others.[63] This political flavour had much in common with that of the New Right, which, as Parton explains, was wielding increasing influence on the Conservative Party at this time, and so helps to explain why the doctrines of removal and permanence became widely accepted.[64]

Parton also identifies the role played by the Tunbridge Wells Study Group, a collection of self-appointed prominent figures in medicine, the law and social work, who, in May 1973, organised a conference attended by Sir Keith Joseph and senior civil servants. The proceedings supported the cycle of deprivation thesis by stressing the generational aspects of inadequate parenting and identified child abuse as predominantly a problem of the lower social classes. Their deduction was that 'strong consideration should be given to the permanent removal of children from parental care'.[65]

The public outcry against the 'blood tie', the apparent revelation that thousands of children in public care needed substitute homes, the influx of a doctrine supporting the suppression of the legal rights of parents, and a political climate ready to receive such messages, all combined to account for the establishment of the permanency movement. Its rise split social work into two camps, one emphasising prevention, the other permanence. As a writer who was identified with the former, I am not pretending that I can present an objective account. However, recourse can be made to an article by Fox which describes both sides. One she calls '*The kinship defenders*', by whom

> the natural i.e. biological family is perceived as being of unique value to the child and as being, for the vast majority of children, the optimum context for their growth, upbringing and develop-ment. State intervention should therefore be directed to pre-serving, supporting and strengthening the family unit; only in unusual and extreme situations should it be disrupted.

The other side,

> *the society as parent protagonists* . . . advocates the readier removal of children from natural families and the provision of permanent, secure substitute families when natural parenting is unsatisfactory. [This school represents] a tradition of paternal-istic state intervention in the cause of social welfare, which has its roots in the nineteenth century; a tradition in which the values of the dominant class have been imposed on the poor for their own good, and in which the children of the poor have been removed to make a 'fresh start'.[66]

It should be noted that Fox's categories sharpen the differences between the two camps. The 'kinship defenders' never claimed that no children should be removed. On the other side, Jane Rowe points out that many social workers associated with the perma-nency movement were not anti-parent but they were opposed to the ill-effects on children of long-term public care. To them, permanency was a goal, especially adoption, because it meant security.[67] The anti-natural-parent side of the permanency move-ment was expressed more strongly in the press and by the authors already cited than by social workers.

The Children Act 1975

Despite these qualifications, strong differences did exist and Fox was correct in identifying the main features of what can best be called the permanence and preventative schools. They soon found a stage on which their differences could be articulated – the Children Bill of 1975.

The bill had its origins in the Houghton Report of 1972, which made recommendations to improve the practice of adoption.[68] After a Commons debate, a pressure group, The Adoption and Guardianship Reform Organisation, was formed to campaign for legislation. The debate occurred in the year 1973, and adoption issues therefore merged with those of 'tug-of-love' cases, child abuse and permanency. A Labour MP, David Owen, initiated a private member's bill. However, Parliament was dissolved and, following a Labour victory, the same Dr Owen, now as Minister of State for Health, was able to formulate a government children's bill. Part One contained proposals to improve the coverage and practice of adoption agencies, and to reduce the powers of natural parents, in certain cases, to refuse consent to adoption orders. Part Two introduced the new order of custodianship, under which substitute parents, in certain circumstances, could gain legal custody over children outside of adoption. Part Three, amongst other provisions, gave local authorities increased powers to assume parental rights over certain children.

Parton sums up the bill by saying it 'attempted to give far greater control to local authorities over the lives of children in their care, to allow for an easier severance of parental ties and give greater security to children in their substitute homes'.[69] Not surprisingly, the permanence school gave it their full support. The preventative school – now a coalition which included the Child Poverty Action Group, the National Council for One Parent Families, Gingerbread, Mind and BASW – welcomed the proposals to improve adoptive practice and to clarify the standing of substitute parents. But it made a threefold opposition to the government's intention to make permanence a central part of child-care policy.

Firstly, it argued that the permanency doctrine rested on false premises. The view that children could only be emotionally stable if placed permanently with one set of parents was examined and found wanting. Studies to show that social workers did not place undue influence on the 'blood tie' were cited and doubts were expressed about the high estimates of children in care needing adoption. Secondly, it pointed out that the Children's Bill made no provision whatsoever to improve the material conditions of parents most vulnerable to losing their children, despite the compelling evidence of a link between poverty and child separations. Prevention received not a mention. Thirdly, the bill was seen as placing natural parents at a great disadvantage when compared with adopters, custodians and local authorities. Indeed Fox, who retained a neutral position, conceded that a proposal that parents could lose their parental rights to the local authority after their children had been in voluntary care for 3 years represented a new innovation in law in that it meant 'that a parent can now be deprived of his rights not because of any culpability on his part, but merely because of the passage of time'.[70]

Despite the spirited opposition, the bill became the Children Act 1975. Not just the New Right but both the main political parties had moved to concentrating child-care policy on the removal of children rather than on the removal of the social disadvantages which put them at risk. The preventative school had lost and some of its supporters compared the new Act with the Poor Law.[71] These comparisons were overstated, for the 'society as parent protagonists' were usually motivated by what they saw as 'the best interests of the child' rather than by the punitive deterrence of the Poor Law. A better historical comparison could be made between the permanency movement and the child emigration of yesteryear. Both tended to take children from poor families and hand them to more affluent ones, both glossed over the adverse effects of cutting children away from their biological roots, and both placed little weight on reforming social conditions so as to help parents retain their children. The Victorian emphasis on rescuing and permanently removing children had returned. Permanency was in the ascendancy.

Prevention impaired

SSDs in the 1970s were subjected not just to the growth of permanency doctrine. More investigations into child abuse, or non-accidental injury, were leading to what Parton calls a 'pervasive fear of "a Maria Colwell happening here"'.[72] The combined effect changed social-work practice. Following a DHSS circular, most departments set up child-abuse registers and area review committees and installed special training for social workers.[73] Indeed, Fuller and Stevenson observed, 'there was more bureaucratic activity at central and local government levels concerning child welfare than at any time since 1948'.[74] Along with plans to detect child abuse, many departments drew up programmes to implement permanency. Specialist fostering and adoption units were created to find permanent homes for 'the children who wait'. Some even made a policy decision that no child entering care under 10 years of age should remain for more than 2 years and then had to be either rehabilitated or put with permanent substitute parents.[75] In order to stop parents upsetting plans for permanency, SSDs became more keen to assume parental rights, so that the number of resolutions passed in England and Wales rose steeply from 12,000 in 1973 to 18,400 in 1979. Departments were also having more recourse to place of safety orders and care orders via courts, so by the end of the decade a higher proportion of parents had lost a say in the lives of their children than at any other time – even than under the Poor Law.[76] The practices were conveyed by social workers much influenced by the British Agencies for Adoption and Fostering (BAAF), which ran courses and issued publications on terminating parental contact.[77] Prevention was out of favour amongst many social workers and replaced 'by a style of social work with families which is more defensive, less prepared to take risks, and relies more on statutory intervention'.[78] The emphasis was now on permanence and the severance of family ties and, for all the protests that they were not anti-parent, it could not but bring social workers into conflict with parents.

The effect of the above trends was to impair prevention in the following ways. Firstly, the social work enthusiasm for prevention was dented. Indeed, social workers working under managements which accepted the Goldstein, Freud and Solnit exhortation that, except in very short separations, 'each child placement be final and unconditional', found the scope for prevention to be minute.[79]

Secondly, the new trend was accompanied by a style of casework which did not fit easily into preventative forms of social work. As SSDs became preoccupied with child abuse so they became influenced by the work of an American specialist, Henry Kempe. Parton explains that Kempe's medical model 'assumed . . .

that child abuse is an illness of sufficient unity to be put into a diagnostic category in its own right and that the pathology resides primarily in the parents'.[80] The model, accepted by the DHSS in its circular of 1974, was spread in conferences, where, as Fuller and Stevenson describe, 'Pens and notebooks in hand, attentive audiences crowd into such sessions which have been widespread throughout the country'.[81] The medical diagnosis held that abusing parents, once identified, should be subjected to treatment which, if it failed, should be followed by the surgery of cutting them off from their children. Translated into social casework practice, the advocates assumed that not only abusing but also inadequate parents could be spotted and offered treatment plans, with the implication that unless improvement occurred, alternative long-term plans would be made for the children.

This kind of authoritarian social work in which the expert professional intervened decisively did not completely dominate the life of SSDs. As mentioned, other social workers were trying to get to grips with an approach which could counter poverty. Family therapy and contract setting were yet other approaches seeking a foothold at this time. Nonetheless it was forcibly conveyed and had an adverse impact as far as prevention was concerned. The medical model with its bias towards personal symptoms and individual responsibility deterred social workers from considering the effects of environmental and structural factors on parents' behaviour. Hence the parents could find themselves under threat to change their behaviour without any corresponding help to do so. Further, subsequent studies have shown that the 'symptoms' of abusers may appear in parents who are not child abusers but who are socially deprived.[82] Consequently the medical model approach was in danger of wrongly drawing people into the welfare net. Not least, it often meant that social workers were not planning jointly with parents about the future of children but were imposing decisions made at conferences of professionals. As Jordan explained, they were acting 'in terms of controlling children's futures, rather than planning'.[83] This control aspect built up amongst families who fell into the orbit of SSDs a fear that social workers were officials 'who took your children away'. It was a reputation which stood in direct contrast to the media stereotype of the soft social worker who worshipped the 'blood tie'.

Thirdly, prevention suffered as SSDs gave it less priority in resource allocation. In their review carried out for the DHSS Fuller and Stevenson noted: 'in 1979, an analysis of professional journals showed that the establishment of posts for fostering and adoption was by far the most significant single development in social work specialisation . . . Comparable posts for the rehabilitation of children in care to their families were nowhere to be seen'.[84] Similarly the Study Commission on the Family observed: 'the development of substitute care in foster homes and adoption homes has expanded recently following the 1975 Act. It takes place at the expense of day care services, and also at the expense of expanded advice centres and cash grants to natural families'.[85]

In no way is the present writer trying to undermine efforts to stop cruelty to children or to hinder social workers in their desire to plan carefully for children's futures. The argument offered here is that this needs to occur within a context of a high commitment to prevention and of the promotion of the social conditions and social services which enable parents to look after their own children. Some of the American permanency projects did stress both sides. The well known Oregon experiment sought permanent homes for foster children and succeeded in doing so for 72 per cent of its sample, yet 26 per cent of these went back permanently to natural parents for whom the chances of rehabilitation had been considered small.[86] In Britain this side of permanence was neglected. SSDs did not appoint specialists in rehabilitation. Resources for removing children were allocated at the cost of preventative work.

Thus two distinct but related child-care trends emerged in the 1970s. One, egged on by a moral panic over child abuse, led to an emphasis on removing children for fear of another Maria Colwell. In some cases children who otherwise might have remained safely at home if supported by preventative services were removed into care. Indeed, in a number of cases, children were quite wrongly removed, and the MP Raymond Fletcher was moved to protest that fear of being blamed 'seems to have caused social workers to over-react and the rights of parents are being trampled on'.[87] The other trend was the permanency movement, which put stress on giving children long-term security through cutting their legal ties to natural parents and settling them with substitute parents. The combined outcome was that removal and permanence overshadowed prevention and rehabilitation. The value of prevention was undermined; it received less priority both in terms of social work practice and in the allocation of resources. More generally welfare spending to enable families to retain care of their children became less of a social and political objective. In the 1970s therefore both public and social work attitudes contrasted with those of the previous decade – and prevention was the loser.

The Voluntary Contribution

How did the voluntaries react in the period when statutory prevention experienced major setbacks in the face of reorganisation, the re-emergence of poverty and the new focus on permanence?

Reorganisation and the voluntary movement

The National Council of Voluntary Child Care Organisations (as it was now called) issued a cautious welcome to the Seebohm Report and the Local Authority Social Services Act of 1970. However, through its journal, it expressed the fear that the new SSDs, by being responsible for so many different kinds of clients, might lose their expertise with deprived children.[88] The societies thus anticipated some of the disadvantages of amalgamating services and so resisted the proposal, which was being bandied about, of a voluntary Seebohm to unite different kinds of voluntary services. Their resistance was important, for during the following decade they did not follow the trend towards generic social workers and so were still able to concentrate on the cause of children.

Although the voluntaries did not amalgamate, the creation of local authority SSDs did bring home the necessity to reorganise within each voluntary agency. SSDs were now so large they could operate a wide variety of residential units and so had even less call upon voluntary establishments. True, the voluntaries continued to run community homes and community schools (as defined under the Children and Young Persons Act of 1969). True, in the mid-1970s the Church of England Children's Society still had 67 residential and day-care units while Barnardo's employed 1,300 residential staff. But the writing on the wall was becoming clear and the writing expressed as figures showed that the number of children cared for by voluntary bodies in residential and foster homes in England and Wales dropped from 18,403 in 1962 to 9,507 in 1974.[89] The voluntaries could no longer compete with the local authorities as equal partners in the provision of child-care resources. They had to reorganise in different directions.

Selected services and selected areas

During the 1970s the voluntaries opted to concentrate their resources on specific activities. Two main examples stand out. They possessed child-care expertise in adoption, for already they had become leading adoption agencies. Now they could ally that expertise to the SSDs' desire to make more permanent placements for children in public care as well as for those still in the care of the voluntary bodies. Younghusband records that while Barnardo's was steadily reducing the number of its children's homes so its 'adoption work was increasingly concentrated on hard-to-place children, and a phone-in service was started in Leeds to answer any query related to adoption'.[90] The National Children's Homes began to develop teams for the same purpose and co-operated in the somewhat controversial advertising of children for adoption on TV. The Church of England Children's Society went along the same path but, interestingly, the numbers placed continued to decline. Thus in 1967 the Society placed for adoption 192 special needs children while in 1977 it was down to 85.[91] The voluntary bodies had identified a new need but its extent was smaller than had been suggested.

In addition, the voluntaries acknowledged they could not offer comprehensive services in a geographical sense. Barnardo's, as Packman says, 're-organised itself completely and ceased to attempt national coverage, concentrating instead on seven urban areas of acute child care need, and developing new forms of help'.[92] The director of the Church of England Children's Society explained:

> We are re-organising, with teams concentrating in geographically smaller areas to meet specialised needs in brick-and-mortar-centres . . . The Society shall continue to look for foster homes for the children in our residential establishments and shall continue to provide an alternative service in adoptions, but

the main thrust now is towards working for the community within the community.[93]

Prevention

What were these 'new forms of help'? For a while the voluntaries appeared unsure of themselves as, to cite Younghusband, they 'moved beyond a concentration on the deprived or neglected child; first to his family, then to the environment'.[94] Gradually their efforts came together in four main directions, all of which had a preventative element. Agencies began to co-operate with SSDs in order to run *intermediate treatment schemes*, the aim of which was to provide imaginative activities for young offenders as an alternative to custody. Next, *day care* for the under-fives was expanded. The closure of residential nurseries and some children's homes freed plant and personnel at the time when the Finer Committee on One Parent Families was recommending 'a considerable expansion in day care services for children under 5'.[95] Like the other child-care voluntaries, the Church of England Children's Society moved in this direction and in 1976 published a report on its day-care centre in Cardiff. It argued that by taking children at risk of abuse or family break-down it was averting receptions into public care. But not all the families were in that position. A number were battling with lives marred by 'poverty, inadequate housing, sickness, and perhaps worst of all, social isolation'. Thus the aim was not just preventing receptions into care but also 'helping families towards a greater degree of self-sufficiency and stability'.[96]

The voluntaries also began to *apply the ideas of prevention and rehabilitation to those residential units* which had once seemed the very fortresses within which rescued children could be kept from their parents. In Scotland Dr Barnardo's took a lead concerning children's needs for 'primary bonds', i.e. for bonds with their relatives. It stated:

[Barnardo's in Scotland] take on the responsibility for over one hundred children. All of them have *families* in which they have lived and grown for certainly seven years and some much longer. It would be as barbaric to deny these primary bonds and their meaning to our clients, as it is to separate elderly couples, when they need to go into residential care.[97]

In response Barnardo's attached to residential establishments social workers charged with the purpose of working with the children's families. Their efforts to bring natural parents into the process of prevention may not have been typical of all the voluntary child-care agencies or even of all the staff in Barnardo's, but it was indicative of the readiness of the voluntaries to begin to incorporate the concept of prevention into the very heart of their organisations.

Lastly come *community projects and family centres*. The National Children's Home established its first family centre with a purpose-built unit at a cost of £200,000 in Birmingham. Subsequent centres converted existing property as a cheaper means. In 1975 its Lambeth centre was opened, with the philosophy that 'early action may avoid the later need to spend much more money on caring . . . in residential institutions'. As an example of preventative work, it was said that a lone father could leave his child all day there rather than placing him or her in public care.[98] The other national child-care agencies pursued a similar path. In the mid-1970s the Church of England Children's Society turned an old TV studio into a family centre in Leeds and backed a community project on a council estate on the outskirts of Bath. Towards the end of the decade some of its day-care centres were turned into family centres. The Society later recorded: 'During the late 1970s the Society began to expand its preventive social work by establishing a number of family centres whose common aim was to help children at risk of suffering deprivation or of becoming damaged or delinquent'.[99]

In contrast to the previous decade, therefore, the voluntary bodies embraced the concept and objective of prevention. They acknowledged that they could not compete with SSDs by offering countrywide services. Instead, as Fuller and Stevenson state, they 'shifted their emphasis (albeit with some resistance) to schemes of community care, many involving innovative local programmes of service to deprived families'.[100] It followed that, although specialist residential establishments and home-finding teams continued to receive a large share of the voluntary bodies' resources, their numerical expansion was in work which helped families within their own communities. For example, at the end of the decade a Church of England Children's Society report included a section headed 'Going Local With Preventive Care', and recorded that of the 5,366 children helped during 1980, 3,993 had been through 'family centres, day centres, holiday schemes and in their own homes'.[101]

The new developments were picking up ideas from a variety of sources, such as community work and the government's Urban Programme and Community Development Projects.[102] Not surprisingly their preventative approach often displayed confusion and uncertainties about both purposes and methods. Nowhere is this better revealed than in Ian Sparks' frank analysis of a Barnardo's project in the deprived Blackhill estate in Glasgow. Starting in 1972, it ran play groups, holiday schemes, youth clubs and groups. It ended in 1977 and Sparks comments: 'The decision to close was a great surprise and shock to most people in Blackhill'.[103] It appeared that the project's aims were never clearly settled but they included some pressure to raise the educational potential of the under-fives and some to improve the self-image of the community. Strategies were never clear, fluctuating between building up open youth clubs and concentrating on small groups, and when two of the staff who lived in the area established contacts and 'were helping to prevent family disintegration', there was some opposition from the local authority that they were doing work best left to statutory social workers.[104] For all the disappointment, the project did show that its workers could be accepted by local residents and that a voluntary body was prepared to learn from its experiences. In similar fashion projects run by the other child-care agencies were also clarifying aims and strategies and identifying the skills required for undertaking prevention in local communities.

The 1970s truly marked a turning point in the history of the major child-care societies. During this period they accepted what had already been perceived by some in the decade before – that in the era of state welfare they could no longer be the major providers of child care services. In response the voluntaries made some crucial decisions. They opted not to seek amalgamation with different kinds of other voluntary bodies, and, in consequence, they could still concentrate on children and their families, in contrast to the SSDs. They decided to foster their expertise, which fitted into the prevailing statutory philosophy of permanence, in order to offer a service the SSDs could use – finding homes for the 'hard to place'. Yet simultaneously, and perhaps most significantly, they also began to face up to the challenge of prevention, not by offering a casework service to a large number of scattered families but by establishing projects in selected localities. This step tended to place the child-care societies in socially deprived areas and so signified a readiness to acknowledge the re-emergence of poverty. It also laid the foundations of promoting skills that took account of environmental as well as individual problems.

The Meaning of Prevention

Despite the problems encountered by prevention, its meaning was enlarged during the 1970s. The SSDs took over as the local authority *agent* with the main responsibility for prevention. The child-care voluntaries accepted that they also were agents of prevention. Just as important, some social commentators were arguing that, as the cause of families' problems frequently rested in societal rather than individual forces, then the agents of change had to comprise, to cite Brown and Madge, 'the full range of central and local government departments and major programmes of social and economic intervention'.[105]

Under the child-care officers the *scope* of their preventative practice had been extended from deprived children to those subject to cruelty and neglect and then to those likely to be delinquent. Similarly the *objectives* of prevention widened from preventing children being taken from their families to preventing them from suffering in their own homes. Even if not so rigorously pursued, these objectives were still officially stated in the 1970s.[106] But the scope and objectives were also reformulated in two directions. Firstly, Sir Keith Joseph saw the scope as embracing the children of inadequate parents and called for 'preventive work', whose objective was to prevent the children repeating the mistakes of their parents. Secondly, and in a different direction, as the destructive effects of poverty on family life became more evident, so a core of social workers in both the statutory and voluntary sectors wanted to draw the children of the poor into the preventative ring. Their objective was not just to avoid having to remove them from their homes but to enable them to avoid within their homes the emotional and physical sufferings associated with grinding poverty.

The *targets* or *subjects* of prevention in the heyday of the children's departments were sometimes the parents and sometimes the children, although there were also indications of concentrating on the family as a unit or system. The focus on the family was strengthened in the years following reorganisation, for generic social workers were expected to give families most of their attention. But some did maintain a more specific orientation. For instance, intermediate treatment practitioners tended to concentrate on teenagers whom they wished to keep out of custodial institutions. In addition, new ideas about the nature of social problems led to greater prominence being given to other targets. The cycle of deprivation thesis led to the deduction that the life-style of a whole core of so-called inadequate people had to change. By contrast the growing popularisation of a structural explanation of poverty – along with the links made between poverty and child separations – led its adherents to claim that the target for change was society itself. In short, they argued that the most significant boost to prevention would be a more equal society in which a fairer distribution of power, status and resources would free some families from having to behave in ways which entailed unsatisfactory care for their children. Thus not only did prevention endure many problems in the decade following Seebohm but its meaning also became more complicated as it extended the range and variety of its targets.

Stages of prevention

In Chapter 2 attention was drawn to the tactics used by the preventative agents. In this chapter the tactics can be included in an analysis of the stages of prevention, the concept of which was derived from its use in the medical world. *Primary* prevention entailed stopping the emergence of a disease, as, for instance, when the installation of efficient water systems virtually eliminated cholera and typhoid; *secondary* prevention meant the treatment of an identified illness like the application of drugs to cure pneumonia; and *tertiary* prevention meant limiting the effects of an illness or even reversing its course.

Within the arena of preventing children having to leave their families or of enduring unsatisfactory experiences within them, Parker states that 'primary prevention is thought of as comprising those services which provide general support to families and reduce the levels of poverty, stress, insecurity, ill-health or bad housing to which they may otherwise be exposed'.[107] In terms of preventative tactics the approach is to ensure to all families those basic necessities which make good parenting possible. The advent of the post-war welfare reforms can be regarded as a major step of primary prevention in that it gave more families access to a better standard of living. Yet the 1970s saw the publication of investigations which revealed that primary needs were still not being properly met for certain sections of the population. For instance, the limitation of housing provision was revealed in the association between poor housing conditions and families whose children were received into public care. Perhaps even more surprising was the failure of the health services. Parker pointed out that 'the ill-health of the parent was involved in 25 per cent of all admissions of children to care in England and Wales in 1976'.[108] In other words the tactic of primary prevention was failing to remove certain families from social distress which could lead to suffering and even separation for their children. Significantly, during the 1970s, successive governments failed to acknowledge the link between social provision and primary prevention. The Children's Act of 1975 stands as a landmark of a government which chose to pursue policies which facilitated the removal of children from their families while refusing to strengthen measures of primary prevention.

Secondary prevention is help offered once problems have actually arisen within families. Parker explains: 'At this stage services are liable to be restricted to those who are assumed to be at "special risk" or whose circumstances warrant special priority'.[109] The SSDs met a number of setbacks in their preventative mission in the 1970s, yet many social workers worked hard in the realm of secondary prevention. Some would have continued to use the old child-care skills of supporting and encouraging parents to cope through stressful times. Others developed a welfare-rights approach both as a means of alleviating the sufferings of the poor and of bolstering their self-confidence by equipping them to negotiate with social security officials. These different tactics count as secondary prevention when they were aimed at families identified as having specific child-care problems.

Another tactic of this stage was finding an alternative to care or custody. Consider intermediate treatment, which the National Children's Bureau study defined as 'a range or combination of programmes and provisions aimed at bridging the gap between the two extremes of compulsory removal of the young person from his family and community and of leaving the young person in his environment without any controls or treatment provisions'.[110] IT was sometimes used by courts as an addition to a supervision order. SSDs, probation departments and voluntary bodies also began to draw into IT schemes youngsters considered to be at risk of delinquency even though no formal order was made. Although no wide-scale research was yet available, early indications seemed promising. Thus a follow-up in Norfolk of seventeen children who had had long records of delinquency found that 2 years after their IT orders only one was in residential care.[111] As a result IT schemes received enthusiastic backing in some parts of the country, although in others a lack of cash meant they were slow to get off the ground.

IT serves as a good example of secondary prevention. It offered an alternative to custody or care to youngsters identified as showing problems. Yet for all its apparent success, IT was not without its critics. One criticism was that it seemed to pin the blame for delinquency firmly on the youngsters and their families without considering the part played by their environment.[112] Another was that sometimes it drew in youngsters with no or few offences, and by bringing them into the 'crime system' actually precipitated rather than prevented delinquency. This kind of dilemma was increasingly to face those social workers practising secondary prevention. It entailed identifying people as having something wrong with them in order to offer them a service. Yet this very identification, it was suggested, contained elements of making people feel abnormal. Thus the early years of the SSDs witnessed the growing appreciation of the role of secondary prevention along with a concern that it might also contain some drawbacks.

The third stage, of tertiary prevention, aims 'at avoiding the worst consequences of a child actually having to spend long periods in substitute care'.[113] Two major approaches stand out. One is to ensure that the form of substitute care is of a high quality in order to minimise the effects of separation. The other is to rehabilitate the children to their parents. Yet research showed that the latter was woefully neglected by social workers in the 1970s, with Thorpe's study revealing that rehabilitation was only considered in 5 per cent of cases.[114] Against this, Thoburn's research in Britain confirmed American studies that determined efforts by social workers to maintain links between natural parents and children in care could promote many returns home.[115] In the 1970s therefore rehabilitation emerged as a neglected yet potentially effective form of tertiary prevention.

The discussion of prevention in terms of stages may give the appearance of neat divisions where none exist. Thus day care could be employed at all stages. It could be seen as a universal service providing necessary socialisation experiences for all children in the primary stage. It could fit in the secondary stage when used to help a family identified as having child-care problems to get through a crisis, or it could be utilised at the tertiary stage as a bridge to enable natural parents to receive back the care of their children. Nonetheless the concept of stages does constitute a useful tool for examining prevention. Looking back on the 1970s one can see that the government failed to maintain primary prevention while SSDs gave insufficient attention to tertiary prevention. Some social workers did pursue secondary prevention, notwithstanding a lack of resources, criticisms of their work, and a dawning appreciation that its practice posed some dilemmas.

Decade of disappointment

Prevention in this period was not fully pursued at the primary, secondary or tertiary stages. Given that the era was preceded by the Seebohm Report which highlighted the importance of prevention, the advocates of prevention must have been disappointed that the early years of reorganisation were accompanied by setbacks, confusion, pressures, criticisms and conflicts, all of which were detrimental to prevention. The setbacks derived from the reorganisation itself, which resulted in increasing demands on social workers who were then less able to concentrate on prevention. The confusion was spread unwittingly from the impact of Sir Keith Joseph's promulgation of his cycle of deprivation. Social workers who had built up a practice based on compassion and support found it difficult to reconcile their casework principles with the new implication that somehow they should be controlling a breed of inadequate families. The pressures came from those families who found their lives shattered by poverty and turned to the new SSDs for aid. The criticisms spilled out from a media which blamed social workers for the sufferings of young children at the hands of their parents. The conflicts occurred with the advocates of the doctrine of permanency. Prevention was thus undermined both on the grounds of practicalities ('there are not sufficient resources') and of priorities ('protection and permanency must come before prevention and rehabilitation'). Hence the title of this chapter, 'Problems for Prevention'.

Given these changes, it may be no surprise that prevention as measured by the numbers being kept out of public care and custody should reveal some disappointing trends. In England and Wales the number of children in the care of local authorities rose from 87,400 in 1971 to over 100,000 in 1977.[116] Parker further points out that not only did this indicate an increase from the days of the children's departments, but that children were also staying in care for longer periods. Moreover these trends were occurring at a time when the child population was declining in number.[117] Again, the number of young males given custodial sentences by the courts remained high. In 1977 such sentences were made against 6,800 males under 17 years and 19,600 aged 17 to 21.[118] These figures cannot just be attributed to the failure of the personal social services to undertake prevention. Factors outside the power of social workers were at work: social deprivations were undermining some families, a rising divorce rate was accompanied by an increasing number of children committed to care under court matrimonial proceedings, and some magistrates appeared more willing than before to make custodial sentences. Nonetheless the supporters of prevention must have been disappointed that the preventative promise heralded by the planting of the new SSDs had not come to fruition.

Yet the disappointments should not be overstated. This volume is partly about tracing the history of prevention, and the 1970s, for all its problems, did give rise to new developments. The new SSDs had to take over the legislative duty for prevention which had rested on the smaller children's departments. With their more extensive facilities, the SSDs were able to use day care as part of a package for enabling parents to cope with their children. Intermediate treatment took off as another alternative to care and custody.

Along with the so-called rediscovery of poverty, some social workers evolved skills to help families whose security and unity were threatened less by individual psychological defects and more by the effects of social deprivations. Not least, the decade witnessed the child-care voluntary societies debating their own futures and opting to seek a preventative role for themselves.

4. Prevention at Present

The 1980s opened with the Child Care Act 1980. However, this was a consolidation act and made no new provisions for prevention. The case for prevention had still to be restated and this chapter will show that, despite opposition and setbacks, prevention did make progress during the 1980s.

For Prevention

Pressure-group activity

Just as pressure groups had led the campaign to implement the Seebohm Report, so they did in an effort to re-establish prevention. But they were different kinds of pressure groups and included the long established One Parent Families, the Family Rights Group – which had been formed in opposition to the Children Bill of 1975 – and consumer groups such as Justice for Children and Parents Against Injustice (PAIN). In a flurry of activity they drew attention to cases where natural parents had suffered injustices. One Parent Families published *Against Natural Justice*, which listed examples of children being wrongly removed from their families and of local authorities which passed parental-rights resolutions under section 2 of the 1948 Act (now section 3 of the 1980 Act) without sufficient evidence and, in some cases, without even informing the parents.[1] Similarly the Family Rights Group cited instances where SSDs terminated contact between parents and children without good reason.[2] Meanwhile Justice for Children took up the 50,000 names by then listed in child-abuse registers. It established that minor incidents could lead to names being included, often without the parent's knowledge, while their very inclusion then increased 'the chances of the state intervening to remove the child from its parents'.[3] One couple found themselves on the register because of their child's injuries, which were later

proved to be due to brittle bone disease. In reaction they formed
PAIN for parents like themselves.[4] Together all the pressure
groups argued that matters were weighted against the parents and
that frequently they did not get a fair hearing in court or from
SSDs. They pointed to the nature of *guardian-ad-litems* – implemented in the 1980s from the Children Act 1975 – who were
intended to provide independent evidence where parents and local
authorities were in dispute in court. Yet the guardians tended to
be chosen from panels of statutory social workers, though from
neighbouring authorities, and thus could not really be said to be
independent.[5]

As well as criticising defects which led to the wrongful removal
of children, the groups also campaigned for more positive preventative action. The Family Rights Group urged that the statutory
duty to undertake prevention be executed by local authorities as a
whole, and not just by SSDs, so that housing and educational
services would make a fuller contribution. SSDs, it recommended,
could boost prevention by expanding day-care and home-help
resources. In common with One Parent Families it campaigned for
the principle that parental rights be only removed via a judicial
hearing where parents were legally represented. In common with
the National Association of Young People In Care it called for a
government review of child-care legislation. In common with the
National Foster Care Association it publicised the notion of 'shared
care', which, in contrast to permanence, retained a partnership
between parents, substitute parents and local authority.[6]

The campaigns often provoked counter-attacks. Some SSD
directors objected to what they saw as a crusade on behalf of
natural parents against departments which were only trying to
protect children. In an article about the rise of these pressure
groups a spokesperson for the British Agencies for Adoption and
Fostering reasserted the view that at an early stage 'in a child's life
you have to put its interests before its parents'.[7] However, it is
worth interjecting that, during the mid-eighties, agencies like FRG
and BAAF acknowledged much common ground between them.
Despite the counter-attacks and despite their shoestring budgets,
the pressure groups did make a public impact. For instance, they
played a major part in the campaign which led to the Health and
Social Services and Social Security Adjudications Act of 1983,
which gave natural parents a right of appeal to the courts when

local authorities cut off complete access to their children. Their
emergence and growing influence is hard to explain. All that can
be said is that they provided a focus for some lawyers who were
moved by the injustices suffered by natural parents, for social
activists who witnessed some of the adverse consequences of
social-work decisions upon families, and for natural parents who
wanted to fight back against a system which seemed to hold all the
power. Whatever the explanation, these child-care groups not only
rendered assistance to many families but also took the lead in
bringing the case for prevention back to the public.

Pressure from within social work

Meanwhile, in 1983, social workers formed a Special Interest
Group in Prevention and Rehabilitation in Child Care within
BASW. It revived the old argument that prevention was cheaper
than removing children by drawing upon a study by the Barnet
SSD which compared the costs of preventive work with a sample
of families with the costs of keeping them in care. Even allowing
that not all could be prevented, it demonstrated a saving of £1.3
million per year.[8] The group pointed out that, if applied nationally, an economic case could be made for expanding preventative
services.

The group then turned to exposing the limitations of theories of
permanency and, in addition, showed that in practice their placements often were not very permanent.[9] The group's vigorous
chairperson, Jane Tunstill, even challenged the sacred cow of 'the
welfare of the child' concept, which had frequently been cited by
the permanency school as the justification for keeping a child in a
stable foster or intended adoptive home even when it was possible
to return him or her home. Tunstill agreed that the child's needs
were vital but argued that his or her welfare was not necessarily
best served by staying with substitute parents, that children who
could not return home might yet prefer to retain links with their
parents and, moreover, that the welfare of the child was not being
fully considered if SSDs were not providing services which offered
the option of prevention or rehabilitation.[10]

In 1984 Tunstill declared that it was paradoxical that SSDs had
developed codes of practice on access and fostering but not on
prevention.[11] The group therefore devised a model code, which it

submitted to BASW for endorsement in the hope that it would encourage SSDs to do likewise. Thus through its publications and conferences the group made progress towards its aim of 'reintroducing the related concepts of prevention and rehabilitation to a position of priority in the minds of policy makers and practitioners'.[12]

Official reports

The cause of prevention was not just pleaded by independent pressure groups and small organisations of social workers. Official reports also added their weight. In 1980 the Conservative government asked the National Institute for Social Work to set up an inquiry to 'review the role and tasks of social workers in local authority social services departments and related agencies'.[13] The ensuing Barclay Report, named after its chairperson Peter Barclay, was published in 1982. It devoted space to clarifying the nature of and justifying the value of social work and then made such suggestions for improving its practice as establishing an inspectorate or raising standards of training. But its major theme was that SSDs should practise community social work, which it defined as 'social work which . . . seeks to tap into, support, enable and underpin the local networks of formal and informal relationships which constitute our basic definition of community'.[14] While offering no organisational blueprint, it reckoned that community social work would be more accessible to the public and would make greater use of local resources than the prevailing system.[15] A three-person minority report reasoned that its implementation would require more than a change of social-work attitudes and proposed that all SSDs decentralise into area teams covering up to 30,000 people, with patch teams of social service staff covering up to 10,000.[16] Social work then really would be close to the community.

The community social-work ideas were totally rejected by one member, Professor Pinker, and they met a mixed reaction outside. But whatever the differences, the Barclay Report was of significance for prevention. It accepted that 'social services departments, through their social workers, have a responsibility for creating, stimulating and supporting networks in the community which may prevent the occurrence of some social problems'.[17] The first official review of local authority SSDs not only challenged the lack of priority which they had been awarding to prevention but it also claimed that one of the many advantages of community social work was that it would facilitate prevention amongst all client groups.

The Barclay Report dealt with a whole range of social-work activities. The inquiry set up by the Social Services Committee of the House of Commons arose specifically because of the 'growing debate about the rights of children and the rights of parents' and concern about the decisions being made for deprived children.[18] Chaired by Renee Short MP and published in 1984, the report ranged over many child-care matters but prevention was its key theme. It declared: 'While there is a general acceptance that more could and should be done explicitly to prevent children entering long-term care . . . there is as yet regrettably little indication of any concerted strategy which could translate pious thought into action'.[19] The committee blamed the lack of preventative action on managers who lacked the 'organisational commitment to prevention to parallel that to fostering and adoption';[20] on social workers who gave it too low a priority;[21] and on society which 'does not take kindly to money spent with uncertain results on socially incompetent families, although vastly greater sums spent on rescuing the victims of such circumstances are apparently less begrudged'.[22]

In order to facilitate prevention the Short Report urged local authorities to develop services like child-minders and daily fosterings to enable parents to cope with their own children.[23] It commended the idea of a social-work manager with special responsibility for rehabilitation, which was a statutory duty 'pursued with insufficient vigour'.[24] It wanted such legislative changes to protect natural parents as the abolition of local authorities' powers to remove parental rights without a court hearing[25] and a duty placed on them to rehabilitate all children in their care and not just those admitted under voluntary procedures.[26] It also gave support to the idea of a family court as the setting to decide the future of children.

As the work of a committee of MPs, the Short Report received much public attention; and the public's attention was drawn to prevention for it made more recommendations about this than any other topic. Not even the Seebohm Report had given prevention such priority. Moreover it was the first major official document to pose a serious challenge to the doctrine of permanency. In strong language it warned that the application of the doctrine meant that 'the courts and parents are being bounced into accepting adoption'.[27] It asserted that the emphasis on permanency, by which was meant adoption, had led to a disregard of practices which either enabled parents permanently to look after their own children or to retain links with them while in long-term care. By identifying the features which impaired prevention and by stating quite specifically how it could be promoted, the Short Report made an enormous contribution to the case for prevention.

The Barclay Committee, composed mainly of social-work figures, may have stirred up the social-work world. But the government made no steps to speed the implementation of its proposals. The Short Committee represented the views of Members of Parliament and thus probably carried more weight. Certainly the government accepted the Short plea for 'a major review of the legal framework of child care' and an interdepartmental committee speedily published, in 1985, a *Review of Child Care Law*.[28] Its 223 recommendations cannot be summarised here but it must be noted that it gave prevention the major billing in the following ways. Firstly, it called for a more positive approach to prevention, with less emphasis on keeping children out of care and more on local authorities having 'a broad power to provide services to promote the care and upbringing of children with their families'.[29] To this end it backed the concept of 'respite care', under which parents could place their children for short periods while still retaining the prime responsibility for them. Should the placements continue for over a month, however, it would change from respite to 'shared care', which was equivalent to the present mode of voluntary care, with placements ending on parental request.[30]

Secondly, desiring to protect natural parents, the working party agreed that the local-authority power to assume parental rights should be abolished, so that any compulsory removals would have to be via the courts.[31] Pointing out that access restrictions imposed by SSDs upon natural parents often made 'long term fostering or even adoption a foregone conclusion', it proposed that local authorities had to make clear any wish to deny access at the start of care proceedings, so that the court could make the decision. Any later alterations in access would be subject to challenge in the courts by parents.[32]

Thirdly, in order to reduce the number of children in care, the working party advocated various changes, so that, for instance, non-school attendance could no longer be a sole ground for making a care order while restrictions would be placed on the use of place of safety orders and interim care orders whose accelerating use was causing SSDs to make 'unwarranted intervention' into the lives of children.[33] In addition, it agreed that local authorities should have a duty – unless contrary to the children's interests – to return all children in care to their families, and to this end should be empowered to pay for children to visit their parents, while parents should be given the right to apply for the discharge of a care order.[34]

The publication of the review met a generally favourable response. The preventative school did express some fears that the proposals could unwittingly increase numbers in care. The attractiveness of respite and shared care could encourage more parents to use public care, but once drawn into the welfare net, they might find it difficult to leave a system geared towards treating children rather than returning them. Some social workers felt the report failed to make a link between legal requirements and social-work practice and did not, for example, specify how often social workers should visit natural parents. Maurice Hawker, the director of Essex SSD, criticised it for ignoring the importance of professional practice.[35] BASW regretted that it omitted any discussion of family courts,[36] and the Family Rights Group criticised it for failing to make proposals to counter primary poverty. But these criticisms were in the context of much praise.

Together the *Review of Child Care Law* and the Short Report indicate an important change from the official thinking that had dominated the Houghton Report and the 1975 Children Act. The earlier documents had majored on legislation to remove children, the latest ones on the need for legislation to enable parents to keep or receive back their children. Moreover the review had outlined its recommendations in such detail that rapid legislation was a possibility, should the government so decide. When added to the Barclay Report and the various pressure group publications, the Short Report and the review completed a formidable case for action to facilitate prevention. Not since the 1960s had the tide of opinion moved so strongly in favour of the preventative school.

Against Prevention

The new recession

Just as the case for prevention was being revived, so Britain descended into an economic recession which bore comparison with that of the 1930s. Falling trade, a balance of payments crisis, rising inflation and falling investment led to an upsurge in unemployment which reached 3¼ million persons, 13.5 per cent of the workforce in 1984.[37] The Conservative government's response was monetarist policies, which included cutting taxes on higher income groups, attempting to hold down wage claims and cuts in public expenditure. Whatever the merits of this approach, and it did check inflation, the outcome was more unemployment. In addition, the levels of supplementary benefit and child benefit were pegged and the numbers in poverty, i.e. those living below, on or just above the basic rates, rose to over 16 million by 1983.[38]

Rising unemployment and poverty resulted in more referrals to local-authority social services. Yet simultaneously they were facing financial restraints. For example, the Rate Support Grant Settlement for 1985–6 reduced the central-government contribution to local-government expenditure from 51.9 to 48.7 per cent. The government also imposed cash limits on local expenditure.[39] Thus, far from expanding services to meet pressures, some local authorities were hard pressed to maintain existing standards. Local-authority housing was particularly hard hit, so that in 1982 the number of new units achieved plummeted to a record low of 49,200. A survey published by the Association of Directors of Social Services for 1985–6 revealed that only the London boroughs had increased expenditure; elsewhere growth was static or in decline.[40] New initiatives did occur but often at the expense of cuts elsewhere. Most marked were reductions in day-care services in nearly half the SSDs.[41] Ironically they were being made at the very time when research was confirming the link between day care and keeping children out of care.[42] A survey by the Association of Metropolitan Authorities concluded that 'services are contracting in some authorities and others are certainly not able to cope with new demands'.[43]

More poverty was combined with services unable to cope. The implications for prevention were twofold. Firstly, the quality of life was lowered for sections of the population. In 1984 the number of homeless households in England reached an all-time high of 83,000. Outside the city centres large council estates were also marked by high levels of unemployment, few public amenities, poor transport systems and growing housing problems of dampness and disrepair. Such conditions weighed the odds against parents who were struggling to provide satisfactory home and community experiences for their families.

Secondly, the declining circumstances served to underline the connection between social deprivations and the risk of family break-ups. Packman and her colleagues studied two large samples of children to whom 'serious consideration' was given to admission to care. They recorded in 1984 'that substantial numbers suffered from a variety of financial difficulties' and were 'under considerable stress from poverty, poor health and strained and broken relationships'.[44] A year later Tunstill cited research in one authority showing over 80 per cent of children in their care as coming from poor families.[45] Mention should also be made that certain ethnic-minority children were disproportionately likely to be in public care. One reason was that their families were especially vulnerable to social deprivations, though the existence of racist attitudes within the social services could also be a factor drawing them into public care.[46]

Thus the cumulative effects of the recession intensified social deprivation and so increased the chances of more children suffering unhappy and unsatisfactory experiences. Yet the local authorities were unable to respond with improved preventative services. As the Short Report wryly commented, 'preventative work was all too often an early casualty of financial pressures'.[47]

Academic opposition

Economic conditions were hampering prevention. Moreover the prevention school was not having it all its own way in the battle of words. The Barclay Report had contained powerful pleading to make prevention, in a wide sense, a major function of SSDs. Professor Pinker in a dissenting note, and in subsequent articles, objected not so much to the objectives of prevention but to the community social work which Barclay saw as one of the means of conveying prevention. He disliked both the notion of community as a basis for social work and the proposal to organise social work from neighbourhood bases. He doubted whether local communities could sustain 'patterns of informal care' as an alternative to professional help.[48] He claimed that the patchwork model of organisation would 'put the future of social work in jeopardy' and he foresaw it mobilising local groups for radical political ends or, at the other extreme, being used to generate informal help in order 'to justify drastic cuts in statutory funding'.[49]

Instead of community social work, Robert Pinker claimed that 'our present model of so-called client-centred social work is basically sound but in need of a better defined and less ambitious mandate'.[50] He placed his faith in a professional elite of highly trained caseworkers to concentrate on clients whose needs or malfunctioning definitely drew them to the attention of the SSDs. 'I am an elitist', he declared, 'and I see the eventual formation of a general council and the professionalisation of social work as useful means to that end.'[51]

Clearly the professor held the broad notion of prevention inherent in the community approach to be counter-productive, threatening and dangerous: counter-productive in that local families would not want help from neighbours,[52] threatening in that 'the idea of preventive social work on a local basis would seriously threaten the right to privacy'[53], and dangerous in that it allowed the state 'to intrude too far into the private worlds of individuals, families and local communities'.[54] Instead of focusing on communities, social work should be 'reactive rather than preventive in approach and modest in its objectives. Social work ought to be preventive with respect to the needs which come to its attention: it has neither the capacity, the resources nor the mandate to go looking for needs in the community at large'.[55]

Pinker's arguments, motivated by a desire to uphold social-work standards, are exaggerated as well as flawed. Much of his case depends on erecting Aunt Sallies which he then knocks down. He enjoyed demolishing the report's rosy concept of community as something which would 'resolve all our policy dilemmas'.[56] In fact, the report acknowledged many of the limitations of a community approach. Again, he attacked the advocates of community social work for setting in motion a process that could become a framework for left-wing or right-wing extremists. Yet no member of the Barclay Committee even hinted at desiring such ends. Further, experiments in community social work made known *before* the Barclay Report contained evidence to undermine his fears. They suggested that communities did possess helping networks which social workers could stimulate and tap. Moreover, far from diminishing the skills of social workers, as Pinker anticipated, neighbourhood-based work appeared to enhance them. Not least, the experiments did not justify the accusations that a neighbourhood approach was not acceptable to those in need, that it endangered privacy or that it extended state intrusion. Indeed, it could be argued that their preventative successes saved parents from revealing personal details in court and freed them from state action to take over their children.

In defending the client-centred model of social work, Pinker overlooked the fact that the Barclay Committee was set up precisely because the old model was seen to be failing. For instance, it had been realised that the concentration on clients who had to approach SSDs meant that not only did social-work intervention occur too late but it conveyed a stigma which worsened the clients' plight. Again, as Jordan explains, Pinker fails to explain how his casework agency could cope with the increasing number of deprived people whom the recession was forcing to turn to the SSDs.[57] Whatever the merits of Pinker's criticisms, he had nothing to offer in terms of making prevention more effective.

Pinker rendered a valuable service in pinpointing some of the difficulties faced by community social work. But his words of foreboding also weakened the Barclay case for SSDs to have a broad preventative remit. In times of cut-backs his plea for restriction was likely to find favour, and may explain why the community proposals of the Barclay Report never received any official implementation via central government action.

At least Pinker wanted to retain a restricted preventative function for SSDs. David Billis of Brunel University, more extremely, stated that '"preventive" social services work is a misleading and harmful notion' and so 'raised doubts about the validity of prevention in social services work'.[58] For a start he considered that welfare bodies were faced with a 'considerable dilemma' if 'Time spent working with breakdown situations (such as residential care) must compete on theoretically unfavourable terms with the more attractive goal of prevention'.[59] Next he argued that homelessness, ill-health and low income should be met in their own right instead of 'subsumed within some giant preventive umbrella'.[60] Rather welfare agencies should concentrate on social break-down, which he defined as arising if 'an individual is either already in an institution or, if no action is taken, is judged to require some form of institutionalisation within an explicit period of time'.[61]

Billis is right to criticise woolly definitions of prevention. But he does not make a watertight case against the social services undertaking its practice. What if the notion of prevention does provoke dilemmas? Priority disputes will exist whether prevention is pursued or not. Further, the existence of a preventative role in the 1970s certainly did not make it the favoured outlet for expenditure. Again, few would deny that housing departments should house the homeless and health services should treat the sick. The prevention school has merely argued that sometimes the personal social services can help children avoid distressing experiences, not that they should replace basic services. Not least, it must be said that Billis's choice of a social break-down function for welfare agencies is also problematic. If agencies concentrated on institutions, they would be providing services which are now often considered to harm inmates. Yet even his definition of social break-down contains a preventative side. If clients are to be institutionalised 'if no action is taken', then the implication is that sometimes officials will take appropriate action. What is this, if not prevention?

Far from being a harmful concept, the historical review of prevention has illustrated its usefulness and importance. It will be recalled that, following the Children Act 1948 some children's departments allowed applications for reception into care to be handled by clerks. They just processed the requests, for they appeared to use only the notion of removal. Once child-care officers, who held a concept of prevention, took over, the flood of children entering care was diminished. Significantly the same officers considered it a dilemma *not* to have a clear mandate to undertake prevention while simultaneously working with break-down situations, and it was they who pressed for it to be specified in legislation. Further, it should be clear that the concept of prevention is closely linked to a widely held value, namely that it is usually best for children to stay with their own parents. The present review suggests that this value is upheld most forcibly when welfare agencies have a clear concept of and commitment to prevention.

Pinker and Billis were not the only academics to cast doubts upon prevention. Dingwall, Eekalaar and Murray wanted more state intervention in child-abuse cases.[62] Their arguments, though, were ably countered by Parton, who pointed out that 'they gave no serious role to prevention'.[63] So academics raised challenges as to what extent SSDs should undertake prevention just at the time when the influx of referrals and cuts in expenditure was making it difficult for them to do so. But, in contrast to the previous decade, the case for prevention was being just as well articulated. The SSDs were beginning to develop the will for a greater extension of preventative work even if they did not always have the resources.

Social Work: Negative and Positive

Negative image

Local authorities discharge their preventative duty through their SSDs. But whether those in need of help will accept their services depends much on their image of social work. Despite the anti-social-work hysteria whipped up by sections of the press in the 1970s following the Maria Colwell tragedy, a national survey in 1981 found that 48 per cent of respondents had a favourable impression of social workers, while, of those who had actually had contact, 60 per cent were satisfied with the help received. Yet 8 per cent considered that social workers were 'too ready to remove children'.[64] The evidence was that hostility existed amongst a minority who feared the removal of their children.[65] As the Barclay Report concluded, 'relationships between social workers and families whose children are in care, or are seen as being at risk of being received into care, against their parents' wishes, are coloured by fear and suspicion'.[66]

This negative image of social work is most vividly portrayed by some consumers. Graham Gaskin, who spent his childhood in care, has written bitterly about his experiences.[67] Not so well known is an account by Pauline, who lived with her husband in poor conditions and whose child was removed by the SSD on suspicion of abuse. Her second baby was taken and sent for adoption despite her objections. On the day she gave birth to her third a nurse took Pauline for some tests. In her absence social workers removed that child. Later Pauline demonstrated that she could cope. She remarried, won back two of her children and bore a fourth, and from her position of family strength worked to help others. But her experiences left her hostile towards social work. She wrote: 'It is horrible when you bring a child into the world and it is living with someone else. You are called an unfit mother and they say you aren't capable of looking after any more children".[68]

No doubt the fear and hostility stemmed from some of the practices associated with the permanence movement, as described in the last chapter. Jordan thus warned:

> The danger is that social workers will adopt a policing style which issues a number of statutory warnings and threats, and then acts decisively to secure the transfer of parental rights, first to the local authority and then to substitute parents. The fact is that such an agency would overwhelmingly be taking children from poor and disadvantaged parents and placing them with better-off parents.[69]

True, permanency practices were not presented so stridently in the 1980s, while many social workers would not act in the way described by Jordan, but examples of unjust removals were still occurring and the damage was done. The results were unfortunate. Carole Satyamurti observed that some clients felt they were regarded, and indeed were treated, as demeaned people who were unable to perform socially responsible roles.[70] Clearly such families believed that association with social workers conveyed a sense of stigma, which Allen, in his study of stigma in social work, describes as meaning 'the social disgrace . . . which attaches to different conditions'.[71] Stigma has a powerful deterring effect; indeed Pinker states that it is the 'commonest form of violence used in democratic societies'.[72] The conveyance of judgement and threat thus makes some needy parents reluctant to approach social workers. As the founder of PAIN put it, 'People are terrified to ask for help because they feel their child might be taken away'.[73]

The Seebohm Committee had hoped that users of the SSDs would feel no more stigma than when using state schools. Their vision has not been fully fulfilled. Visits from social workers to assess parental capabilities and the possibility of removal can transmit to parents and children feelings of guilt and condemnation which reinforce rather than relieve social problems. Herein rests a major challenge for the preventative social services, namely how to concentrate help on vulnerable families without imposing a sense of stigma. For social workers the question is whether they can counter the negative image of social work.

Positive image

Even social workers may hold a poor image of some of their services. As a recent research review put it, 'Virtually all social workers appear to view admission to care very negatively'.[74] Hence the prevention school has tried to keep children with their parents, while the permanence school has tried to by-pass public care into, preferably, adoptive homes. Of late, however, some authors have called for a more positive image of care.

Residential care has long been subject to criticisms. But David Berridge contends that the best establishments can be a base for children who want to maintain links with parents and for that small number who want to identify the institution as their home.[75] Susan Loveday, who followed into adulthood children from the homes of the Children's Society, noted that establishments could keep together siblings who might otherwise have been split assunder.[76] Along with other departments which are promoting a more positive view, the Strathclyde Social Work Department published a review which argued that its establishments' purposes were 'assessment, rehabilitation, preparation for new families, preparation for independent living and care, control and treatment'.[77]

Foster care has also discovered renewed support. Jane Rowe and her colleagues' study of long-term fosterings, while pointing out some of the advantages of adoption, declares 'that it would be a serious mistake to assume that *all* long-term foster children could or should be adopted'.[78] Suzan Theze of the National Foster Care Association has articulated the role of a foster-care occupation with the 'social skills of maintaining and strengthening links with the child's own family'.[79] As Fuller and Stevenson make clear, this kind of foster care is in 'conflict with the view of those who advocate permanency planning' and is a reaffirmation of a form of local authority care.[80]

These arguments for residential and foster care share a common element in that both have contributed to the notion of shared care which emerged in the *Review of Child Care Law*. The hope is that parents would regard care as a positive resource which they choose to use. Jordan has now taken up this theme of positive care to extend the notion of prevention. Prevention viewed just as stopping children entering care, he argues, makes parents unaware that public care can be 'a means of achieving long-term improvements in family relationships'.[81] If both social workers and parents esteemed care more highly, it could be used more fully for the children's well-being. The crucial element then becomes the nature of care, and Jordan insists that positive care is only achieved if it enables parents and children still to maintain their relationships. The meaning of prevention, where parents can not themselves offer long-term homes, then becomes, to cite Jordan, 'to prevent the loss of meaningful links between the child and his parents, friends and community'.[82]

Jordan, and those of like mind, are not only extending the meaning of prevention, they are also changing that of permanence. In the 1970s it meant being placed permanently with substitute parents with no links with natural parents, in order to give security from disruption. But if permanency now allows the inclusion of natural parents, then a new term is required, and June Aldgate has come up with 'inclusive permanency'. Citing research findings to demonstrate that links with parents do help children while in long-term care,[83] she even disproves the much voiced fear that natural parents automatically disrupt placements. She also points out that the recent implementation of custodianship (from the 1975 Act) offers a new kind of legal security for foster parents while still allowing contact with natural parents. Not all contemporary researchers would go as far as Aldgate but the balance of evidence seems to support her conclusion that 'the retaining of bonds with families of origin and the successful making of attachments to permanent alternative families are compatible concepts'.[84]

The positive image of public care has been bolstered by studies that stress the achievements of residential and foster care. Now authors like Jordan and Aldgate are arguing that even long-term public care can be positive if children retain links with their natural families: positive because it benefits the child, is more acceptable to parents, and is not inconsistent with security for foster parents.

In the final chapter I shall express some doubts about the feasibility of positive care but few will doubt its desirability. Steps are thus being taken to give care a positive rather than a negative image. The negative image of social work made some natural parents fearful of co-operating with the social services. In so doing, it has impaired prevention. By contrast, the image of positive care is one that implies sharing care with natural parents so that their children can either be rehabilitated or they can maintain relationships with them even if removed permanently. The breaking of the negative and the promoting of the positive will depend very much on the activities of social workers, for research studies suggest that their skills and attitudes have a crucial influence on the involvement of natural parents.[85] The next section will explore to what extent SSDs and their social workers did respond to the challenge of prevention in the 1980s.

The Response of the SSDs

During the 1980s SSDs were still subject to pressures about child abuse. More investigations, especially those concerning the tragic deaths of Tyra Henry and Jasmine Beckford, led to more criticisms of social workers. Documents from the DHSS and BASW extended the definition of child abuse and specified the procedures to be followed in investigating, supervising and removing children.[86, 87] Incidents of sexual abuse also received publicity, often with the innuendo that social workers were not active enough in stopping children being molested by relatives. As Laurance observed, 'the defensiveness of social workers fearful of a child battering case and its attendant publicity, can result in them putting all their efforts into getting control of the child'.[88] It seemed like the 1970s, only made worse by the economic recession. But the position was different in the 1980s. SSDs were now established bodies, while, as shown, a strong case for prevention was being articulated. This section will therefore discuss how SSDs developed in four spheres crucial to statutory prevention: policies, organisation, avoiding custody and relationships with natural parents.

Policies and procedures

Throughout the 80s SSDs continued to make available family aids, day fosterings, day care, small grants and individual support. It was never enough but it helped some parents in their child-care tasks. Preventative innovations occurred. In Birmingham a day-care centre numerically demonstrated its success in keeping out of public care children referred because of abuse or neglect. Importantly, its staff did so not by treating the parents as 'pathological' but by enabling them to fulfil their parental roles.[89] The Strathclyde Social Work Department devised a scheme of contracts with parents and children with severe school-attendance problems. Failure to keep the conditions could result in short periods in an assessment centre. Early indicators were that the majority of children were avoiding what at one time had seemed inevitable long-term removals from home.

However, continuing services and new innovations do not constitute a preventative policy. The Special Interest Group on Prevention and Rehabilitation examined the child care documents of twenty-seven SSDs. Of these, fifteen did regard prevention as an integral part of their work, a quarter failed to give it a mention and the remainder saw it as a kind of appendage. It seemed that compared with the previous decade more departments were making prevention a major goal. But many lagged behind and few awarded it a specific managerial priority or devised codes of prevention comparable to that given to fostering and adoption. The group concluded, 'we were not impressed by our study that prevention usually forms the baseline of departmental work with children and their parents'.[90]

Decentralisation

As long ago as the nineteenth century the Rev. Thomas Chalmers was trying to counter deprivation in Glasgow by applying the 'principle of locality'.[91] Thereafter the Settlement Movement, the community association movement,[92] and, more recently, some community workers[93] have worked within small localities, which could be described as communities in the sense of comprising a small number of people who held similar interests there, or neighbourhoods in the sense of embracing a small geographical unit whose physical boundaries were generally recognised.[94] During the late 1970s a number of writers began to draw upon the concepts of community and neighbourhood as a remedy for what they saw as the limitations of large SSDs. Led by Professor Roger Hadley, they criticised departments for being too centralised, too professional and too remote.[95] One result, they claimed, was that prevention was impaired because social workers lacked decision-making powers at local level and were too removed from the neighbourhoods where preventative action was required. A few SSDs then did experiment by decentralising into patch teams and, no doubt influenced the Barclay Committee, of which Hadley was a member, to call for community social work. It is difficult to say how many SSDs took up the Barclay suggestions. Some have actually become more centralised. However, a study made in 1983 of sixty-five departments stated that '28 per cent of those changing, reported department-wide moves to patch-based working'.[96] So decentralisation was under way and it is appropriate to cite some examples and to consider its relevance to prevention.

Decentralisation followed no single pattern. Some local authorities also decentralised other services, such as housing, as well. Some SSDs moved all their functions to patch offices while others left day-care and residential services at higher levels. In some SSDs it was thought that decentralisation would save money, and most thought that going local would promote prevention. In one authority the initiative of one officer led to a patch team being formed in Normanton, but nearby Featherstone did not go patch, a fact which allowed Hadley and McGrath to compare them.[97] In East Sussex the drive originated from top management, which wanted to develop 'a strategy of preventative care in the community'. Thus the whole department was divided into forty-five patch teams serving populations of about 16,000.[98]

As well as Normanton and East Sussex, other accounts of patch systems have been collected and some early conclusions can be drawn from them.[99] Problems have been met. Some patch workers found it difficult to reconcile the demands of statutory cases, like child abuse, with non-statutory work in the community.[100] Others feared the community approach would dilute their child-care and mental-health skills.[101] Some councillors worried that patch teams would win extra resources to the detriment of areas without patch.[102]

But despite the setbacks, decentralisation does seem to have brought a number of benefits. The accessibility of patch offices to their localities has meant, as Hadley and McGrath instanced, that the Normanton team knew 'a larger proportion of those at risk' than the Featherstone team.[103] The teams were well placed to meet local inhabitants and John Rea Price, director of Islington SSD, recorded: 'The locally based teams soon found . . . quite unexpected resources of self-help and competence drawn from communities which had traditionally been labelled as deprived and dependent'.[104] In turn, the recruitment of local residents probably encouraged social workers to regard clients in a different light, so that, as Bennett explained in another patch team, consumers were also seen as resources.[105] In terms of prevention these benefits meant that social workers could often intervene before problems intensified into crises and also could draw upon local resources for help. Most accounts agree that prevention was facilitated and, in Normanton, Cooper records that 'closer community contact paradoxically has halved the number of statutory cases while doubling the number of referrals for help. In our view this is a clear indication of the existence of a preventive strategy'.[106]

Decentralisation represented a significant organisational step for the departments concerned. It meant that their patch workers now viewed neighbourhoods as the focus through which they assessed need and conveyed services. For some, it meant adopting a new approach, which Thomas and Shaftoe term 'localisation', that is 'the process by which a worker consciously and deliberately makes himself known, visible and accessible within a wide range of local networks'.[107] Patch was a pioneering initiative and for most of the SSDs it was undertaken as one of their responses to the call for a renewed emphasis on prevention.

Diverting delinquents

The Criminal Justices Act of 1982 owed something to the Conservative government's wish to uphold law and order by making available stiffer kinds of sentences.[108] Yet influences for a different kind of policy and practice were at work. Just as the Criminal Justices Bill was proceeding through parliament so was published

Donald West's longitudinal study of 400 young people. Of his many conclusions, two can be mentioned. The connection between poverty and delinquency, he observed, 'points inexorably to the need to include anti-poverty measures in any coherent policy of delinquency prevention'. Further, his recognition that custodial institutions just turned delinquents into tougher delinquents led him to recommend 'community-based programmes' which at least avoided some of the 'alienation, stigmatisation and contamination' of being sent away.[109] His words were confirmed by other studies, which showed that institutional treatment had little success in stopping delinquency.[110]

As the National Association for the Care and Rehabilitation of Offenders made clear, the number of detention-centre orders and youth-custody orders imposed on juveniles showed no sign of slacking.[111] Some academics began to ask why. Thorpe and his colleagues gave particular attention to the number of care orders imposed upon young offenders. They discovered that for a third the order had been imposed at their first court appearance, that 70–90 per cent were inappropriately placed in residential institutions, and, most surprisingly, that in 83 per cent of the cases the order had been recommended by social workers.[112] Other research revealed that the very making of a social enquiry report for the court by a social worker actually increased rather than lessened the chances of severe treatment.[113]

Clearly court appearances and custodial sentences were doing little to help offenders. Moreover the custody element was expensive for local authorities which had to foot the bill. A number therefore set up schemes to divert youngsters from entering the juvenile-justice system and, if that failed, to divert them from custody. There were four main elements in these schemes. First came the reduction of prosecutions. Some departments were able to co-operate with the police to reach agreement on what action to take on youngsters thought to have committed offences. Secondly, there was a reduction in the number of reports written by social workers for the courts, and, thirdly, close liaison with magistrates to share the reasons for the diversion approach. Fourthly, the existence of non-custodial alternatives for youngsters who could not be dealt with by the aforementioned ways was considered. The alternatives included work-experience placements, day-attendance centres and community-service work, but the best known was intermediate treatment. By 1985 over 3,000 places were being provided by statutory and voluntary agencies for youngsters aged 16 and under. At times controversy raged over IT, and its own practitioners sometimes differed over objectives and methods. Nonetheless it had been established and local studies suggested that, at least, it was more successful in cutting offending rates than residential approaches.[114]

The diversion strategy was sometimes brought together into what were called juvenile liaison bureaux. For instance, the Northampton Bureau, in which five welfare agencies co-operated, liaised with the police in all cases of juvenile offending, so that in 1984 it diverted 81 per cent of all cases from prosecution. It was prepared to offer services to some of these youngsters while being careful not to draw into the welfare net families whose circumstances did not warrant it.[115] Of eleven local authorities which pursued diversion strategies, Professor Norman Tutt wrote: 'The number of young people appearing before the courts has been cut significantly and custodial sentences sharply reduced without any recorded increase in juvenile crime'.[116]

Delinquency diversion should not be presented as *the* great preventative success. Some local authorities did not promote diversion, and some could not afford alternatives. The Association of Directors of Social Services pointed out that the upward trend in custodial sentences continued nationwide despite 'the development of alternatives undertaken by Professor Tutt, NACRO and others'. ADSS went on to make a case for children's hearings based on the Scottish system, which brought the whole family together in a more informal setting than the court.[117] Nonetheless it must be said that during the 1980s a number of local authorities enlarged their alternatives to custody and implemented plans to divert delinquency. They were taking prevention seriously.

Rehabilitation and work with natural parents

Rehabilitation of children to their natural parents was one of the weaknesses of SSDs in the 1970s. What has happened in the 1980s? In a study of foster children published in 1984 Rowe and her colleagues commented: 'The most remarkable fact about our study's children's family contact is the lack of it . . . There were only 31 youngsters (21%) who had even casual contact with a parent during the previous year'.[118] Marsh and his team interviewed children in care, their parents and social workers and noted: 'In fact the parents were often rather unknown qualities . . . In general, the process of ending care was not accorded much attention by most social workers'.[119] The National Children's Bureau has been following the progress of 185 children in the care of eleven local authorities, and Vernon discovered that although the social workers were not anxious to admit them into care, once they were accepted there was no 'enthusiasm to move them back out of care'.[120] The Dartington Research Unit projected from its study that nationally 7,000 of the 44,000 children admitted to care each year are 'destined for a long stay, and a withering link with their parents and families'.[121]

If rehabilitation depends on continuing family links, then clearly social-work practice is falling short. The studies indicate that often social workers interpret admission to care as the final failure of the parents and then underestimate their wish and potential for receiving them back.[122] Others thankfully turn to other priorities once a child is safely in care.[123] The parents were often poor, isolated and devastated by the loss of their children. If not encouraged to visit, there was a danger of them giving up altogether.

There is no doubt that forging contact with natural parents is still a neglected part of prevention. Yet hopeful signs do exist. In 1984 the Islington SSD issued a statement of Child Care Policy which not only stressed its intention to 'ensure vigorous plans for the rehabilitation of children back to their own families and communities' but also stated that it would only assume parental rights in rare cases.[124] Some social workers are committed to rehabilitation, and there are instances of them stimulating parents to form into groups in order to develop an approach to prevention and rehabilitation.[125] Again, Rowe and her colleagues did find exceptional cases of SSDs with a policy of encouraging parental contact and even using volunteer drivers to this end.[126] More recently, Greg Kelly reported from one study that 42 per cent of the foster children had frequent contact with parents, a proportion higher than in most previous investigations.[127] The message to emerge is that parents often do wish to maintain contact with a view to receiving their children back but their wish needs to be

supplemented by the skills and commitment of social workers if it
is to become a reality.

Conflicting trends

The SSDs' response was thus a mixed one. A few made detailed
policy statements about prevention. A number decentralised their
social work teams but others did not. Successes in diverting delinquents were achieved by some but not by all. Rehabilitation still
received low priority but there were exceptions. Even research
studies reflected these conflicting trends. Vernon and Fruin implied a degree of prevention from social workers, who 'admitted
children to care very reluctantly'.[128] Yet Millham concluded: 'If
preventative work was going on, none of our 450 children was
getting it'.[129]

Two factors contributed to the differences between SSDs. One
was that, even when convinced of the case for prevention, they
were still subject to strong pressures to rescue children. In theory
social workers should be able to protect children in danger while
also enabling those who can possibly stay with their parents to do
so. In practice the difficulty of deciding what is 'danger' and what is
'possible' is much more complicated. Reactions to the Jasmine
Beckford investigation illustrate the point.[130] Some SSD directors
advocated more admissions to care as a safety-first measure.
Others argued for more resources for prevention.[131] As one analysis
put it, 'The overall impression is of two opposing trends: one
towards community involvement, participation and prevention;
and the other towards an increasing use of compulsion by social
workers in relation to children and their families'.[132] The other
factor concerned variability in availability of resources. Some
SSDs did receive increased budgets during this period, but others
had to cut back. Some were able to launch preventative initiatives,
including family centres, of which more will be said in the next
section. Thus new ventures were not unknown but they sometimes
occurred while other services were being reduced and always in
the midst of increasing demands. The result was variable and
patchy growth in prevention.

During the 1980s therefore SSDs made limited but growing
ventures into prevention. What effect did this have on numbers in
care in England and Wales? In 1980 the number was 100,200. By

1984 it had declined to 78,900, a drop from 7.7 to 6.9 per 1,000 of the population under 18.[133] The decline is not just attributable to SSDs, for other agencies played their part; but deteriorating economic circumstances were placing more families at risk, and so it is reasonable to award much of the credit to the preventative activities of the SSDs, as described in this chapter. Certainly some SSDs made this interpretation. Avon SSD explained a reduction of 481 children in care as due to its 'prevention is better than care policy'.[134] Another department increased its section-one spending by 180 per cent and the numbers of children in care fell by forty.[135] Of course, not all SSDs responded in like manner and the Family Rights Group could point to departments such as the one that in 1981 spent only £3,000 of section-one prevention money compared with half a million pounds in placing children in substitute care outside its boundaries.[136] But, in general, prevention was back and was making an impact. If not in the centre of the social work stage it was at least being awarded a more important part.

The Voluntary Organisations

The Child Care Act of 1980 defined a voluntary organisation as a body, apart from a statutory one, 'the activities of which are carried on otherwise than for profit'.[137] In this volume attention is concentrated on the national child care voluntaries, which, by the 1980s, were represented by the National Council of Voluntary Child Care Organisations. In 1985 it approved a statement of child-care policy which gave a prominent place to prevention. It stated:

> It is important to help children by enabling families to stay together. A positive response to the need for preventive work has become increasingly apparent among member organisations. We believe that the principles and practices which we here summarise will contribute to the prevention of disadvantage, neglect or abuse of children and young people and to the achievement of their individual progress.[138]

The NCVCCO's enthusiastic commitment to prevention contrasts with the lukewarm reception its predecessor had given to the preventative sections of the Children and Young Persons Act of 1963. But time and the voluntary societies had changed. By the 1980s they regarded prevention as one of their main functions, as can be illustrated by describing the work of two of the largest voluntary child-care agencies and by examining an approach which was taken up by nearly all the child-care voluntaries, namely the establishment of family centres.

Two child-care agencies

In common with other voluntary bodies, the number of children in the residential care of the National Children's Home continued to fall. In 1970 it catered for 1831 children in its residential establishments but by 1985 the number had dropped to 816. It continued to find foster and adoptive homes for 'hard to place' children but its growth point was in work with children in their own homes, the number of which was put at over 2,000 in 1985. In terms of costs, residential care still absorbed over half the expenditure in 1984–5, but in terms of numbers and direction, the emphasis was on working with families and communities. Continuing some of the patterns set down in the previous decade, the NCH expanded its work in intermediate treatment so that by 1985 it ran sixteen projects. It developed phone-in services for parents (and others) under pressure. It promoted its expertise in identifying and treating children who were sexually abused. In brief, there was a major drive within the agency towards enabling families to cope with their own children. The rescue and removal drives of the Victorian era had been replaced by an emphasis on prevention.

The Church of England Children's Society – the Children's Society for short – retained some residential units for physically and mentally handicapped children as well as most of its Home-finding Teams to seek permanent families for children 'with special needs'. The major growth point, however, was with community projects and family centres, the latter numbering forty-six by 1986.

The Barclay Report had urged voluntary bodies to undertake prevention and, indeed, had stated that in many instances they were 'better placed than most social services departments to concern themselves with the preventive role'.[139] The Children's Society appeared to take these words to heart. Thus, within its care for mentally handicapped children, the Society was offering 'respite care' to give the natural parents a break, while one centre helped parents with detailed guidance about how to teach specific skills to their mentally handicapped under-fives.[140] Community-living units were installed to enable older mentally handicapped children to live within the community or as a stepping stone to prepare some physically handicapped young adults to move into their own permanent accommodation. Other schemes provided self-contained flats for young people – some of whom had been in public care or even homeless – as a start to independent living without the aid of social-work support. A residential centre for severely disturbed children had the threefold aim of rehabilitation, placement with a substitute family or help towards independent living. In the field of juvenile justice, the Children's Society not only ran IT schemes but also pioneered an alternative to custody centre which offered close supervision and helpful experiences and training to teenagers who would otherwise have been sentenced to custodial institutions. Juvenile justice and *guardian-ad-litem* projects were also set up in order to help youngsters avoid admission to care or custody. By the mid-1980s the Children's Society claimed to be helping about 5,000 children, of whom very few were in residential care. The emphasis was on prevention but prevention with a wide definition. As well as wanting to prevent the break-up of families, the Society wanted to prevent unsatisfactory experiences for disadvantaged children who did stay in their own homes and below par living for young adults who wanted to live away from home but not in the care of any authorities. In short, the Children's Society wanted to prevent the 5,000 children from being devalued and dehumanised by society at large.

The trends just traced in the National Children's Home and the Children's Society were also reflected in the other major child-care organisations. By 1982 only 5,811 children were in the full care of voluntary child-care bodies in England and Wales, and of these 86 per cent had been placed there by local authorities. Residential care was no longer the main role of the voluntaries. Instead, the movement towards helping children within their own families and neighbourhoods, which had taken root in the 1970s, began to flourish in the 1980s. The difference was not just one of numerical expansion. The new approach was becoming more precise in its objectives, its methodologies and its understanding of prevention. Nowhere was this better revealed than in the main growth area – family centres.

Family centres

SSDs created a number of family centres during the 1980s. But whereas for the local authorities family centres were a small part of their total work, for the voluntary societies they came to constitute a large part of their response to social needs and problems. Thus, as this volume moves on to study the preventative contribution of the voluntaries, so it will focus more closely on these kind of community projects.

What is a family centre? Any visitor to one cannot fail to notice a great variety of activities operating under the name. For instance, the family centre run by the Aberlour Child Care Trust in Falkirk (which I have visited) offers day care for the under-fives, drop-in facilities for parents, individual counselling, group meetings for specific types of problems, training for parents and a toy library.[141] But there are common features and Jan Phelan, who made a study of some of the earliest family centres initiated by the Children's Society, has identified three of them. Firstly, centres 'are located in neighbourhoods where there is a marked incidence of factors associated with the sorts of problems that lead to the reception of children into care and family stress'. Secondly, they draw out families' strengths instead of labelling them as problems. Thirdly, their services are 'more accessible to local communities and more responsive to people's felt needs'.[142] To these features can be added those identified by Erica De'Ath after reviewing the written responses of 250 centres. Amongst the most important were working with parents as well as children, an emphasis on user participation and a commitment to increasing the self-confidence and self-esteem of users.[143]

With some features established, some writers felt more able to define the meaning of a family centre. De'Ath stated: 'The phrase "family centre" is increasingly being used as a generic term for any provision for parents and children where a range of services is offered to families living in a defined area and where the centre acts as a base for carrying out many of the activities'.[144] Neil McKechnie of the Association of Scottish Family Centres wrote:

The term 'Family Centre' is increasingly being used to describe community based provision for parents and their children, particularly where there is a high level of parental partnership over such matters as the activities taking place in the building, the control of these activities and the development of new services.[145]

Just as the definition of family centres was being established, so it also became clear that prevention was close to their heart. The wish to pursue preventative objectives was noted in many of the centres reviewed by De'Ath, by those in a study made by Willmott and Mayne,[146] and in most of those run by the National Children's Home.[147] It also emerged strongly in the early family centres of the Children's Society as described by Jan Phelan. She recorded: 'They had a common baseline premise that the best possible place for a child was with his/her own family and community. It was the centre's task to facilitate the kind of package of services and resources that would help families not merely to remain intact, but also to function more effectively'.[148] Phelan adds that as the centres progressed, so they might widen the nature of their activities to cover not just families but also groups for unemployed men, clubs for bored children and tenants' associations. Thus the centres underwent change but the new developments were still regarded as preventative in that they were helping members of families to avoid some of the community disadvantages they would otherwise have faced.

The rapid expansion of family centres was an indication that they had an important role to play in prevention. Yet the expansion was not accompanied by a growth in the literature about such centres and, in the next chapter, I will explain the study I had to undertake in order to establish more precisely their contribution to the community projects. Here it is sufficient to say that family centres became the flagship of the voluntary organisations' passage into the community. They now serve as a sharp contrast with the activities of the same bodies 30 to 40 years ago. Then the childcare agencies were synonymous with residential care and they gave little time or thought to prevention. The change is a remarkable testimony of the ability of traditional organisations to throw off Victorian ideas, not to mention Victorian buildings, in order to forge new services to keep pace with new definitions of social need. During the 1980s various bodies and individuals made a strong call for prevention. The child-care voluntary agencies responded by making prevention one of the chief characteristics of their work, perhaps even the main characteristic.

The Meaning of Prevention

The expansion of the quantity of preventative services during the 1980s has been accompanied by more precise consideration of its nature. SSDs have continued as the local-authority *agencies* entrusted with the statutory duty but other local-government services have shown some sign of appreciating the value of prevention in child care. For instance, some education departments have preferred to send certain disruptive pupils to special schools, whereas before they might have been admitted to public care.[149] Moreover a number of SSDs perceived that they had to create sub-agencies in the form of patch teams to more effectively discharge their duties; and, most noteworthy, voluntary bodies accepted a major role as agencies of prevention. The eighties have also been significant in that some practitioners decided that the juvenile-justice system was the *target* for their intervention. Others looked upon neighbourhoods as the target to be changed. Just as interesting, some social workers redefined the standing of their targets by regarding individuals and families not as clients to be treated but as participants and resources. *Tactics* too became more precise, with the diversion of youngsters away from illegitimate activities, the postponement of their entry into the justice system and, if that failed, the provision of alternatives to custody, all being recognised as measures worthy of more skills and expenditure. A few writers even argued for the more ambitious approach of creating the appropriate framework in society, be it a caring neighbourhood or universal social services, which would enable most families to cope with their own children.

The practice of prevention is by no means in a satisfactory form at present, but in the Victorian era the concept hardly existed and even 40 years ago no one child-care agency had a responsibility for it. Today SSDs and voluntary child-care agencies practise prevention and sometimes receive support from other statutory organisations. The targets, in theory at least, have been extended from just

children and parents to changing agencies, systems, neighbourhoods and even the structures of society; and more varied kinds of
tactics have been pursued as campaigners have won a measure of
public support for their case. Prevention at present is showing
some signs of progress.

Preventing what?

There remains what is perhaps the most important question. What
is being prevented? Prevention has expanded its meaning and so
seven answers can be given. First on the list is the prevention of
children being received into public or voluntary care away from
their families. The implication is that separation is usually a less
satisfying experience than staying with natural families. Some
commentators would add that children's emotional, social and
intellectual growth is likely to be hindered by the experience of
public care.

Second comes the prevention of children entering custodial
care. The new duty introduced by the 1963 Act spoke not of
preventing custody, although obviously this was implied, but of
diminishing the need to bring children before a juvenile court.
From the debates at the time it was clear that delinquency was
considered worth preventing because it harmed the people against
whom offences were committed, because it impaired the proper
development of children and because it placed them in jeopardy of
losing their freedom. In turn custodial care was worth averting
because not only was the resultant separation likely to harm the
children's emotional growth but also because it might actually
reinforce their delinquent tendencies.

Third is the need to prevent the neglect or abuse of children.
From their earliest days child-care officers interpreted neglect as
meaning not just physical cruelty but also neglect of proper standards of health and nutrition. Later the SSDs became preoccupied
with preventing children enduring the kinds of horrors suffered by
Maria Colwell. More recently attention has focused on preventing
sexual abuse. Some cases are so severe that children can only be
protected by removal from their homes, but the number on 'at risk'
registers is so large that SSDs cannot cope with admitting many of
them to their care and so social workers attempt to improve the
caring capacities of parents in order to protect the children.

Fourth comes preventing the effects of poor parenting on children. Neglect and abuse may be the results of poor parenting but Sir Keith Joseph also argued that it could mean children not being equipped with the values and skills akin to the normal population. Academics like Harriett Wilson, while disagreeing with Joseph over the causal mechanisms, also believed that some parents were not allowed to develop their children adequately for the modern world. More recently the *Review of Child Care Law*, while not discussing explanations of poor parenting, has added its plea for the need to prevent 'a substantial deficit in the standard of health, development or well being that can reasonably be expected for the child'.[150]

The fifth role for prevention is to save children experiencing those disadvantages in their homes and communities associated with lack of income, amenities and social experiences. This objective has been particularly voiced by the voluntary child-care agencies in the 1980s. One of the regional directors of the Children's Society has defined prevention as 'Intervention into processes and/or events affecting the individuals and/or groups and/or communities . . . which without that intervention would result in disadvantage and/or harm to that individual and/or group and/or community'.[151] Not only has the definition been widened to prevent disadvantage to children within their community but also to prevent disadvantage to the community itself.

The trouble with this kind of definition is that it becomes so all-embracing.[152] Yet anyone who undertakes prevention knows that it is too complex a matter to be restricted to a single definition. Consider a family known to me. A lone mother struggling in poverty on a neglected estate faced danger to herself and children when a violent lover moved in. In such a case, the 'what' of prevention includes preventing the children having to leave their mother if possible, preventing them experiencing cruelty, and preventing them enduring the disadvantages associated with a low income and poor neighbourhood. Prevention with such families fits into the kind of diverse approach outlined in this section.

Sixthly, we come to preventing children from having to stay in care. Rehabilitation is one of the most neglected parts of prevention, although its legislative roots go back to the Children Act 1948. The Short Report urged that the rehabilitative duty should apply to all children in care and not just those accepted voluntar-

ily. Of late the voluntary child-care societies have urged that
children be returned not just to their families as quickly as possible
but also to their neighbourhoods, for this too is important to them.
Seventhly, it is important to prevent the isolation of children in
care. The Family Rights Group's latest definition is 'to prevent
permanent family separations and where that is impossible to
promote and maintain links between separated family members'.[153]
The theme is that children's time in public care will be less damaging
if they remain emotionally, if not physically, a part of their families
of origin.

This review has now been able to establish the ends to which
social workers and others want to direct prevention. But the terms
they use raise further questions. What is meant by 'neglect',
'abuse', 'poor parenting' and so on? Some academics, like Geismer, have tried to provide measurements for such terms but in the
end they come down to the personal assessments of panels of
judges.[154] It seems there is no scientific measure of such facets of
human behaviour, no more than there can be a completely objective measure of poverty. It is now usually agreed that poverty is a
relative concept, and in Chapter 3 attention was drawn to the
definition that people were poor if their income was not sufficient
for them to maintain the standard of living considered 'common or
customary' in their society. In the same way the terms used within
the definitions of prevention have to take account of the standards
prevailing in a particular society at a particular time. Thus prevention aims to minimise the number of children having to leave their
families, because within our society it is customary for parents to
look after their own children. Again, it wants to prevent children
from missing out on those social, physical and emotional aspects of
family life which are considered beneficial or reasonable for members of our country.

The meaning of prevention entails consideration of its agents,
targets and tactics. In time these become embodied into practices
and policies and sometimes into legislation. But the most significant part concerns the aim or purpose of prevention. Prevention
may thus be regarded:

(a) Reactively or defensively, as those policies and practices which
    prevent children from needlessly being separated from their
    parents and placed in public (or voluntary) care or custody;

and, if separated, from needlessly having to stay in care or being stopped from maintaining physical and/or emotional links with their natural families.

(b) Positively, or promotionally, as those policies and practices which prevent children from failing to enjoy in their own homes, the kind of parenting, the freedom from suffering, the standards of living, and the quality of community life which is considered the reasonable lot of every child in our society.

It is not claimed that the definitions offered here are the last word. Perhaps they will act as a stimulus for more able authors to form more sophisticated definitions.

Key Features

This volume has attempted to trace the development of prevention in child care from Victorian times until the present. From the analysis, it now becomes possible to identify five key features which, in the writer's understanding, are crucial to the operation of prevention.

Prevention as an objective

During Victorian times and the early decades of the present century, both statutory and voluntary agencies were prepared to rescue deprived children but at the cost of separating them from their parents. Responsibility for deprived children was spread amongst so many agencies that none could or would give single-minded attention to the value of prevention. It took the effects of the Second World War and the creation of the modern welfare state to alter the social climate significantly and pave the way for a single local-authority service for deprived children. Local authority children's departments brought together elected members and child-care staff and from their midst a number began to articulate that the preservation of the family unit, of all social classes, was a social value which should be upheld by the practice of prevention. Their efforts largely contributed to the preventative legislation contained in the 1963 Act and to prevention becoming a major objective of children's departments.

The Seebohm Report called for 'a forceful and widespread commitment to prevention',[155] but the confusion arising from the vast reorganisation of the personal social services along with the introduction of competing values, particularly those associated with the concept of permanence, led to setbacks for prevention in the 1970s. It no longer held a central place in the priorities of many social-work managers and practitioners, though, at this very time, the voluntary societies were shedding their vast residential responsibilities and were able to concentrate increasingly on prevention. For the SSDs it was not until the 1980s, when pressure groups, official reports and a new grouping of social workers began to exert pressure, that preventative practice began to gather pace again. The lesson to be drawn is that if prevention is to hold a prominent place, then it must be held as a major objective by organised groups both within and without the social services. As Professor Parker wrote, 'we believe that only by a firm preventive orientation and commitment can the potentialities be discovered'.[156]

The contribution of social workers

To assert that prevention is beyond the powers of social workers alone will provoke no dispute. Nonetheless, this study has noticed repeatedly the crucial role performed by them at the secondary and tertiary stages. After all, it is the social workers of the SSDs and voluntary agencies who work directly with the families meeting difficulties. It is their assessments and recommendations which influence the courts and committees that ponder the fate of children. It is social workers who maintain, or fail to maintain, links between children and natural parents. As Millham pointed out, 'rarely in our study cohort of 450 children did social workers report that the decision to admit a child to care was out of their hands'.[157] In recent decades preventative social work has sometimes held back by disagreements about its value within the ranks of social workers, by a shortage of resources, and by limitations in the legislation relating to prevention. Despite these drawbacks, the fact that SSDs are now claiming that their social workers are making headway in reducing numbers in care serves again to underline the vital contribution which they can make.

Status of users

In studying the history of prevention it becomes clear that the way people are treated by officials is as important as the service offered. Even in Victorian times observers noted that the harsh attitudes of Poor Law officials not only deterred applicants but could promote negative or aggressive behaviour in them. A number of social reformers subsequently perceived that the harm created by this unequal relationship between givers and receivers would only disappear if the population regarded their use of social services as a right based on being a citizen. Following the Second World War, they succeeded in some measure with regard to education and health services. But these services were likely to be used by the bulk of the population at some stage in their life. Social-work services differed in that only a minority approached them and then usually only in time of trouble. The Seebohm Report recognised that people in need were often reluctant to use the personal social services and so recommended a 'community based and family orientated service which will be available to all'.[158] But being available to all did not mean that the new SSDs were relevant to or acceptable to all. Indeed, it was within the new service that occurred the application of Sir Keith Joseph's cycle of deprivation thesis, which – more than ever – marked out clients as inadequates and so intensified their feelings of inferiority. This failure was fully recognised by the next major report on the personal services and led the Barclay Committee to recommend community social work as a means of bridging the gap between officials and users. Certainly, as discussed, the creation of some patch teams has had an effect on altering the way in which social workers treated and regarded clients. Nonetheless some parents still view social workers as a threat and find contact with them akin to a disabling process which reduces their confidence.

The difficulties inherent in the treatment of consumers is seen in the ways SSDs handle the apparently straightforward resource of day care. If such facilities are open to all the under-fives, then local authorities face a great demand. If they limit the number by imposing charges, then the most needy may be excluded either because they cannot afford the fees or because they dislike a means test. But if day-care places are reserved for certain social categories – say single parents or abused children – then users can feel that they are being marked out and stigmatised before others. Enough has been said to establish the significance of the status of consumers in preventative work. Where social workers and their services have the effect of undermining people's confidence, then their preventative efforts can be set back. Where they succeed in winning the willing participation of consumers, then it takes a step forward.

Localisation of services

The localisation of personal social services into small geographical units has occurred both in some SSDs and voluntary agencies. In the former SSDs decentralised into patch teams as a reaction to the increasing size of their departments. In the latter the concentration on community projects followed the drop in demand for residential services and the acknowledgement that the voluntaries could no longer provide nationwide services. In both cases the signs are that localisation has meant a greater capacity for social workers to help families at an early stage of their difficulties and a greater opportunity to enlist local resources, so that prevention has been facilitated.

Combating poverty

At several junctures the analysis has detected the connection between social deprivations and the separation of children from their families. It was most blatant in the Victorian squalor, which made it impossible for some parents to care for their own. On the other hand the improved conditions associated with the modern welfare state not only enabled more parents to cope but also made the practice of prevention a possibility. In the last two decades the connection has again been demonstrated by studies which show that children from low-income families are much more likely to suffer disadvantages at home than those from more affluent backgrounds. Two more bits of recent evidence can be added. In Britain an intensive study of a small number of families by Coffield, Robinson and Sarasby stated: 'One cannot dissociate the divorces, suicides or attempted suicides, the abortions, children in care and accidents, the delinquents, debts and family rows from their lack of money and lack of space, the low status and dirty jobs, the poor education and poorer prospects and their lack of power and control over their lives'.[159] In the USA a study of children in care concluded that the major priority was 'the need to provide money directly to biological parents'.[160]

If prevention is to be more fully and more effectively implemented, then this study suggests that it must include social workers and other staff who focus on prevention and rehabilitation and who work through services which are local to users, so enabling them to participate as citizens rather than being treated as inadequate clients. This social-work activity will need to be set within the framework of a society which is moving towards the reduction of its vast inequalities and social deprivations. But the implementation of these key features will depend on a firm and widespread commitment towards prevention not only from within social work but also from officials, politicians and citizens outside.

If central and local government ever produce a comprehensive strategy for prevention, then the analysis implicit in this study suggests that it must find a major place for these key features. Outside the statutory sector, if the child-care voluntary agencies are to make an impact on prevention, then they too must take them seriously. It is to the contribution of the voluntary agencies that this volume must now turn.

5. The Voluntary Projects

The review of the development of prevention in child care has shown that the voluntary agencies moved from having little interest to the position of being amongst its foremost supporters. Indeed, in the last chapter, attention was drawn to a policy statement by the National Council of Voluntary Child Care Organisations which not only gave priority to enabling families to stay together but also embraced the wider concept of prevention, which wanted to stop children experiencing social disadvantages, abuse and neglect in their homes. But how did this work out in practice? There was little detailed evidence on the matter, so in 1985 the Children's Society released me part-time to study the preventative work of ten of its projects. This chapter will thus differ from the rest of the book in that it presents the findings of a particular study.

The Children's Society undertakes various kinds of prevention but its recent expansion has occurred within the community, with the Society's family centres, neighbourhood centres and community projects. Whatever their differences in name, these centres share a desire to use their resources for preventative work with local families. I will tend to use the generic term 'community project' to describe them, although there is an increasing tendency to apply the term 'family centre'. From the many projects run by the Children's Society I selected ten, mainly on the basis that they were willing to receive me and that no other studies were being made of them. I then spent several days at the projects, observing their activities and also interviewing staff, users and 'outsiders' such as social workers and members of the clergy who knew the projects. The interview approach was adopted because I was keen to present the projects according to the interpretations of the people most concerned with them. I do not pretend that this constitutes sophisticated research, in which a representative sample of centres is chosen at random, and the results backed by objective methods of evaluation. Rather it attempts to convey, in the participants' own words, what the projects do and how they evaluate the work.

Limitations of time and resources meant that this study has had to concentrate on projects run by one voluntary society. However, I have visited a number of centres run by other voluntary bodies. I have also been to ten family centres run by local authorities in order to compare and contrast them with the voluntary sector. My report to the Children's Society contained an account of all ten projects. Restrictions on space mean that only four can be presented here, and even within these I have had to omit some interviews. The shape of the chapter will be to render a short outline of the project followed by the words of the participants. Chapter 6 will then draw upon both these accounts and those interviews which are not recorded here in order to consider the voluntary contribution to prevention.

Baron's Close Young Family Centre

Background

Originally purpose-built in 1974 as a day nursery, Baron's Close became a day-care centre and then, in 1982, a family centre. It is based in the town of Bletchley, part of the new city of Milton Keynes. Its objectives are stated as providing 'a specialised service to help families cope and stay together and enjoy their children. To try to help families to help themselves and be part of the community'.

The centre's staff consist of a project leader and deputy, three senior family-care workers, six family-care workers, a social worker (part-time), secretary (part-time), and two domestics (part-time). The main activities are day care for up to thirty children a week, work with individual families, activity groups for mothers, mums and toddlers groups, a toy library, play schemes and outreach programmes on outlying estates.

Project leader

'Most families are referred to us through the SSD usually while at a crisis or despair point. A lot of these are on the child-abuse register. After the family has been coming here for about 3 weeks, we have a meeting together to work on a contract which is signed by the mother, the key worker from here and the SSD social worker. The first part of the contract is what days they come, what time they come, whether the mother stays with the child. Sometimes we have the mum in for 1 ½ days with the child and the child in half a day on its own; or the child might come in a day on its own and mum might come in 2 days. The second part may say that mum needs to make friends here to build up her confidence or that we may agree to help mum handle her child who is out of hand.

'We start at 9 o'clock in the morning, when some children come with their parents and some without. The children are all under five and are divided into three groups and their activities go on all the time. The parents do different things on different days and the normal programme is that on Monday morning a group of them go to a skills centre, which is about 3 miles up the road. Monday afternoons we run a mums and toddlers group on the Lake Estate. On Tuesday mornings, in addition to normal activities, we have a toy-library session in one of the schools with two members of staff there. Tuesday afternoons we have a mums and toddlers here. This is open to outsiders and is one of the few activities which take families not referred by the SSD. But the room for this is very small, so we usually take families recommended by health visitors, those who don't fit very easily into the large mums and toddlers groups in the area. Wednesday mornings we have a parents' general activities group, which has been going on since 1979. They have family cookery, keep fit, films, speakers from social security. Thursdays we usually have staff meetings and training sessions. Fridays we have a health programme, about looking after yourself.

'The aim of the centre has always been preventative work. As a day-care centre we probably helped just by giving parents a break from their children. Now we have a more planned system, which is concerned with directly helping the parents as well as the child. One of the hopes is that we will change the parents a little bit by making them into better parents and to help them to understand why their children do things that they do. They can find friends here. We are a new town and there isn't mum or a familiar face around the corner. When I came, I didn't know anybody and I know what it is like. They haven't got anyone to turn to, they are separated from families and they haven't got the money to go off and visit relatives, or the reality is that they have lost contact with them. A lot of families over the years have come to us through Women's Aid. Now they are often very damaged people and they have often come from London because the London Women's Aid hostels are full and they are isolated.

'Families like this can benefit from the parents' groups here. The groups are open; we encourage people to go in but by no means force them. Mostly they enjoy the groups. Films on caring for children are very popular. The police have sometimes brought things like 'Don't Talk To Strangers'. Health care and make-up are always popular. We go off on outings, we like to have fun. Our best discussions are often in somewhere like the park. They talk about what it is like being with children on your own, what it's like not having any money, not having contact with your own family, how nervous you are going into places and meeting people. The sort of things that people share in common. Sometimes they are very hairy: people share terrific confidences, as when they have beaten their children and how guilty they felt and couldn't talk to anybody, and it will come out of the blue, and then somebody else will remember that they had done exactly the same and they can support one another.

'It is much easier to help the children because they are ripe to learn and they are usually quite bright children. If the children need individual sessions, we can give that, usually in the last term before they go to school and make sure they are up to coping with school, and we help them a bit with concentration and learning. But children just enjoy learning and getting together and the freedom of being able to play, learning controls which they often don't get at home. We are practically all of us trained in child care and that's the easy part of our job. It works. We are told very often that where the older brothers and sisters have not had the benefit of this kind of situation, the differences at school between them and the children who have been here is very marked.

'I think the centre has helped many families. In one case a very depressed mum was living with a dad who got hooked on drugs. She ended up in a battered wives' hostel not because she was battered but because she had run away. She returned home but the dad deliberately fed his children drugs or left them around where they could pick them up. They took the drugs, both were very ill, and the little one nearly died. Dad got a 4-year sentence for attempted manslaughter. When he was inside, the mother found it very difficult to cope. So the children came to us 2 days a week and mum came on the third day and we kept this up for 2 years. At first we had to collect mum to bring her in on the third day but gradually her confidence built up and in the end she was giving us a lot more than we were giving her. You don't get many pats on the back but one of our staff met mum recently at a workshops' meeting where this mum was actually speaking. This mum, whom everybody said was not fit to look after her children, was on the committee of the workshops and she said, "I would never have coped without the help that the centre gave me", and I know that's true.

'Our efforts have always been helped by a good working relationship with the local authority. I admire them because they are under a lot of pressure from the outside to take children into care. They have often taken a risk and allowed children to be shared between us and the parents where other authorities would have taken the children away and denied them the chance of being kept with their parents. Just lately, after the cases that have been in the papers, they have persuaded mums to let them take children into care just for a short period to give mum a break. But it is better if children come to a place like this, because I feel that once they have been in care, it becomes easier for them to go in again. In some cases it's what was the mum's life when she was young, so it is just history repeating itself.

'We have been to court on several occasions with parents. On one occasion the magistrates were debating as to whether a child should be returned to its parents and they actually came here to see the centre and then decided yes, the child could go home on condition that it came regularly to the centre with its parents; and that family did actually survive, the child is still with mum.

'There are difficulties in the work. We just haven't got the space. And we went through a phase when some of the parents have said such things as 'Oh, I'm not going to let my child go there because that's where the battered children go'. Up until a short time ago we did take a mixture of children referred by the SSD and voluntary admissions and that gave a lovely balance. Now they are nearly all referred.'

Senior family-care worker

'There is poverty around here because social security benefits don't cover what families need. Kids who live on social security are expected to go without a lot. If you are on social security, you are not supposed to want to go out on outings or have the things that other children do. This is why a lot of the times when mums have got the money they spend it on stupid things rather than food, and you can see why. It is not nice to be broke all the time and sometimes they say, "Oh, why shouldn't you have some fun". But I suppose isolation is the major problem around here. It's the way these estates have been built. The people are not asked how they want to live. Then add to that that many of the mums who come here have been in care themselves. They had bad experiences when they were young – sexual abuse, physical abuse. They seem to move from a dad who was physically abusing them to a husband who does it. There's a lot of violence around, that's frightening. Most of these people suffer so much rejection that in the end they think they are not worth being cared for or about.

'So what can we do about it? Well, we had a family in this week where the man's last wage packet was about £40. They have got one baby and one child who had a birthday yesterday. The mother was desperate. Rather than give them money we did up a food parcel for them. We try to help out with clothes. People bring in second-hand clothes and we sell them off for a few pennies. We pay parents' bus fares to get here and help them to work out their money to try and make it go round. An organisation called Money Advice hold little surgeries on the estates and we also get them to come here. Then parents can book an appointment and come and talk confidentially about whether they are getting enough benefit or whether they can claim for clothes and bedding.

'We are trying to change parents' attitudes towards their children: helping them understand why children react the way they do or what different stages they are going through; to give them a better idea why a child constantly wets the bed by looking at why and going through it to see things that are going on at home. We try to get over the importance of play. It is a learning system for the child. A few minutes' thinking of an activity for them gives you 2 hours' peace. We encourage parents to think of activities they can do at home. They say "Sand? Don't want that all over the house". So you have to put over that sand doesn't have to be messy and if you put an old cover on the floor, you just chuck it out at the end. We have a toy library and sell materials cheaply there: paint, making dough out of flour and water. Most of them are astounded what you can do with children with cheap materials.'

User 1

'Me and my wife separated. She took three of the children and I was having problems looking after the other two. They were 9 and 3. The older one is a problem child. I've had a lot of trouble with him — he is too old for here but he did come to the play schemes and enjoyed that. Anyway, I was having a job looking after them 'cos I was working. I was mini-cabbing and a girl I picked up told me about this place. She introduced me. I felt nervous when I first came but they calmed me down and helped me through. The staff try to bring parents into the family centre and try to help out. I went around trying to play with the other children. Different kinds of parents come in. I'm friendly with some of them now. It's like a family here really.

'My girl came when she was 3. She used to come 4 days a week and she's just left. It really has got my girl ready for school. It learns them quite a lot like painting, slowly learning things, to speak properly. It brought her out a lot. When I first brought her in, she had problems with speech and it's brought her through and now she speaks pretty clear. It has helped us a hell of a lot coming here. If I didn't come here, I wouldn't know where I was. It could have come to me not having them I would have thought.'

User 2

'I can't see. Not since I was 21 because of a tumour on the brain. I have never seen my children or my husband. It was difficult from the word go in one sense. I have got two children; one is 8 and one is 4 now. The social worker said it would be a great help to get him off my hands for a couple of days a week me being as I am. They got me into this nursery to give me a bit of a relief for a few days because it can be a bit of a handful when you can't see.

'We parents get together here as well. We have a discussion or if someone has a problem, we try and sort it out. And we have little outings. We talk about the children, like some have got older children so we talk about that. Or some are having trouble with a boy-friend at home. I'm good at listening to them and sometimes listening helps more than giving advice.

'So I've made a lot of friends here. Even the staff are all my friends. When my boy leaves here, I shall be lost. I shall still come. I cannot flip round to everybody's houses. It's awkward when you can't see and I don't think people feel comfortable coming into my home. It's different here. I come in and make the tea for them all and we get on fine while we are here.

'If I had had to stay at home all the time, I don't know what would have happened to the children. I know what would have happened to me. I would have gone up the wall. The children would not have got on so well. The staff have really pushed my children to get a high standard themselves and to be independent too. They taught them colours and my son will say "I'm not putting the green jumper on, I want the blue one on".

'I still want to come here when my son starts school. Even if it is just on Wednesdays with the parents' group, more than anything else I would like to keep that one up. I would be lost without the nursery. The nursery was the first contact I had with outside people here because I don't come from this area, so without the nursery I have got nobody.'

SSD area social-work assistant manager

'We tend to use Baron's Close mainly for families within 3 to 4 miles' radius. The transport situation is not good, so often we have to provide it ourselves. We fund so many places at the family centre and fund places not just for children but also for parents – which is a comparatively new idea. The procedure is that our social workers have to put in a request to us giving their reasons as to what they think the family centre has to offer. In most cases there is an element of the child being at risk, if not of physical abuse then certainly of neglect. Baron's Close is particularly good at work with parents who are not motivated; the staff have considerable patience and will do all they can to win their confidence. This is important in an area where there may be inadequate mums who are very young parents themselves but have not got the back-up of friends and relatives. They need mothering themselves. They are also good with mothers who are on the defensive or who are aggressive. They offer a lot of care for the mothers and the children and their way of working is to offer a model which the mothers can follow.

'In one case we were very worried that a mother was not properly looking after a 3-year-old child. She was not accepted in her community, she was very rejecting of authority and, because of violence in the home, the child was received into care a number of times. Originally the mother went to one of our local-authority family centres some miles away but she could not settle. Again it was the authority thing and the image of local-authority places as places for people who batter their kids. So she went on to Baron's Close where we wanted the staff to help her cope with a 3-year-old who was constantly having temper tantrums. The mother was accepted by the staff and she has accepted what they have to offer. She has worked extremely well there. It is still going well and further receptions into care have been averted.

'The centre can also help us to get children back home. In one abusing family a child had died and another been severely injured and went into care. When the mother came out of prison, the staff at Baron's Close did a lot of work with her. Her marriage broke up while she was inside and she remarried later. Eventually the child was returned to her. So Baron's Close is successful not just in keeping children out of care. It is a base to provide links by which to return children from care to home, and there are very few cases where it hasn't worked.'

The Gerard Avenue Project (GAP)

Background

GAP has operated since 1984 in a former children's home in a street in a neighbourhood in Canley, a post-war council-house development consisting of some 10,000 persons on the outskirts of Coventry. The objectives of the project are given as

To provide an alternative to custody for juveniles. To divert youngsters from court by increasing the rate of cautioning. To support those youngsters at risk of reception into care, in their homes. To provide the project resources in a manner which is conducive to community development work and enabling the local residents to use the facilities.

The project staff consists of a project leader, two project workers, a part-time clerk and two community programme workers (part-time). The centre is open during the day-time for anyone to drop in, to use the washing machines or to obtain welfare-rights advice. Youth-club work and sport is undertaken with youngsters of junior and senior age, and one club exists just for girls. A motor-cycle project operates most weekdays and a toy-library service is available. During the holidays extensive play schemes are run.

Project leader

'I was appointed in 1983. It was important to me to recognise the way the juvenile-justice system works and the effect it has on why young people get sent down. If you keep kids out of court, then ultimately you keep them out of custody, because one of the reasons for them getting sent down is frequency of previous court appearances. The second major need was to look at practice. Traditional IT has many failings in terms of bussing kids from their own communities to participate in one night a week group work. It gives rise to the notion of holidays for hooligans – why should it be that youngsters who commit these terrible offences get the benefit of videos and all the rest of it whereas their neighbours who do not offend do not? We tried to formulate a notion of practice that would enable us to work within the community and so recognise all the various areas of young persons' lives that they felt were important.

'These were the ideas we put together. We have been able to locate ourselves within the juvenile-justice system and so influence the things that are happening around us. Essentially the three key areas are the point at which the police decide whether or not to prosecute, the writing of social enquiry reports by social workers and probation officers, and the putting together of an alternative to custody where courts are considering that. We've been to speak to the local superintendent and explained that we are not here to stop you doing your job but we are here to try and increase the rate of diversion. We recommend more cautions for kids and then, when the police still insist on prosecuting, we seek alternative solutions. We have got the police to reverse a number of their decisions to prosecute. We have spent this year showing that we can divert some kids without the feared likelihood of them coming back just a few weeks later because they have been let off. On the basis of our experience we've written a paper suggesting a model for a citywide juvenile-liaison bureau comprising the police, probation service and SSD.

'We have at GAP a weekly meeting which the probation service also attends and we look at every young person who has been arrested. We then back a recommendation on behalf of the SSD sent to the police whether we feel they should be cautioned, prosecuted or no action taken. We also decide whether or not a key worker should be allocated and whether a home visit should be done. We work on the basis of minimal intervention. If it appears that the youngster is not likely to receive a custodial sentence, then we recommend that the SSD team or probation service write the social enquiry report. We would be advisory to them and in particular act as a consultant over what recommendation to make. We try to ensure that the lowest tariff recommendation is made and that this is well worded, so as to be logical to the magistrates. There is still an issue over supervision orders, for some probation officers in the city will gladly recommend a supervision order for the first minor offence because they are taking a welfare line. Here at GAP we take the view that a supervision order should be reserved as a high-tariff disposal. With youngsters for whom there is a likelihood of a custodial sentence, we will try to write the report ourselves unless it is allocated to a district social worker or probation officer. Then generally we'll co-work and try to have a heavy influence. There has not been any case where we have wanted to recommend something and the social worker disagreed. The report is then presented to the court. We usually attend if we think there is a risk of custody or if we've recommended an alternative that involves the resources of GAP.

'In the 2 years before GAP started there were twelve to thirteen youngsters given custodial sentences in this area. In the last 2 years there has been one. There has also been a massive reduction of about 80 per cent in the use of supervision orders, which I think is a reflection both of us looking for alternatives that make more sense when we go to court and also with this notion of encouraging social workers to go down tariff and to regard supervision orders as high-tariff options.

'The Project's work with juvenile offenders is very discreet. We do not take referrals and we do not miss any kids, because we are notified of every arrest. With kids who are at risk of being received voluntarily into the care of the SSD it is very different. We do attend all weekly team meetings and allocation meetings at the SSD, so we are aware of all the new cases that come into the district team. We have tended to respond to those cases where there is clearly something we can offer, or where we think the department is going to make a wrong decision. We have worked with a number of young women whose parents have been up to the district office of the SSD insisting that their kids are taken into care. We have done that by offering everything from individual work to involvement with the groups and schemes we run at the project. But we are a small team and must not duplicate social-work activity that is done elsewhere.

'Turning to the neighbourhood activities, when I started here, I had hopes of us forming a local tenants' association and work of that nature which has never really materialised. The focus has been around this building and around play schemes. We have tried to use the nearby youth centre as an example of establishing a framework whereby we can bring in the local people with a view to enabling them to have greater control over local resources. We have tried to get the whole community to participate in the summer play scheme, which catered for 500 or 600 kids. Last Christmas we had a party for the under-tens where 200 kids turned up. We try to ensure that people do not see us as having favourites and only working with people who've been in trouble. It is often a tightrope trying to meet the more general needs of the neighbourhood and catering for your priority client group. It is important though to recognise that GAP is an IT centre that works from a neighbourhood context rather than the other way round. If we do that, it is necessary to prioritise the use of the building with regard to that client group, which consists predominantly of young males. Sometimes their loud swearing, running around the building and stuff like that does put other people off from using the building. But they are the primary group.'

Project worker 1

'Other places have a systems management of juvenile offenders. The difference here is that we work within a neighbourhood and so offer facilities to youngsters who are not identified as delinquents as well as those who are. Few youngsters are referred to us by the social services; most we meet at the youth club or by word of mouth. After all, only those youngsters going through the courts are likely to receive IT. But others may have similar needs. Further, because we work on this basis, those youngsters who do come here do not get identified by the community as going to a place which is for kids who are in trouble. Instead they are just going to that place where the kids go.

'Twenty five per cent of my time goes to the motor-bike group. Another quarter on statutory work. Also I run groups for regular users, such as the football group, and I've set up occasional weekends going walking. I try to spend some time with kids who are hanging around the project, but because this has not been consistent, it has not been satisfactory.

'When we started here, the youngsters who had been in most trouble could be categorised as doing auto crime. So we thought the best way of dealing with it was to set up a motor-cycle group. It was only limited by the amount of time I could spend on it, so we made application to and got two part-time workers from community programmes. The aim was to offer to youngsters who are interested in motor bikes the chance to do it as enjoyable leisure, to learn to ride and maintain bikes. By statutory work I mean those who come to our attention via the juvenile bureau for non-school attendance, for a court report, or who are referred by the social worker who wants some back-up for a particular boy. The statutory cases are not the bulk of our work and we would not want that. We like to form activity groups into which the statutory referrals can participate. Thus two boys have been referred to the football group but most come because I put up a notice in the youth club.

'Concerning the youngsters who spend a lot of time here, I feel we can't offer them enough. They want to be better off and I can't do that. But we can offer them the opportunity to sit and talk, or to go, say, on a sail-training course. We provide a route to certain resources. I rarely approach them thinking I've got to change them but rather I offer an education so that they can learn things from their own experiences and so make more informed choices. But the prospect for many is long-term unemployment. We are the first-aid workers of an unequal society. But we still have a role to play, can still show what choices are open.

'Consider a family we know well. Mum has come to the play group, the daughters to the girls' events, the sons to the football group. A few weeks ago mum came in and said: "I've got a real problem with J (her son). The minute I go out he gets hold of my lighter fuel and inhales it with his mates. He won't talk to me, will you talk to him?" I wrote a note to the boy saying I was not going to tell him off but would he come in for a chat. He came and I gave him some pamphlets about solvent abuse. The next day I came in and there he was with half a dozen of his mates. He was saying, 'They won't believe me, they think I'm telling lies". So with the whole group I was able to go through the same information about abuse and from what I hear the whole thing has changed. It's not a panacea but it is a natural contact which offers a more palatable way of dealing with an issue with local youngsters than can be done by a panic.'

Project worker 2

'In any week I do juvenile liaison work, attend to welfare rights enquiries, do on-going work. I spend time with the users of the building and I work a couple of nights a week, usually with some girls.

'The management committee of the local youth club has appointed two sessional workers for new initiatives with girls' work. It was exciting because we got some of the local girls to interview for the workers. I became involved because the facilities at GAP are so much better than at the youth club and they could use our video or photographic equipment. It evolved into a lot of support work for the sessional workers. Then, coming from that, girls were saying to me, "We would like to play some sport, the boys get all the action and we would like to give it a crack". So I said we could meet and play some sports on a Sunday night. It is giving girls space to talk about what it's like to be a girl. It is also useful to me. If we pick up a girl at GAP and she is at risk of custody or care, we have very few systems we can fit her into. Given that we are trying to avoid individualising or labelling, if I can evolve some activities that girls can become part of, it means my work with those girls is enhanced.

'Turning to families, a man came in this morning with whom I work jointly with the district social worker. It is easier for him to pop in here than to hike all the way up to the district team with his two kids. He came in before Christmas saying he had baby-sat one night for his ex-wife and she hadn't come back, so he got the kids, no money, no tenancy of the house and a lot of debts. I felt I would try to sort out the finances. The district team was concerned that he wouldn't be able to cope for long. But he's coped really well and that's partly because we are here, and if things do get on top of him, he can come across. He lives right opposite. I think the knowledge that there is an agency here that's not a statutory agency has been very useful to him.

'Although we are not a statutory body, I would never apply a friendship label to describe my relationship with people. I cannot be a friend because in the end I am paid as a professional worker. I was walking around the shops this morning and about five people stopped and said, "Have you done this or can you see me about that?", and you think, yes I am really into this community. But there are times when I am in a very difficult position when I have been a community worker to a family and yet also been very concerned about the children and have had to say, "I am sorry about this, but I want to see the children". So it is a tightrope. Luckily what happened with that family is that they weren't hostile to me; they could place it in the context of the other things I had done and they recognised that I had to be concerned about the kids.'

User 1

'People call Canley a tramps area, the doss place. It's people in snobby houses who say that, they're no better than us. But it can be depressing, no work, no money. In the evenings we go to the youth club until 8.30 then to the pub. But we're skint and you've got to sip a pint to make it last the whole night. Or we'll hang about the shops trying to keep warm.

'We've all been in trouble with the police but some more than others. One of the troubles here (at GAP) is that I think those in the most trouble get the most privileges. They (the staff) are friendly but they pay more attention to others. This is a place to keep warm, to doss, to bring in your mates and have a chat and coffee. But they do put you out too easily. I got banned for breaking a window.

'I'm on the committee and because we are older we're treated as responsible and allowed to have the keys for the youth club and have a game of pool. It's good to know that they think you are responsible people. If too many come in to the club, I think that's a bit hard to handle, so I lock up. But most of the time there's only five or six so we're all able to get something to do and nobody gets bored and starts smashing things.'

User 2

'We do spend a lot of time here and we have a laugh. But often we're bored. We've been asking them for quite a time to get some music instruments, a guitar, keyboard, drums. They say they will but we haven't heard anything since. I'm not saying all this necessarily keeps you out of trouble with the police because at night there is nowhere to go and we don't get into trouble. But it keeps us off the streets and that is good and they try to help you out as much as possible.

'You get loads of different people visiting this place to use the phone, the washing machine, hiring out the camping equipment. It's good for all the people around here. In the summer you get women bringing their kids in here because they have a nursery and put the climbing frame and swimming pool out the back.

'Things ain't going to change for me, so I'd like to see this place open until nine o'clock at night. You could go home, get something to eat, get a bag of chips, and come back. We wouldn't rob this place because we'd be robbing ourselves.'

User 3

'I first met a social worker when I first got into trouble. I did about four burglaries. The first probation officer I had was wicked; she didn't like me at all. Said I was the gang leader. It was my first appearance and I got sent down for 3 months. I got into trouble again then I met N (project worker) at the social-services place. I was one of the first to come here. What I like about the people at GAP is that you can see them any time in the week and get to speak to them. A probation officer you see only once a week. When I met N, I'd got into trouble, he became my mate, he came to court with me.'

User 4

'I hadn't had much to do with GAP, then a woman came to my house and said about this 2-week sailing trip. We went from Southampton to Dartmouth then Cherbourg and Amsterdam. We had storms, I nearly got washed overboard. We had to go up the masts. I was scared but it was great. You must work together as a team. It makes you grow up. I got an excellent report. We were sponsored by GAP. I could never have afforded it. I haven't really thanked GAP for it.

'When we came back from the trip, five or six girls wanted to do sport. Now we meet every week. You feel as though you are helping to get other people in. The lads like to think it's their GAP but we're showing them it's for everybody. I'd be lost without it now. I've got a temporary job as a cleaner but there is not a lot to do around here at nights.

'The leaders are a great bunch, really helpful. They know what they are doing. The lads here are a pretty rough bunch. I thought it impossible to keep them under control but they do; and the lads have changed, they don't seem half as bad as they used to. It's K (project worker) I really talk to. You can talk to her about boy-friends, family problems. I can talk to K better than I can to my mother, you really get your feelings out. I've got trust and confidence in her because I know she's not going to go around talking about it. She's near my age, she's not married, she's got time. I don't see her as a social worker. She is more like a mate. When I first came here, I had an image of social workers all sitting in little offices. Instead there was music blaring out and kids running around. I sometimes think I'd like a job here. I wonder if I've got it in me. I think I have.'

User and volunteer

'There's isolation around here. This has been part of my difficulty, because I'm divorced with two children. I've got a hyper-active child. He's six, he's partially deaf and has to have a special diet, which causes financial problems. I've also got a teenage girl.
'I heard about GAP through the first play scheme they held. When I first came in, I thought how friendly they all were. That was important to me, because I was very shy. I got involved in the arts and crafts and acted as escort on the trips. I know so many people here now. My child met other children here and that burned up his energy and my daughter joined the girls' group.
'I've got involved in a women's health group which meets here. GAP lets us have a room and allows us to use their video. Now we are going out into the community to tell women about things like cervical cancer, post-natal depression and so on. Now I'm also trying to start something for one-parent families. You have children 24 hours a day without a break so you need your own organisation.'

Community policewoman

'Predominantly I come into GAP to see the staff. I also see the lads and have a fairly good relationship with them. They see me differently from the bobby in the car and call me by my first name. I have nicked a number but, as I have been fair with them, it doesn't sour it. You get a different attitude being on the community, because you know the people. You learn that a lot of the kids are defensive and aggressive in their language and that helps you go in with a different attitude.
'GAP is valuable in terms of the relationships it has with kids and because it gives them somewhere to go. It is somewhere they can bring their problems and talk with people. The SSD here have such a case-load that they just haven't got the time. In GAP youngsters can get much more of time input.
'GAP has motivated youngsters, motivated them to take responsibility, for instance, as to using the keys for the youth club. They know they must look after those keys. It is a discipline. Look at B (a teenager). He has now kept out of trouble for 12 months and no doubt there are pressures on him to take to crime again. He

comes here a lot, so some of this must be attributable to GAP's work with him. They have had their failures and some kids they have got nowhere with, but you expect that.'

Schoolteacher

'They have tremendous contact with people. I get some feedback from the boys. They keep on going to GAP, that is the best measure. One of the benefits is that it is on their doorsteps. Unlike the social services, they can just pop around the corner and it is there just when it is needed. And anyone will talk to you. It's not a matter of "Oh that's nothing to do with me, go and see so-and-so". This means people get confidence.

'We've benefited from GAP because we are now more aware of the problems in the area. In the past we dreaded these roads. We've been able to relate to GAP and through it to the area; and through them we might find out why a kid is behaving badly perhaps because his old man or mum has gone off. Our attitudes have changed.'

SSD social worker

'Obviously the SSD has ties with GAP. If we are working with the same child, we pool information. For instance, one boy had come from a secure unit and was living in a children's home in Canley. I got together with GAP and we drew up a plan. I started taking him to do photography at GAP and he related well to the people there. In the end it worked out very well – rehabilitation.

'There is a dynamic about GAP. They have ideas about what they want to do, they stick to them, and it works. They've helped the police see that it is not just a matter of little vagabonds roaming the streets and nicking cars. They've enabled the police to see that it goes deeper than that.

'You do hear criticisms of GAP. I've heard people complain that kids are running in and out there all the time. But you get criticism in any community and the people who do it don't bother to knock at the door to find out what it is all about. GAP has been very successful and other SSD districts ask why they can't have one.'

The Roundhill Project

Background

The Roundhill (formerly Southdown) Project was run in the first leader's home from 1976 to 1983. It then moved into a small purpose-built centre. The project now serves two council estates, with a total population of about 5,000 persons. The stated objectives are 'to prevent children from being removed from families unnecessarily, to lower levels of delinquency, to provide or enable youth and community facilities'. The staffing consists of a project leader, a project worker, two part-time project workers (who share a post), two secretaries employed on a sessional basis, a part-time warden, and a part-time coffee-bar worker via an MSC scheme. The main activities are before-school clubs, after-school clubs, junior boys' and junior girls' clubs, infants' club, senior youth club, mother and toddlers group, a mothers' group, keep fit, judo club, a meeting for the elderly and various sporting activities.

Project leader

'I was brought up on this estate and I'd been in trouble for various reasons, drug-taking, burglaries. When I became a Christian 11 years ago, I became very aware that there were other youngsters in the same position as me. When the first project leader came, he asked me to get involved in the youth club. After a year of being a volunteer, I was taken on full-time. I had no qualifications but I studied and after some years became project leader.

'The centre is open from 8.30 am until 10 pm most days. It is used by local mums and children, who come in for various clubs. This open, drop-in nature makes the centre available to people. It is also providing the centre with a non-stigmatising atmosphere; people can come in at any time for any reason, it may be to talk about how they can give up drugs, about the fact that they have got no money or no food, or it may simply be to have a cup of coffee, to play table tennis or just to talk to some of the workers.

'We also do a great deal of sport, which gives alternative prestige. Some kids are given the label of failure at school, but sporting activities enable some to excel, which is important in terms of self-development. The sport and the clubs are also an alternative to getting into trouble, to walking the streets, to drifting into delinquent behaviour. It is a valuable place to get to know youngsters. Your average social-work relationship which is over a desk produces a kind of guard in people; they become very defensive. But when you are engaged in an activity with a youngster, the barriers go down.

'Another aspect of neighbourhood is that P (project worker) and I live locally, so we are available, people can approach you at any time. Also people can see your family and the fact that you have difficulties. So they don't view you just as a capable helper but as a part of their community. A related advantage is the time we have been here. We form relationships with younger children that carry on, so that when they are teenagers going through troubles, we already know them well.

'The emphasis on community is also seen in our reliance on volunteers, with about twenty to thirty here most weeks. They are local people who live on the estate. We have encouraged people who have had difficulties such as unemployment or crime in their own lives to become volunteers, so that they see that they have something positive to offer. To help volunteers, we set up a training scheme in which they keep diaries and record their work, which is discussed in tutorials, and they attend a residential weekend. At the end of the year they receive a certificate.

'To illustrate our work with individuals. George came in to play pool. He's part of a group that were abusing amphetamines. He's married with children, in and out of prison. I tend to gravitate towards such people partly because of my own past, partly because it's a big need. He owed a lot of money to pushers who were threatening him. He recognised that his family was cracking up and that his wife might leave. We gave him some practical help to get the pusher off his back. He then began to talk about how to give it up. I gave him social-work advice, community-work advice and suggested he try prayer. He did give up drugs for about 4 months. Then he relapsed. Now he's going through a good stage, his family is holding together and is going on holiday with the project.

'Al came in with the group using amphetamines. He's also married with children. I did not relate directly to him but later he told me his decision to give up using them was related to the ethos of the centre. He now runs the coffee bar under an MSC post. Interestingly, he has also started to open up his own home to other local people.

'Of late the project has been changing as the Children's Society does not want to put in so much money into a small area. So we are encouraging local people to take over. We have a Users' Committee and that is taking on more power to control the centre. This will change into a Management Committee which will be responsible for the centre, for saying who the workers are and what they do. We will not be so much involved with work with individuals – except for J (project worker), who has a specialist preventative role – but more in training local people to run clubs and cope with delinquency.

'I am obviously biased but I think it has been a success. We know that care orders and juvenile-crime rates have gone down and we know young people who would have ended up in institutions but are still here. And we get a lot of positive feedback from local people.'

Project worker (part-time)

'My main responsibilities have been for the women's groups, youth work and counselling local families. A Tuesday group tends to be for women with young children because we have a creche run by two local women. It makes its own rules and insists that no one can miss a session without good reason – they have a high commitment and there is a waiting list. The statutory agencies have referred women who are facing financial problems, who are under stress, or whose children are at risk. This tends not to be stigmatising because the woman usually knows about the group already, knows women who are in it, and does not feel it is threatening. The Wednesday group is more for women whose children are at school. They discuss, say, problems with the DHSS, how to claim for their teenage children. It is more of an open group, bigger but more fluctuating, with about fifteen members.

'The value of the groups is that it gives women confidence in their own abilities. It has taught them their own skills and to deal with life's problems. It has helped them to share difficulties with other women. Because the groups are a means of introductions and friendships, it leads to them forming links which are maintained outside the centre, and so they help each other independently of the group.

'I also work with families outside the groups. A husband approached me when he was devastated by his wife leaving. He was suicidal and unable to cope at home. I remember finding every cupboard steeped in filthy washing. Together we plodded through the washing, the ironing and all the practical things. He was able to share his pain with me. In the end he managed the home and children incredibly well.

'We knew the eldest daughter of that marriage very well. She truanted a lot and I encouraged her to attend school. I feel the activities of the project compensated for what she lost at home. After she left school, she was accused of a serious crime at work. She had a traumatic time at court. She was found guilty and sacked and unable to get another job. We managed to get a grant to employ her at the project for 2 years. She had felt totally undermined and to put her in a position of trust was crucial to restoring her self-confidence. She has now developed so much that I can hardly remember her as she was. She can still be extremely silly but she has got a tremendous understanding of other people's needs and has become competent at her job within the centre. She has now left because she's found a job in town, which is great, but she stays on as one of the leaders of the senior youth club.'

Project worker

'I was introduced to the project when I was still at school. Later I went on the trainee leader scheme and my interest increased until they asked me to join full-time in 1981. I am very much a local person, born and bred on this council estate. This has made it difficult in that youngsters whom I knew came under my control at the youth club. But it helps because I know so many families and the area.

'As I am going away on a course, I am in the process of handing my responsibilities over to local people. These are the infants' and girls' clubs and the general running of the centre. I recently did a time and motion study and found that a lot of my time is spent on ensuring that things happen here, that clubs run smoothly, that volunteers turn up, and answering the calls of people who come into the centre for things like welfare rights. Now I must ensure that this will continue in my absence.'

User 1

'I never got on at home and then got sent to detention centre. I met Margy at a hostel and we moved into a council house here. She already had one child and soon we had four – all under five. We found it difficult on the dole and I got into debt – £500. Margy came to the mums group at the project. I popped in, met everybody, played for the football team. But the relationship between me and Margy dwindled. She went to live with someone else. I tried to keep all the kids together but I couldn't give them what a mother does. In the end I turned to drugs. J (project worker) and the others were helping. When the school complained about the two kids being late, they took it in turns to take them. J was magic. Sometimes she met the kids. She took all the washing to her place as I never had a washing machine. Helped me on the financial side and tried to get me off drugs. If it wasn't for her, the kids would have gone into care a long time before. But I was hooked. One night a mate and me got through £50 worth. I sold all my stuff, you'll do anything to get it. But I didn't sell the kid's beds. J reckoned we had to go to social services because she could not withhold the fact that I was on drugs. It was getting too much for me and once I hit the kids. So they went into care.

'I've stopped the drugs now. I go to the centre every day. I don't know what I'd do if I didn't go there. D (project leader) is there and you can tell him anything and he'll keep it between ourselves. You can trust D, you can't trust social workers. When I've got all my debts sorted out, perhaps I can get a job.'

User 2

'I had a violent marriage – cracked ribs, split lip. And no money. My mother met J at the shops and she offered to call on me. We were friends from then on. She talked to me and my husband. I came along to the project. I now go to the mums group and keep fit. I'm always popping in and out there because you can always go there. Anyway, eventually we divorced but I still need help. J is always there. I even phone her at night. She came to court for the access hearing. My ex-husband now has access and this is done at the centre because of the violence. I know the children are safe there. J is like a mum to me. She advises you how to go about things, like if you want to change your solicitor. But she gets you to do it. She likes everybody and everybody loves her. I know a 4-year-old boy and he told me that J is his best friend. I'd love to be like J.'

User 3

'I was in the house with two small children. Divorce is like losing someone through death but it goes on. I was on tablets and living on social security. The social worker from social services suggested I went to the project. A neighbour took me along. I was shaking but it was really good. They bothered to include you, you didn't get stonewalled. In the group we do lots of silly, nice things. Like the jacuzzi at Bristol. For us it is a step out of our circumstances. We slog our guts out 7 days a week trying to keep everything together and just to have 5 minutes without the children is really good. I've gained a circle of friends. We look after each other's children. I'm a lot more relaxed. I don't take tablets and I don't need a social worker any more.'

Volunteer

'I've lived in this area all my life, although a lot of my childhood was in a children's home. After I married, I was having trouble with one of my sons and went to child guidance. She suggested I went to the mums group at the project. I didn't until I met a girl who said, 'I go to this lovely group, why not come?' I went, they all seemed friendly, and that's how it started for me. That was 8 years ago. I go into the project every day, I can't stay away. I like everyone connected with it. My sons had been nagging me about doing judo but we couldn't afford it at the Sports Centre. D (project leader) said we could have Saturday mornings and recommended an instructor. He thought the club was a place for rough kids but said he'd give it a go. I applied to the Sports Council and got a grant for mats. Five parents helped, the club started and has been very successful.

'Now I'm chairperson of the Users' Committee. We have been worried about the abuse of equipment so called a meeting – about fifty came – and agreed that every club must delegate two leaders to look after things, to keep the café clean and to report breakages. That has improved things. It has changed me. I used to have an inferiority complex, walking along with my head bowed, thinking everyone was looking at me. I don't do that anymore. I find I can help other people too. I've a friend going through a marriage problem. She wants to share it with me. I'd like to get even more involved. I've applied to do a leader's training course.'

Junior-school teacher

'When I first came to the school, it struck me that it needed to be part of the community. In my class over a quarter of the children were from one-parent families and many found life a real struggle. I heard from the children about the project and I realised that its staff were important to the neighbourhood and the children. Many go to junior club. It is not just the deprived ones, because the project is reaching out to the whole community. The parents know the children will be looked after there, they have tremendous trust in the project; and the club before school is useful to us, for that slots beautifully into the school day. When the staff come to take assemblies, it is like having old friends in, you feel the buzz around the children.

'The project is a great help with youngsters who are on a short fuse. I think of one who would react with fists, words, anything. He was suspended and if he had not had the project to go to, he would have got into all sorts of trouble with the law. I now talk to boys there with whom I did not get on well at school. We can talk because we have another link beside school.

'Not everybody speaks well of the project. Some parents wonder if it is a place for glue-sniffers and drug-takers. Some complain about the noise. But for most it's very important because you can go there for help. Children can talk to the staff there and pour out their problems, they'll be listened to. Sometimes adults don't have time for children but I've never known anyone in the project who won't give time and themselves.'

SSD social worker

'The two estates served by the project have the highest rate of juvenile crime and the highest rate of referrals to the SSD in the city. So the fact that the project provides somewhere for kids to go and a wide range of group activities must take pressure off us. The staff prevent people being drawn into the social-services network, either by reassuring us about a family or providing a solution without us having to touch the situation.

'It prevents children going into care by providing alternative activities to kids getting into trouble. It provides a focus for kids who have started going down the road and need some sort of supervision. One teenager who was put on a supervision order became a helper at the project and, as far as we were concerned, Roundhill did the supervision. It has provided an alternative to reception into care for a lot of children, but also by forming bridges it sometimes makes periods of temporary care more acceptable to families.

'The staff at the project get on well with everybody but they are also professionally skilled. From a SSD point of view they understand exactly what approach we have to take. They have the ability to respect other people's points of view and, not exactly being laid back, but of letting other people get involved and making decisions for themselves. You can rely on their work to be of a very high standard. Their attitude to how people should be treated and dealt with is always right and proper in terms of not going behind people's backs and always wanting to be straight with people about what is happening. In that sense they are very good for social services because they insist on certain standards.'

The Walcot Centre

Background

Situated in a prefabricated hut in the grounds of a school, the Walcot Centre was opened in 1980, with close co-operation between the Children's Society and the local authority. Walcot is an estate, mainly of council housing, to the east of Swindon and with a population of about 4,500. One worker concentrates on Penn Hill, an estate of about 8,000 population to the north of the town. The centre's objective is 'to involve local people in projects which are designed to improve the life chances of children from the areas in which we work'. To reach this end, the centre runs a nursery group called Acorn, a Clinic Link group, a First Time Mothers' group, Family Link Volunteers, a toy library, play schemes, coffee mornings, welfare-rights advice and keep-fit sessions.

The centre's staff consists of a project leader, project worker (under-fives), neighbourhood worker, neighbourhood worker (Penn Hill), neighbourhood worker (part-time), welfare-rights worker (part-time), administrator (part-time) and three nursery nurses (part-time).

Project leader

'My work as project leader is mainly concerned with administration and groups. The groups range from the staff team, the training groups of volunteers, to a new group we are starting for claimants. Occasionally, when somebody else is not available on a particular crisis, I will see local residents directly but generally I work through staff and volunteers. We have full-time staff, part-time staff and volunteers. The former would take on more complex cases like complicated welfare-rights matters and things at the organisational level, whereas the volunteers do personal and family crises. Sometimes the volunteers have faced severe problems themselves, like a woman who lost a baby through a cot death and was helped by being in touch with a group. But there are a diversity of volunteers and that has the advantage of a diversity of approaches.

'The project has been based on AIR, Accessible, Informal and Reciprocal. Accessible does not mean that the centre is open 5 days a week. It means that someone is available. There are now networks of informed individuals who through training or commitment have knowledge of community and social services and who are identifiable within their own streets. Informal means that we respond without an appointment – no need to fix a time in coming here. Reciprocal implies that people can give something back. If you visit the centre, it is hard to know who are the staff, the volunteers and the users, because everyone is mixed in together.

'There is something about being local and accessible which means that we may be more likely to deal with crisis situations than a local authority SSD in the centre of town. Often the centre staff are the first port of call. This means we can be preventative in terms of keeping children out of care. But we do more, in terms of empowering local residents, increasing self-confidence and self-esteem, and increasing the involvement of local people in identifying their own needs.

'But major changes are taking place. When I first arrived, the staff took responsibility for providing all the services and making sure, for example, that people held keys for the mothers and toddlers groups. The staff will definitely not do that now. The role of the staff with such groups is to attend committee meetings and to ensure things are discussed but not to be involved in the nitty gritty. If local people want activities to happen, then we will provide support but we won't actually do it for them.

'The plan is that there will be local management committee made up largely of volunteers and users, although funders will be represented. The way I would like to see it developing is that accountability of staff at the centre would be to the chairperson of a local management committee and the Children's Society role would be in consultancy, support and training. In terms of ownership I'd like that to be with the local committee. I would not be based in the centre but we would have a network of staff within the town in a variety of teams of which Walcot would be one and Penn Hill another. The Walcot Centre would still have full-time and part-time workers, although the Children's Society would not be funding all of them. One of the things we have done is to develop a strong committee that can continue the work. The advantage of the plan is that it will give more responsibility to local people. The disadvantage is I wonder if we are asking people to do too much in too short a time and with too small resources.'

Project worker (under-fives and families)

'My main responsibility is the Acorn Project, in which I lead a team of four. In the beginning I worked closely with the health department in the baby clinic and set up a group called Clinic Link, which helped isolated parents with young children to make friendships. During one of these sessions the health visitor expressed her concern that many families did not attend the clinic. Our ideal became a special play group with high-health input where children could have developmental checks and where parents could share in the play and growth. The Children's Society and the health department agreed to a 2-year pilot scheme. Acorn was born.

'All the families attending the Acorn Project are referred through doctors, health visitors or social workers, because they have fallen behind in development owing to hospitalisation, illness, lack of stimulation or poor parenting skills. At least half the children have been at risk of coming into public care, owing to possible abuse or poor physical care.

'Acorn is for children 20 months to 3 years old and the group opens 2 days a week. We start with free-play sessions and parents work alongside staff, helping their child by naming objects in a book, fitting shapes in a puzzle, or helping to build a child's confidence in climbing and balancing skills. The parents have a rota where they help the cook prepare the midday meal and learn about cooking and the nutritional value of the food children eat. The parents take coffee-breaks together; this enables them to build friendships in the group. If parents have problems, are feeling low or upset, the family worker is available to talk things through.

'We have formal teaching for the parents in the sense of discussing films on child development and behaviour. The doctor and health visitor are available to talk to parents individually about children's health problems, contraception, breast-feeding or parents' health. We have fun things too like parents having their hair done or beauty treatment at the local college or going to the local ice-skating rink.

'We are preventing children coming into care, preventing abuse, preventing them falling further behind in development. One parent here was sent by the social services as a last chance before they took her children away. She left the children alone for hours on end, shut in their rooms, with no stimulation, no warmth, clothes not changed, poorly fed, their bottoms all raw. I thought she was going to be so hard. But she's lovely, she really likes coming. We cannot force mums to come but we have only ever had one who dropped out. Mums come to support each other. One mother was in and out of psychiatric hospital and the other mums were really supportive; they looked after her children so the husband could visit her. Mums who left a year ago still meet together on their own, go to their children's parties and so on. In the summer we hold play schemes and the old mums come back. The fact that the mums come from the same neighbourhood means that they keep on seeing each other and they go on to the same play groups and school together.

'We have a family where the children are actually in care and we are helping the parent to learn the parenting skills needed to have the children returned to her. The foster parent brings the children into the group and the mother feeds, changes and cares for them and learns about the play and stimulation children need. The twice-weekly access encourages the parent/child bond to remain strong, so if and when they return home, it will be less traumatic for everyone.'

Neighbourhood worker

'Married at 16, divorced and remarried, I've spent years staying at home looking after my children. Taking my younger girl to school, I saw the Walcot Centre and went to keep fit. From the outside it looked like some old hut but it was amazing inside because it was so friendly. I met a lady here and we became good friends and we went to J (former leader) and expressed our concern about isolated mums in Walcot. We thought she would do something but she said, 'What are you going to do?' We called it Neighbourhood Care Volunteers (later changed to Family Link). Eight of us decided we wanted some training first. We got so much from the training – self-awareness and listening skills. We then contacted outside agencies for referrals to visit. Some of the referrals were devastating to us. I had a mum in a top flat threatening to throw her baby out of the window. I went with her to the housing officials. Me! I had only ever been to pay the rent before. Well, when this man knew I was from the Walcot Centre, he shook my hand and asked if I wanted tea. His whole approach was different from what I was used to. And it was successful. At the end of the day she had her house.

'Eventually I became a full-time worker. What Family Link can provide is one of the most important things in preventive work, that is time. It could be in the evenings, at weekends, sometimes I spend near enough the whole day with a one-parent mum who's bruised her children. Social workers are very restricted in the time they can give. This mum had lost confidence, there was no bedding, just a mattress which a kid had wee'd on night after night. The mum was so depressed, I had to spend time with her and we became good friends. Gradually the little boy went to school with underpants on. Before she hadn't got up to dress him. I used to go there in the mornings to give her a knock. This is preventive work. I want to do something before the child gets battered.

'I am now doing a CSS (Certificate in Social Services) course. It is a chance in a million for a mum on Walcot but I must not forget my own experiences.'

Neighbourhood project worker (part-time)

'A number of things have helped me. One is living on the estate. When I go out on my bike, it is a matter of "hello, hello, hello". Another is that I know what it's like for my husband to be unemployed. Sometimes you see women outside the school all tense because their husband has been laid off and you can say, "There is someone in the Walcot Centre that deals with welfare rights, come and see them". Some people just cannot cope with money, with children, with life in general. Like me, they are not very good at making the housekeeping money last from Friday to Friday. You learn it is all right to have to go to jumble sales for your clothes. Also now we pass clothes around. It is sharing clothes and it is sharing a problem. I see mums standing at the school gates, their faces full of problems, and I can see me standing there 6 years ago. That's how I was, so I can offer them the hand of friendship.'

Welfare-rights worker (part-time)

'I was suddenly on my own in Women's Aid with two children and had to claim supplementary benefit. Being paid on Monday, by the weekend I didn't have enough for food and heating. So I have got some insight into social security. Now I work 12 hours a week doing welfare rights. I also represent at tribunals and am chair of the Welfare Rights Forum. We are the only welfare-rights organisation in Walcot, so we are very busy. People even call at my house for advice.'

Administrator (part-time)

'I have been here since day one. The users had the feeling that they were joining people who were one of them. The economic climate was different then. It's all so different now – you can't have this, you can't have that. I do regret this new branch-out approach. People think we are going to leave them in the lurch.

'The project has done a tremendous amount of good. It has given the people that use the centre a sense of being more confident and more self-sufficient. They are people who may not have a lot of this world's goods but they are really worth something and they contribute a lot in friendship and help in the community.'

User

'My child wasn't thriving so the health visitor suggested I came to Acorn with her. I didn't think it would help but it has. She is pottying herself now but foodwise she is still not right.

'Last night about 11 we put a fan on to heat her room – we can't afford heat all the time – and took her up with a bottle. She began screaming. I was tired, I could really have hurt her but something in me said "No". I can understand how some parents do it. When I woke up this morning, I didn't want to come to Acorn. I was fed up and tired. I rang S (project worker) and she said "Oh, come in". So I did and now I feel better when I talk about it instead of bottling it up. I wouldn't want my child to go into care. If the centre shut down, there would be a lot of bad things happening to the kids.'

Community medical officer

'I come in to Acorn once a fortnight, the health visitor once a week. We are looking for children for whom something is wrong in their development, perhaps due to a lack of stimulation and this does not necessarily mean they are abused. Very often it is a matter of parents in difficult circumstances who love their children.

'Everybody who has been involved says Acorn should go on. This work is saving thousands of pounds. We have been able to spot special education and health needs at an early stage and later the children have been able to settle into ordinary play groups and schools. We know several families whose children would have been in care but for the support here – from the parents as well as staff.'

SSD social worker

'We refer families to the centre, particularly those on the child-abuse register and those with financial problems. It is important that the centre is not part of a statutory body. We've got statutory responsibilities and the families see us as "If I don't co-operate, you are going to do what I want". And that is reality. Families at risk need the kind of support that is non-threatening and agencies that can spent time working with them. That is what the Walcot Centre does. It can really raise people's sense of worth. It does so by encouraging families to take on responsibilities for particular tasks. Originally they share with the families in their difficulties but gradually they withdraw. Our caseload and referrals to our department have diminished as a result of the Walcot Centre being there.'

The Other Projects

As mentioned, six other community projects were included in the study. Lack of space means that their interviews cannot be recorded here, but the full script has been lodged with the Children's Society. However, they constitute an essential part of the investigation, and the analysis and conclusions made at the end of this chapter and in the one that follows are based on these six centres as much as on the other four. Indeed, reference will be made to them and hence it is appropriate to include their background here.

Beckhill Family Centre

Opened in 1985, the centre is located in a Leeds Council estate with a population of under 2,000 and where 66 per cent of the households have a child under 5. The centre's premises consist of a two-floored maisonette in the upper part of a block of council accommodation. Although the Centre is in its early stages, the staff have initiated two mothers and toddlers groups and run the centre on a drop-in basis. In an internal document it was stated:

Our aim is to encourage 'user' participation on decision-making and to develop the individual's confidence, skills and abilities and so encourage self- worth. We aim to foster a good working relationship with other agencies, to facilitate and initiate the development and use of groups and also to be aware of and responsive to the needs of families and their children with particular reference to single parents. We also aim to build up networks of mutual support.

To achieve these aims, the project has the following staff: a project leader, two part-time project workers and a part-time administrator.

Maltby Family Centre

One of the Children's Society's first community projects – it started in 1977 – the family centre has shop-front facilities in Maltby, a mining community in South Yorkshire with a population of 17,000. The stated objectives of the project are to 'Give greater control to people. Develop their confidence and abilities. Make agencies more responsive to people's needs. Foster spirit of mutual and self help'. The family centre's staff consists of a project leader, project worker (young people), community worker (welfare rights), community worker (play), project secretary, handyman (part-time) and a toy-library organiser (part-time).

The staff make a distinction between activities the centre provides directly and those it supports or encourages. Among the former are a welfare-rights advice service, the young unemployed group, the Worzel Gummidge after-school club, play schemes and the minibus loan service. Among the latter are play groups, mothers and toddlers clubs, a toy library and the handicap support group.

Millmead Neighbourhood Centre

The centre, which opened in 1981, is based in a detached three-bedroomed house on a council estate on the edge of Margate. Under the first project leader the centre's objectives 'were designed to provide a low key, first line prevention service for families and children'. Under the present leader, who started in 1984, the objective is 'to improve the quality of life for children and families on the Millmead estate'. The staff employed to further this aim are a project leader, neighbourhood worker, part-time administrative officer, and two part-time domestics. Amongst the activities held at the centre are an advice service, keep fit, First Steps and Centre Link for mothers and children, a Twilight Club and Friday Club for children, a computer club, adult education.

Shoebury Family Centre

After periods in two other sites, the family centre moved in 1985 to two adjoining council houses. It serves council estates with a total population of around 27,000 people some 5 miles from the centre of Southend, although concentrating on two smaller areas within these estates.

The objectives of the project are 'the complete development of individual and family so that they can survive in their community' and to 'prevent children being taken into care and to enable families and individuals to grow and develop so that they may successfully function within society'. The staffing consists of a project leader, two project workers, an administrator, a part-time clerical worker and a part-time domestic. The project's activities include a nurture group and mothers and toddlers group, after-school club, play schemes, and support for local participation in youth clubs and tenants' associations.

Swansea Family Centre

Having worked from two previous sites for several years, the project secured its present premises in 1985. It serves a community of three council estates on the outskirts of Swansea. An internal document recorded that 'It is with the aim of breaking a deprived cycle that we are placing a great emphasis on preventative social work' while a recent official definition of the centre's objective declared it was 'To provide and facilitate a supportive element by which the local community members will enhance their leadership skills and their ability to form a firmer network of services for children on the estates'.

The activities run at the family centre include mothers and toddlers groups, play groups, after-school clubs, the pre-adolescent group, the youth training scheme. The staff consists of a project leader, three project workers, a secretary (part-time) and caretaker (sessional). A further project worker is pioneering work on another estate some 8 miles away.

Walsall Family Centre

The family centre has been run in two linked council houses since 1984 in an outlying pre-war council estate whose population is 3,128. The aims of the project are:

To reduce stress in families and to encourage good parenting and child care skills by a broad education programme. To prevent avoidable family breakdowns and the need for committal to or reception into care. To provide a welcoming environment which will encourage informal contact/visits by people from the local community. As other needs are identified to work with the local community to meet these as far as possible from within their own resources.

The family centre is headed by a project leader with one other full-time project worker and a part-time secretary. Also housed within the centre is a Manpower Services Commission scheme run by the local community association. It employs a leading hand, a mothers and toddlers' organiser, a drop-in centre organiser, a hairdresser and three part-timers.

Between them the project workers and MSC workers run an advice service, mothers and toddlers groups, play groups, keep-fit club, slimming group, a men's club (the Hooligans), an after-school club and a football team. Services are also provided for pensioners and the handicapped, while the centre is open for local residents to drop in.

Three Models

The accounts of the voluntary projects convey a complex variety of activities within a small number of centres. Yet they should not be regarded as somehow separate from the larger trends in prevention which were described in earlier chapters. For a start they were part of the response of the voluntary agencies to the growing call for more preventative action. In common with some local-authority departments, they also expressed the belief that prevention could be more effectively achieved within a neighbourhood setting. Moreover, like the statutory workers described earlier, the project members were having to grapple with problems that had their roots in poverty and inequality and hence some began to think in terms of how they could facilitate greater equality. The projects were thus a response to and a reflection of larger social forces which were influencing the social services in general.

But the projects, small as they are, are able to add something to existing knowledge about prevention. Thus from an investigation of their approaches it is possible to identify three different types or models of community projects.

The client-focused model

The Baron's Close Young Family Centre stood out as different from the other nine projects. Yet my visits to centres run by other voluntary societies and to those of the local authorities confirmed that its approach is not uncommon. It displayed the following characteristics:

(a) *Specialised activities.* While not excluding other activities, most resources were devoted to one service and one client category, usually care and training for the under-fives and their parents.
(b) *Referred clients.* Access to the service usually depended on a referral from a statutory body, particularly the SSD. To be referred, to cite one SSD officer, the family usually had to be 'at risk if not of physical abuse then certainly of neglect'.
(c) *Restricted neighbourhood outreach.* Local residents were not normally expected to walk in and avail themselves of facilities. Indeed, some of the referred clients were not from the im-

mediate neighbourhood but were bussed in from outlying districts.

(d) *Professionalism rather than participation.* The running of such centres rested largely in the hands of qualified staff. Local residents did not occupy leading roles as volunteers, committee members or full-time staff.

The model thus concentrated professional help on a small number of clients referred for severe problems – hence its name of the client-focused approach. It has obvious advantages. The leader at Baron's Close explained that it attracted high quality staff. Concentration on a few families allowed a planned programme for each one, using such skills as counselling, play therapy or group work. The gathering together of parents with similar problems enabled them to share in each others' difficulties. Further, the existence of day-care resources meant that sometimes the projects could respond to a family crisis by providing safe care to avert an immediate break-down. But the client-focused model also held some disadvantages. The emphasis on referred clients could give the projects a negative image – 'that's where the battered children go'. This, combined with the small span of activities and a 'closed door' policy to those who tried to walk in, meant that the people of the neighbourhood did not regard the centre as belonging to them. In turn, the closed nature and the domination by professionals tended to exclude the participation of local residents in availing themselves of and running the centres.

The neighbourhood model

The majority of the projects were located in small areas of high social need where staff attempted both to serve and to draw upon the life of the neighbourhood. Its characteristics can be itemised as follows:

(a) *A broad range of activities.* A variety of groups and activities were on offer. They included advice services, youth clubs, play groups, tenants' associations, mothers and toddlers groups, sports teams and even meetings for the elderly. They were designed to suit differing age groups and differing interests throughout the neighbourhoods.

(b) *An open door.* Staff tried to create a welcoming atmosphere and to establish the practice that callers did not require an appointment or referral but could just 'drop in'.
(c) *Neighbourhood identification.* Centres were presented as advocates for and with the neighbourhood. Sometimes festivals were held to boost the image of, or campaigns run to improve services to, the locality. Staff took pains to distance themselves from statutory services, so that the projects could in no way be seen as a threat to vulnerable local families.
(d) *Local participation.* The neighbourhoods were regarded as the source of much of the person-power of the projects. Volunteers, numbering up to fifty a week, were recruited not from distant suburbs but from the immediate vicinity. Sometimes unqualified residents worked their way to become full-time project staff. Usually those running activities were eligible either for a committee for their specific club or for a users' committee which voiced local opinion.
(e) *Flexible staff roles.* Given the wide variety of activities, project staff had to adopt many roles. They acted as service-providers who directly ran some clubs, as stimulators who supported self-run groups, and as counsellors who related to individuals with problems. These diverse roles meant that staff tended not to see themselves as professional specialists but rather as community generalists, while residents looked upon them as resourceful friends.

The neighbourhood model offered distinct advantages, which will be elaborated upon in the next chapter. Here it suffices to say that the projects tended to be extensively used by the local populace, that users were not publicly stigmatised, that staff acquired enormous local knowledge and that many of the helping capacities of the neighbourhood were utilised. On the other hand staff admitted that the widespread involvement of local users could lead to conflict between them, while the many activities resulted in intense work pressures for staff. Not least, project leaders found that, while SSDs were prepared to give grants on a *per capita* basis to client-focused centres which took referred cases, they were less likely to back those neighbourhood projects whose users included many who would not normally be clients of the SSDs.

Community-development model

Some project staff commented that the emphasis within the neighbourhood approach on staff directly providing services lessened the responsibilities given to residents. The alternative was what they called the community-development model. The project leader at the Millmead Neighbourhood Centre explained it thus: 'We have a community development philosophy. We are trying to enable people to exercise more power over their lives and to enable them to develop facilities and activities which benefit them and their families and actually tend to assist them in having more meaningful and purposeful lives'. Like the neighbourhood approach, the community development model also featured a broad range of activities, an open door, a neighbourhood identification and local participation. Added to these, it had the following characteristics:

(a) *Indirect work.* The staff deliberately withdrew from running services themselves. They wanted to stimulate residents to organise their own clubs, play schemes, play groups and so on.

(b) *Not social work.* The staff were at pains to dissociate themselves from traditional social work. Not only were they reluctant to take referrals from SSDs, but they did not see it as their role to undertake casework with individuals.

(c) *Collective action.* The hope was that residents would act collectively to improve the quality of their lives. Some staff dismissed the word 'prevention' as being too negative and asserted that it was associated with reacting to individual crises. They wanted to promote movements to improve environments and circumstances and to change the kinds of depriving social conditions which lowered the quality of life for some families and, indeed, led to children being admitted into public care.

(d) *Local control.* 'Local control' was a key term voiced by the advocates of community development. They hoped that eventually users would make the management decisions about how centres should be run. It should be added, though, that progress was slow and in few centres did consumers play a major part in controlling expenditure and staff; and, in discussions, it emerged that some of the advocates considered that the skills of full-time staff provided by the Children's Society would always be necessary to support residents. They believed that deprived localities could not raise large sums of money, so that if the Society withdrew its cash, then centres would have to drastically cut activities. The modified version of community development to emerge was one in which an outside body, such as the Children's Society, guaranteed an input of resources over which local residents had control to use as they saw fit.

The benefits to be gained from the community-development model were seen as fourfold. Firstly, it met the desire of local residents to define their own needs, problems and solutions. Secondly, the concentration on neighbourhood rather than individual needs conveyed no stigma. Thirdly, it enabled residents to develop their own skills and confidence in order to have a greater say in shaping their own environments. Fourthly, there was less pressure on full-time staff, as they were relieved both of the organisation of services and of intense counselling of individuals.

But staff and consumers were also ready to pinpoint certain drawbacks. One project leader admitted that the transferring of the running of activities from full-time staff to local volunteers had led to some lowering in quality, as the latter found it difficult to cope with the many demands of organisation and keeping control. Another thought it had been pursued too quickly, with the result that local users had been overwhelmed and then disillusioned. Further, the fear was expressed that powerful residents might take over some activities and then exclude more disadvantaged members; and some users and volunteers were worried that, as staff changed to a community-development role, so their help to individuals would decline. Lastly, project members occasionally wondered if community development was part of a 'political game' used as a 'cover' by which management could justify reducing expenditure on particular centres.

Models do not reflect exactly what happens in practice. They are attempts to group together certain characteristics in order to distinguish different trends. In reality the three types of project overlapped and, indeed, one project might contain elements of all three models. For instance, at the Walcot Family Centre the leader held a community-development philosophy, one of the organisations took direct referrals more in keeping with the client-focused model, and another provided services on the neighbourhood basis. Again, some of the advocates of community development were in projects which did have staff running services for the community. Lastly, some of the neighbourhood type centres were in the process of moving towards the community-development model.

What can be said with some confidence is that the majority of the projects fell within a neighbourhood/community-development continuum. This reflects a deliberate choice by the Children's Society, for a statement by its consultant for community projects explained that its family centres should be regarded 'as a response to locally defined need and the fact that they are open and accessible to all. They reflect a commitment to participation and local involvement in both the work and management of the centres, and this is characterised by a belief in reciprocity and mutuality'.[1]

The Children's Society's projects were thus clearly of the neighbourhood/community-development kind. Whatever the differences between these two models, both gave priority to concentration on the neighbourhood rather than upon a few referred clients, and so for much of the rest of this volume they will be classified together and the discussion in the next chapter will be about projects of this kind. The question whether the projects run by other child-care voluntaries are also in the same camp now arises. My contacts with the National Children's Home leads to the assessment that it contains a larger number of the client-focused type. Nonetheless it is also true that both the National Children's Home and the other major voluntary child-care agencies also include a large number of the kind of projects which fall into the neighbourhood or community-development descriptions. The voluntaries are thus developing neighbourhood projects as one means of promoting prevention. The next chapter will therefore identify more precisely just how these projects do facilitate prevention and whether or not they differ from work undertaken in the statutory sector.

6. The Voluntary Contribution

What is the contribution of the voluntary sector to prevention in child care? This chapter will attempt a partial answer by analysing the work of the ten community projects listed in Chapter 5. It will identify their key features, consider how these have facilitated prevention, and discuss the differences and similarities between statutory and voluntary preventative social work. But first it is necessary to say something about the impact of the projects.

Does It Work?

Some of the projects have published figures to demonstrate the decline in the numbers of receptions into public care, in the number of custodial sentences and in the amount of delinquency in their areas.[1] It was beyond the brief of this volume to conduct a statistical evaluation of the outcomes of the centres, and its conception of prevention anyway is broader than stopping admissions to care and custody. However, this study is in a position to record the views about outcomes of the projects' users and associates. Over thirty users were interviewed. Their opinions should be taken seriously, for, as one SSD director has explained, it is people not statistics who benefit or fail to benefit from services, so 'the views of the consumers . . . become as relevant, if not more so than the crude financial measures of success'.[2] Nearly all spoke positively about their involvement. Some were convinced that their children would no longer be with them but for the direct help of project staff. Some described how their own participation had boosted their confidence and so enabled them to function more effectively as parents and citizens. Some of the users were interviewed at the suggestion of project staff and some I approached as they walked into the centres. But they could be said to be biased in favour of the projects, so I also sought the views of outside social workers.

Views of social workers on projects

The interviews with the social workers as recorded in the last chapter show them speaking highly of the preventative outcomes of the four projects. This was confirmed by the six whose interviews were not given. The social worker associated with the Swansea Family Centre commented: 'It is definitely the case that some children that would otherwise have been brought into care have been able to remain at home'. The social worker who knew the Millmead Neighbourhood Centre considered that it prevented 'problems getting worse rather than in immediately preventing children coming into care . . . it leads to a general improvement which is hard to measure but which leads people away from contact with statutory services'. At Shoebury the local NSPCC inspector attributed a halving of the number of referrals to him largely to the influence of the family centre. Similarly the SSD team leaders at Maltby and Walsall attributed a drop in the number of cases to their departments to the work of the family centres. All agreed that the projects helped counter the effects of isolation and poverty and so, to cite the social worker who knew the Beckhill Family Centre, functioned to 'improve the quality of people's lives to the extent that these things are much less likely to happen'.

The words of the users and social workers confirmed my observations that the projects were particularly active in five of the seven forms of prevention, namely children were being prevented from experiencing public care, from custody, from neglect and abuse at home, from poor parenting, and from severe social disadvantages in the home and community. The remaining two forms of prevention were less in evidence. But three of the centres gave some emphasis to rehabilitating children who had been removed from the neighbourhood. Moreover, a few examples did exist of centres being used as meeting places for parents and their separated children while project staff sometimes kept in touch with youngsters who had been removed in order to lessen their isolation from their former life.

Limitations

There is a danger of making the projects sound like a Mills & Boon novel, all romantic with happy endings. Far from it. The project workers frankly admitted that they could not cope with some of the families they encountered. Examples were given of children who entered public care and of teenagers who were 'sent down' despite all their efforts. Again, team members acknowledged that, for all their open-door policy, certain residents felt excluded. Sometimes adults felt put off by the aggression of teenagers, and at other places the focus on mothers made the teenagers feel unwanted. Further, the project workers often felt they were being called upon to deal with problems whose causes were far beyond their powers to solve. Unemployment, poverty, inadequate housing conditions arise from structural inequalities within society as a whole, yet they were presented as personal problems by callers at the centres. The full-time, part-time and volunteer workers at the projects could offer advice about welfare rights, could equip residents to negotiate for themselves and could take up issues with public bodies. But too often these interventions were not sufficient to remove the stresses or the social deprivations which were undermining the lives of some families, and they felt helpless as they received the distress and pain of the losers and victims of present inequalities.

Lastly, even if the projects are held up as examples of promising forms of intervention to prevent difficulties and disadvantages, it must be added that they were small in their outreach and number. The projects often did serve many people in the areas around their centres but they would never claim to reach all those in need. Thus the play leader at Maltby was pleased when a play scheme attracted 200 children but he added that the locality still contained over 1,000 other children in the same age range. Again, the major child-care societies, such as the Children's Society, are among the largest of voluntary organisations, but the number of projects they run nowhere near provides coverage for the whole country. Most needy localities do not possess preventative projects. At present any value their work possesses rests not on the extent of its coverage but more on the identification of promising ways to achieve prevention.

But the promise is that the ten projects were making a deliberate and often effective bid to execute prevention. It is in no way being claimed that the Children's Society's projects were unique. Indeed, from visits to other societies and from published articles it is clear that other voluntary projects do similar work.[3] Rather the claim is that voluntary projects of this kind do have a significant contribution to make to prevention, and this chapter intends to explore the reasons for it.

The Essential Framework

What factors enabled the projects to make their preventative impact? Clarification can be found by discussing the essential framework of the projects, the prevention it facilitated and the means or tactics which were employed. From the material collected it becomes possible to pinpoint five factors which nearly all the projects held in common and which thus can be called their framework.

Voluntary

It is easy to overlook the obvious fact that the projects belonged to voluntary organisations. Yet the voluntary nature was frequently noted by both users and the local-authority social workers associated with the centres. As the under-fives worker at Walcot put it,

It's a great advantage being voluntary. We're not education, we're not social services, we haven't got any labels. It's all informal, we're all called by our first names. Lots of the mums had terrible experiences when they went to school . . . They don't like social workers, they worry them because they think they are going to take their children away . . . But we are not a statutory body and so can be informal.

This statement shows how the voluntary aspect was perceived by users in two ways: one was the informality of the centres, which contrasted with the formality, the routine, the bureaucracy of official bodies; the other was the non-threatening nature of the centres. Statutory bodies were unfortunately often seen as threatening even when offering similar services to the voluntary ones. The fear of children being removed or teenagers taken to court was deeply entrenched in the minds of many users. By contrast they rightly perceived that the voluntary projects possessed no such powers.

Openness

The projects, with one exception, were characterised by their openness, so that residents felt free to walk in. Mornings generally started with mothers making tea or youngsters gathering around the pool table. This open-to-all approach did not mean that projects never took referrals from outside agencies. Some were prepared to take a limited number. The Swansea Family Centre, for instance, took referrals to its play groups and youth clubs from the SSD, the NSPCC and from schools. Yet the staff insisted that the open atmosphere was not lost because groups also contained members who just walked in, because staff did not obviously distinguish between referrals and others, because the walk-in members often had the same kind of problems, and because the overriding atmosphere remained as an informal place which welcomed anyone.

Neighbourhood orientation

The community projects, with the exception of the client-focused one, attempted to serve whole neighbourhoods. Their activities were not restricted to one client category. Even those projects which developed an affinity with one age group never tried to exclude others. Moreover the activities were geared to everyday participants. A hairdressing service, football teams, youth clubs, mothers and toddlers, were available to people on the basis of being members of the neighbourhood. It followed that the centres were people-orientated rather than problem-orientated. One resident described how she first went to the Walcot Centre: 'I saw a notice about keep fit and I wanted to lose weight. So my sister and I came along and I've been involved ever since'. The woman, who did have certain personal problems, later became a part-time worker there but initially she walked in to partake of an ordinary community activity.

Neighbourhood-type projects tend to attract large numbers.

The leader at the Walsall Family Centre estimated that within 14 months he knew between 90 to a 100 families. At Roundhill a survey found that 84 per cent of children at the local junior school and 20 per cent of adults had been to activities at the centre.[4] Thus the projects were neighbourhood-orientated both in the sense of being well known and also well used by the community.

Local participation

Perhaps the outstanding characteristic of the voluntary projects was the attention given to bringing in local residents. This had three aspects. Firstly, there was the recruitment of volunteers. With the exception of the one client-focused centre, all the projects drew heavily upon volunteers for the running of services. At the Swansea Family Centre over fifty volunteers played their part each week. Volunteering was taken seriously, with the projects providing training and, in some cases, payment. Given the small number of full-time staff and the large number of activities, it can be recognised that volunteers were not a frill but rather an essential part of the framework of the projects.

Secondly, local participation was further expressed in some residents becoming staff members. At Maltby a resident with years of work experience in a local factory became the full-time worker amongst young people. Three part-time and one full-time posts were filled by women from the Walcot estate. The project leader at the Roundhill Centre had started as chairman of the youth club. An MSC scheme at Walsall allowed the employment of seven adults from the surrounding streets. Almost without exception these staff members had lived within the local neighbourhoods for many years and, in some instances, had first approached the centres for help with their own problems.

Thirdly, local participation was also expressed in residents exercising collective responsibility for activities. Sometimes they formed committees to take over existing services, as happened at Swansea in regard to an after-school club. Sometimes they formed new committees to initiate activities, as occurred with a play scheme at Millmead. In addition, participation was also found in user committees, which made decisions about what kind of activities were run within the premises and which were expected to take on increasing responsibilities.

User-participation has not been a feature of social services in Britain. Barry Knight concluded his study by stating: 'In Britain, far from deprofessionalising the social care industry, the trend has been in the opposite direction. More stress has been placed on qualifications, career ladders, formal bureaucracy, statutory responsibilities, and centralisation of administration'.[5] The American 'poverty programme' of the 1960s gave publicity to the 'participation of the poor', yet even here doubts have been expressed as to whether there was any indigenous leadership.[6] Against these trends, the degree of involvement found in the voluntary community projects is impressive. Large numbers of volunteers did participate. Indigenous leaders did emerge. Local committees did run specific services. Local participation was thus a prominent plank in the framework and one that strongly influenced the course of the projects.

Staff style

The final brick in the projects' edifices was the style displayed by the staff. One word employed frequently by users, volunteers and social workers to describe them was 'friendly'. A desperate lone mother who had turned to the Millmead Neighbourhood Centre, where she burst into tears, explained that the project worker 'sat me down, sorted me out with a cup of tea and a fag . . . it seemed friendly, a place you could come in'. The social worker who knew the Maltby Family Centre was echoing the sentiments of other social workers when he commented, 'We know people always get a friendly welcome at the family centre and so some prefer to go there'. Similarly the local headmistress near the Shoebury Family Centre explained that the authority of teachers and social workers created a barrier between them and many residents, whereas the unofficial nature of the voluntary project 'enabled them to be seen as friends'.

No doubt the staff found it easier to convey friendliness because, unlike local-authority social workers, they did not have to enforce statutory regulations or act as agents of the courts. But, in addition, they also did so by becoming local participants, i.e. they deliberately sought to engage in local activities alongside residents and users. A member of the street in which the Walsall Family Centre was located observed of one of the staff: 'They love J.

Although she is official in one sense, they don't look upon her as a social worker. It's because she mixes in with us all. People don't notice she's doing a job because they think of her as a friend, more like one of them. She entered into the carnival, there she was in a grass skirt and it was freezing'. A city councillor attributed the success of another project team to the fact that 'they're able to get down to the grass roots. They're not aloof, they can speak their language, they can be a part of them, they can merge with them, and therefore people don't feel as if they are going to some solicitor or some Citizens Advice Bureau type'. There were examples of staff playing in the local football teams, of going to the same pubs as residents and, where they lived in the area, of sending their children to the same schools. They were subjective participants rather than distant observers.

Not least, many of the project staff displayed a strong commitment towards their jobs, the centres, the neighbourhoods and the residents. It was displayed in the long hours they worked, the zeal and enthusiasm they conveyed, and in the long-term nature of their employment. In eight of the centres the present project leaders had been associated with the centres from the very start. This is not to say that no changes occurred and that no disastrous appointments were made. But, in general, staff were characterised by a determination to persevere. Thus their friendliness, engagement in local life and perseverance fused together into a style which marked out the performance of the staff; and staff style joined with the voluntary nature and openness of the centres, the neighbourhood orientation of the members and the emphasis on local participation to form a project framework which shaped the nature of the preventative work undertaken there.

Facilitating Prevention

The framework allowed the projects to develop common aspects, which encouraged prevention through the following means.

Approachable, available, accessible

The projects were marked out by being approachable, available and accessible. They were approachable in that residents were ready to ask for help, like a young woman at Walsall who said, 'I hit my daughter and I did bruise her hard. I came round here and I sat and cried to J (project worker). I can talk to J'. They were available in that someone could usually be found even in the evenings and at weekends. They were accessible in that – unlike some of the SSD offices, which were miles away – the centres were close to the people they served. Thus while at GAP I witnessed an agitated man walk in at 9.30 am on a snowy morning. His separated wife was threatening to snatch the children and he wanted advice quickly. He got it because the project was accessible to him.

Approachability, availability and accessibility were important aids to prevention. At Roundhill a distressed woman felt able to approach the project leader late one night for help with her cohabitee, who, following police allegations of sexual abuse, was threatening violence against himself and others. Elsewhere, when staff were encouraging truants from school to stay at the centres as an alternative to court action, it was the availability of the project which made it possible to win their co-operation. In general, families under stress were ready to turn to help which was near at hand.

These preventative assets did not occur by chance, but were made possible by the framework. The openness of the centres made for approachability, the use of local residents as staff and volunteers made for availability at all hours, and the neighbourhood orientation ensured that centres were accessible. Prevention was thus facilitated.

Time

A caller at Walcot stated: 'The staff have always got time for you even if they are busy . . . if you are really worried about something they will always stop whatever they are doing'. She reflected a general view that the project staff were able to devote much time to people in need in two directions. Firstly, they gave time in intensive periods of stress. A husband deserted by his wife, a woman facing violence from her husband, a family overcome by debts, were able to see staff every day for a period until some kind of normality was restored. Secondly, they could give regular time over longer periods. At the Beckhill Family Centre I observed an isolated Asian mother and a lone mother with two children who regularly dropped into the centre, where staff always greeted them warmly, sat to chat and played with the children. Clearly their positive, unhurried attention was one factor enabling the women to survive through difficult days.

Why could the staff give time? It was not that they had little to do, for they worked long hours and were under many pressures. But they certainly had more time for individuals than their local-authority counterparts. The explanation rests in the framework of the projects. Being voluntary projects, staff were not constantly attending to urgent statutory enquiries. Further, the emphasis on local participation meant that often the centres contained a number of volunteers, who freed the full-time staff to concentrate on callers who required a large time input.

Breaking the client image

One of the most significant features of the voluntary projects was their finding a way of conveying services which did not imply stigma and which did not cast users as inadequate clients. This feature can be demonstrated by outlining the ways in which users regarded the staff, themselves and the centres.

Local residents did not perceive staff as officials who posed a threat to themselves or their children. Nor did they view them as the only source of help. They would also turn to the clerical staff, to volunteers and to each other. At times, too, the staff were treated as people who needed help with their difficulties. Thus one project leader received much support when his wife gave birth to a Down's Syndrome baby. Users most frequently referred to project staff as 'friend' or 'mate', yet it must be said that they were not exactly in the same position as other friends of the users. The relationship had aspects of friendship in its informality and reciprocity. But, in addition, the staff often did possess knowledge and resources which the users did not, and they were willing to pass these attributes on to them. Thus I have suggested elsewhere that the staff are best described as resourceful friends.[7] But whatever the precise nature of the relationship, there is no doubt that users did not define staff as powerful officials, as the only source of help, or as superior beings who needed no help themselves.

Local residents frequently became participants in the life of the centres and hence were able to see themselves as people with something to give. Some thus became simultaneously people who both gave and received aid. Not least, it was obvious that users did not look upon the centres as places where predetermined services either had to be taken or left. Rather they understood them to be places where they could run activities which suited them. To sum up: with staff regarded as resourceful friends rather than as powerful professionals, with users seeing themselves as givers as well as receivers, with the centres perceived as places which responded to local definitions of need, then it was clear that users were in a very different position from those approaching traditional statutory social services. They were not inadequate supplicants turning to experts who were the sole possessors of the answers. The client image was broken.

How did the breaking of the client image facilitate prevention? For a start it encouraged people to use the projects. Entering the buildings did not mean that people felt they would be subject to blame or shame. The outcome was a neat balance between residents who were in desperate need feeling free to enter the projects to seek help while knowing that in doing so they were not being marked out as unusual or despicable.

Next the fact that calling on the projects for help did not cast users in the role of clients acted as a brake to prevent them entering upon welfare careers. As explained earlier, a danger of children (or families) becoming known at an early stage to the social services or justice systems is that they can then pass through a progression of stages which ends in removal from home. The project staff did not label users as clients. Hence not only were staff less likely to channel users into the welfare system but residents themselves were more ready to look upon themselves as resourceful persons who could find their own solutions within their own communities, rather than turning to outside agencies.

The absence of any stigma or shame associated with using the centres helped to counter some of the devastating effects of their imposition. If people in difficulties are treated as inferior, there is a danger that they react with an aggression or with a withdrawal, which increases rather than lessens their problems.[8] On the other hand the evidence suggests that even families on the verge of break-up can be helped if the aid is conveyed without judgements that parents do not care about their children.[9] The voluntary projects appeared to have some success in this direction. Parents who were facing difficulties with their children were accepted into groups where problems were acknowledged and shared and where participants all helped each other. Youngsters who had committed offences were accepted into clubs not because they were delinquent but because they were residents of the local community. Hence a positive rather than a negative aspect of their life was emphasised. Thus instead of undermining users by defining them as 'child abusers' or 'thugs', the projects tended to draw out their coping capacities by treating them as citizens with a right to belong.

Lastly, the projects proved that people previously regarded as clients or low-income residents were often the most able to function as helpers and leaders. Their recruitment as participants obviously boosted their own self-confidence, and examples have been given of apparently apathetic parents finding the strength to stand up to social-security officials or of regaining the motivation to win back their children. But beyond benefit to themselves, they frequently showed that they were the people best able to help others. After all, they knew what it was like to face unemployment, isolation, poverty and delinquency. They could speak from experience. Again, they lived locally. As one volunteer graphically explained,

> Living here is a help. You see people that come into the centre or people that you go out to help and they know that you live around here and that you are not stuck in one of the snob areas. If you live in one of the areas that hasn't got the problems of Walcot the people think 'Oh, you don't know what is happening'.

So with such residents functioning as capable helpers, the old image of inadequate client or apathetic parent could no longer be held.

While this study was being undertaken, Crecy Cannan published an article describing visits she made to a number of local-authority and voluntary family centres. She warned that, in their zeal to undertake prevention, the centres could actually defeat their own objectives by 'stigmatising services'. This occurred when the centres restricted access to certain families and so 'heightened public awareness that the centres were for problem families'; when they imposed such controls as compulsory attendance on parents, which then intensified their feelings of being different from other parents; and when the concentration on the few families meant they were then drawn 'into the general net of child protective services'.[10] Most of the ten centres run by the Children's Society appear to have avoided these dangers. By breaking the client image they developed services which facilitated rather than hindered prevention. Why did this occur? Again the explanation rests in the essential framework of the projects.

The open-door practice meant that no special status was placed on anyone using the centres. To enter the buildings did not imply that the persons were delinquents or child-abusers; they could be calling for a game of darts, a chat or a coffee. Of course the centres did aim to attract and serve residents with severe problems which threatened their family lives. But this service came under the umbrella of other, wider services. The ingredient of local participation further functioned to destroy any belief that there were two kinds of people – the professional expert and the helpless client, the coper and the non-coper. As the leader of the Walsall Family Centre explained about local workers, 'Some have had very severe problems in their own lives. There is no doubt that they are of very great value to the community'. The framework thus created opportunities for residents to prove that possessing problems was not a barrier to being a user who contributed helpfully to others. People with problems were more than just problem people. In addition, the style adopted by staff also broke down social barriers. They insisted that the capacity to help was not restricted to them and, indeed, as members of the local communities showed that they too had their weaknesses. Distinctions between experts and clients were thus removed. Thus the essential framework of the projects served to break down the client image.

Knowing the areas

Most projects were characterised by a neighbourhood orientation. Rather than concentrate on a small number of referred clients, they tended to maintain activities which interested a large number of families. This aspect of the projects' framework enabled project members to gain knowledge about residents and resources which helped to facilitate prevention.

The project staff and volunteers mixed with a large number of families at activities held at the centres. They also walked the streets and participated in community life and so got to know families who might not even enter the centres. Staff who stayed in their posts for long periods saw children grow and change, attended local weddings, witnessed new families moving in. They thus accumulated much knowledge, which enabled them to make more accurate and positive assessments about families who were being subjected to scrutiny by statutory social workers. The latter often come into close contact with such families only at a time of trouble and fraught relationships. Consequently their assessments can be based on limited and negative observations. Rowe in her study points out that social workers 'quite often misinterpret natural parents' behaviour at the time of admission . . . we have some painfully vivid examples of cases where parents were considered rejecting or uncaring because the problems they were facing had not been properly understood'.[11] By contrast the project staff were able to perceive their positive as well as their negative characteristics. They were thus better equipped to assess whether families could or could not cope, whether children really were in danger and how best members could be encouraged to tackle their difficulties.

The close knowledge also enabled project staff to foresee forthcoming difficulties. A worker observed that a youngster was taking a few days off school, or that a depressed mother had not come out of her home for a week. Such incidents served as early warning signs to the possibility that trouble was brewing and, in some cases, prompted staff to intervene at an early stage to prevent it escalating into a family crisis. Recent research in child care reveals that most decisions to admit children into public care 'are made rapidly and often in a crisis'.[12] By acting early to head off the build-up to crises, the project staff were therefore taking effective preventative action and that action stemmed from their knowledge of what was happening to families in their localities.

The appreciation of what was happening to families was also crucial in helping project workers decide what kind of action to take. Marsh and his colleagues in their study discovered that natural parents felt that statutory social workers did not appreciate what pressures they were under from the behaviour of their older children.[13] At least the project workers were likely to know a little more about what the families were enduring, especially if they too

were experiencing the youngsters' aggression, rudeness or delinquency within the centres. This knowledge could then sometimes
be used to suggest some practical ways of relieving the pressure –
perhaps that the teenager should attend the youth-club holiday or
that the whole family should meet together at the centre to discuss
with the project worker just what they were doing to each other.

Their local knowledge thus enabled project workers to understand better and to intervene more effectively on behalf of individual families in need. It also meant that they became familiar with
other helping resources in the neighbourhood. There were examples
of staff being able to call upon a network of local mothers to
support a very depressed woman, on a neighbour to provide
accommodation for a family sheltering from a drunken husband,
upon an elderly lady who several times looked after youngsters
who needed a break from home. Sometimes they found that their
encouragement was enough to motivate kinfolk, especially grand-
parents, to take a more active role in supporting relatives who
were undergoing traumatic episodes. Some academics have expressed doubts about the availability of local, informal resources
in needy areas.[14] But the experience of nearly every community
project, no matter how deprived the locality, was that there did
exist friends, neighbours and relatives who were able to help some
– though by no means all – families to survive times of stress. The
framework of the projects gave staff the knowledge of where to
find that help.

Centres of stability

Many residents called into the centres just occasionally when they
had a specific need to be met. But others attended so regularly that
the projects became havens or shelters. They would echo the
words of a user at the Maltby Family Centre who stated: 'It's not
like an organisation, they are like a family . . . It's like a feeling of
security'. They saw the projects as centres of stability.

The stability and reliability of the community projects were a
further means of facilitating prevention. At Walsall a core of
parents, mostly struggling with low incomes and with demanding
children, when needing to give vent to their problems or when just
wanting some adult company, walked into the project premises,
which became havens from some of the troubles outside. The

Gerard Avenue Project was used by a group of unemployed youngsters who saw it as their club. In lives that often seemed to lack any purpose, the project provided a secure base where they made friendships and activities which were legitimate rather than unlawful.

It was not just the buildings. Sometimes the project staff acted as stable figures for youngsters whose lives were blighted by uncertainty. The staff at the Roundhill Project attracted a number of boys from homes where there was no permanent father or no adult male at all. The boys would attend a number of clubs at the centre as well as dropping into the homes of the staff. They seemed to want another trusted adult to whom they could boast about their school successes, bemoan their detentions, play table tennis or with whom they could just laugh and joke. The project workers had been in their neighbourhood for a number of years and this stability appeared to make them acceptable not only to the boys but also to their families.

The stability of the centres stemmed from the framework, which contained a staff style built around endurance and commitment. The openness of the centres also meant that local residents could feel free to walk in to take advantage of the stability of the projects. The result was that both isolated mothers and teenagers could be diverted away from some of their stresses and boredom, while some younger children could be offered a stable, individualising relationship, which filled a gap in their lives. They would have agreed with the words of a father in Roundhill who described the centre as 'a rock in the middle of the community'.

The essential framework was not all good news. The voluntary nature of the projects meant they sometimes faced financial shortages and uncertainties about next year's resources which far exceeded the insecurities of statutory bodies. The openness and neighbourhood orientation could produce such a volume of callers that staff felt bombarded by the pressures. The distinctive staff style could also pose dilemmas, when, for instance, a member had to decide whether or not to report to the authorities child abuse inflicted by residents who were also friends. But, as this section has demonstrated, the framework facilitated prevention by creating stable projects which residents felt free to use without risk of stigmatisation and where they met staff who could offer both time and knowledge.

The means of prevention

Within the framework and features of the projects the team members utilised certain tactics as their main means of working. Of these, five stand out. The staff depended much on *individualisation or personal relationships* in order, say, to encourage families to hold together at times of stress or to enable teenagers to avoid delinquency and drug abuse. Even in centres where staff wanted to do without therapeutic relationships, they still related closely to residents in order to strengthen their involvement in groups. Working with individuals was central to all the projects and was incorporated into all the tactics.

Some staff defined their major role in terms of *empowerment*. The Millmead leader explained: 'We are trying to enable people to exercise more power and control over their lives and also to enable them to develop facilities and activities which benefit them and their families'. Empowerment sometimes meant transferring information and skills so that individuals could obtain housing, welfare and other entitlements; sometimes it entailed encouraging them to develop personally so that they could take on leadership roles; sometimes it consisted of equipping residents to negotiate with outside agencies, such as the courts or the SSDs, about the future of their children; and sometimes it was about creating opportunities for local people to act collectively either to run services themselves or to act as pressure groups for improved amenities. Empowerment is perhaps too grand a word if it implies that low-income inhabitants of council estates and inner-city areas were somehow armed to transform the social structures which determined their status in society. But, as used by the project workers, it meant encouraging them to challenge the injustices of the ways in which they were treated and of arming them, in small ways, to fight to improve the quality of life in family and neighbourhood.

The voluntary projects were located in areas where parents often met difficulties in raising their children. They responded by offering what they called *stimulation* in order to compensate for these disadvantages. Within day-care, play-group and toddler-group settings, children were stimulated by play, by interaction, by new experiences. This input was regarded as promoting their emotional and social growth. The Swansea Family Centre did much to stimulate not just the under-fives but also junior age children in various clubs and groups, for, as one of their project workers put it, 'they will be the parents of the future and perhaps we can break into the cycle and help them to care for themselves, their children and their community many years later'.

Nearly all the centres put great emphasis on encouraging users to regard themselves as participants rather than merely recipients. Such *participation* did much to reduce the social isolation which reinforced or even caused the problems of some youngsters and adults. The participation of people who had previously regarded themselves as failures did much to boost their feelings of self-worth, and in so doing enabled them to cope better as parents and citizens.

Most staff believed in *diversion* as a tactic to keep families from embarking on what they called 'welfare careers', which could finish with the children in public care. Similarly at Maltby a group for the young unemployed, at GAP a motor-bike group, and at Roundhill the clubs and sports, were deliberately designed to divert youngsters away from the courts and custody.

Agents of prevention

This chapter opened by showing that the community projects, as the agents of prevention, were achieving some modest advances towards the seven ends of prevention. The analysis of the ten centres suggested that any gains owed much to the essential and common framework of the projects. That framework was then used as the source for creating the features which facilitated prevention and which also allowed project workers to employ the tactics most suited to their localities. The whole process can be expressed as in Table 6.1.

Lastly, it is worth referring back to Chapter 4, where a review of the development of prevention in both statutory and voluntary sectors led to the conclusion that there were five key factors in the pursuit of effective prevention. They were a commitment to preventative objectives, the nature of the contribution made by social workers, the status awarded to consumers, the localisation of services, and the combating of poverty. The projects examined in this study were by no means outstanding in all these areas, but from the preceding pages it emerges that they were strong in their

TABLE 6.1 *Voluntary projects as agents of prevention*

The essential framework	Facilitating features	Tactics
voluntary	approachable, etc.	individualisation
openness	time	empowerment
neighbourhood orientation	breaking the client image	stimulation
local involvement	knowing the areas	participation
staff style	stability	diversion

commitment to prevention, in their capacity to engage consumers as participants rather than recipients, and in their readiness to localise services in the midst of small neighbourhoods.

The Voluntary Factor

How different were the voluntary projects from what local authorities did in child-care prevention? Clearly the users claimed that the informal, friendly and unofficial manner of the voluntaries made them preferable to statutory services. Gratifying as these remarks may be to the staff, they do come from people with a close identification with the voluntary projects. More objective views came from the local-authority social workers who knew the centres.

The statutory social workers acknowledged that the powers and resources of their departments gave them a preventative scope outside that of the voluntary sector. Yet they were unanimous that the voluntary projects possessed certain advantages. For a start they pointed out that the community projects were invariably nearer to people in need than their own offices. Next several mentioned that families often preferred the voluntary agency because, as the team leader at Maltby put it, 'the average person with child care problems might fight shy of the SSD especially as there is now a general feeling that social workers take your children away'. They added that callers often felt less stigmatised. The social worker at Beckhill claimed: 'It's an advantage it is not run by the SSD because it might become a place for referring problem families. Social workers tend to see clients as problems and the people who come see themselves in the same light'. Most also said that not only did the project workers have more time for individuals, not only did they relate more closely to the community, but also that they supplied a broader form of preventative resource with their clubs and play schemes. The team leader at Walsall reflected a general conclusion when he said: 'The fact that they are not statutory workers is their greatest strength'.

Important as these social work views are, an important qualification must be inserted. The interviewed social workers tended to be drawn from SSD teams which had not decentralised and which did not have local-authority family centres within their boundaries. They were thus rightly distinguishing the contribution of voluntary projects as against statutory social work run from area offices. But further consideration must be given to whether the voluntary contribution is any different from that of local-authority patch teams and family centres.

Patch teams

As explained in a previous chapter, the move to patch teams by some SSDs did improve their preventative drive by making their teams more accessible, by giving social workers greater knowledge of local resources and by encouraging them to regard clients in a new light. So did any differences distinguish local-authority patch teams from voluntary community projects? Four can be identified. Firstly, the patch workers continued to possess statutory duties and powers. On the one hand they had access to far greater resources than their voluntary counterparts, but on the other they could not concentrate on child-care prevention, for they continued to exercise duties towards other client categories. Social work texts stress that statutory powers to remove and control can be the basis of a positive relationship with clients. This may well be so, but a study by Gardener detected that many clients 'found it hard to accept the workers' dual role of controlling and caring, so were not so open with them'.[15] The point is not that the SSD and project workers were better than each other but rather that differences still existed between them.

Secondly, there are differences in the size of geographical areas. One local authority aimed at a population of 16,000 for its patch teams. Others made teams responsible for two or three neighbourhoods.[16] By contrast the voluntary projects in this study dealt with populations of between 2,000 and 10,000. The patch teams could gain by co-ordinating a larger number of voluntary agencies within their greater populations, the community projects from a closer involvement with their smaller constituencies.

Thirdly, the promotion of wider activities like youth clubs, mothers and toddlers groups and sporting teams had a different position within the two systems. To the voluntary projects they constituted a major reason why people came to their building and were activities to which staff and helpers devoted much time. To the patch teams they were more like extras which they stimulated but which were secondary to their primary task of servicing their statutory responsibilities. Even in Normanton 'the patch leaders felt unable to exploit the potential of their roles as community workers in their patches because of the continued demands of their personal caseloads'.[17]

Fourthly, differences occurred in the opportunities and responsibilities awarded to local residents. The community projects could hardly have functioned without volunteers. Some encouraged residents to become full-time workers and members of committees with increasing charge of the centres. The patch teams did sometimes appoint locals to full-time posts but usually only to lower-grade ancillary or warden-type jobs. They encouraged volunteers but their agencies never revolved around them, and residents played little part in committees which shaped the nature of the patch teams' work. In fact, a recent study of patch in East Sussex revealed that residents felt they were not consulted and 'Most felt they had little or no say in the department'.[18] Both statutory and voluntary sides favoured local participation but the latter did possess greater scope for allowing residents to identify needs, to define means of intervention and to help in their implementation.

Local-authority family centres

SSD centres are known as resource centres and children's centres but are more generally called family centres. In order to ascertain differences between them and the ten voluntary projects, I visited a similar number of local-authority centres. Both kinds made prevention an objective and ran activities like day-care and parents' groups. But on closer examination differences did emerge. The local-authority family centres usually occupied large, well equipped and well staffed buildings, served substantial areas, specialised in referred clients, provided treatment by professional experts, and were entrenched in the world of welfare. The spacious buildings, often former day nurseries or children's homes, contained up to seventeen full-time staff, not counting secretaries, domestics and drivers. They served areas of up to 250 square miles, with one centre typically covering not just its town but also 'surrounding towns and villages' from where users were bussed in. These users were nearly all referred by statutory agencies, with each centre specialising in a service for one major client group – an attendance unit for poor school attenders, IT for offenders, and, most frequently, specified day attendance for mothers with young children who were on the abuse register or who were diagnosed as depressed or even psychotic. The concentration on one type of client had a twofold implication. One was that the centres' staff felt they should not focus on the neighbourhood. One leader bluntly stated, 'The community is not our responsibility'. Others allowed locals to drop in one day a week but still saw SSD clients as their prime target. The other implication was the creation, as one staff member put it, of a local feeling of 'I'm not going there, that's where the social service people go'.[19] Thus users were not regarded as ordinary residents but as problem clients who needed the professional expertise of qualified social workers, teachers and nursery nurses. Such an emphasis did mean that the statutory centres offered highly skilled, well planned, therapeutic aid to a core of clients with designated problems. But it also meant that there was little room for unqualified volunteers, indigenous leaders and local committees empowered to influence the centres. Lastly, the family centres were an integral part of a web of social services in which clients were frequently given key workers within the centres, social workers outside and were often also treated in conjunction with such other agencies as child guidance. Theirs was the world of welfare.

Interestingly two of the statutory family centres were somewhat exceptional. Located in linked council houses, they were more open to the neighbourhoods. Nonetheless both still took a large proportion of referred clients who were expected to attend at stated times. In one users were also transported in from outlying districts and in both the allocation of key and field social workers ensured that some users were drawn into welfare careers. The two exceptions underline the point that the statutory and voluntary centres were not completely different creations. Overlaps did occur. However, differences there were. Whereas a majority of the statutory centres were of the client-focused model and a minority of the neighbourhood model, the voluntary projects had a minority in the client-focused camp and a majority of the neighbourhood or community-development type. The voluntary projects were more likely to be small in size and resources, to serve small geographical areas, to regard neighbourhood as the focus of their work, to draw in a variety of users, to engage local as well as professional help, and to be in the realm of community rather than that of welfare. The existence of such characteristics demonstrates that differences can be identified between the local-authority family centres and the community projects of the voluntary agencies.

The voluntary difference

Brenton, in her recent study, questions how far voluntary organisations really are independent. Some receive nearly all their income from statutory grants and thus have to fit in with 'official priorities'.[20] Voluntary child-care agencies are still in receipt of much voluntary giving yet they too may shape some of their practices in order to win whatever statutory grants are on offer.[21] Thus the role of the voluntaries within the social services is currently subject to debate, and in 1984 the government promised a consultative document on the subject. When it was slow to appear, the Voluntary Organisations Personal Social Services Group issued a paper in 1986 in which it specified six important voluntary functions – advocacy, innovation, maintenance of services to minority groups, direct provision of services, consumer and neighbourhood participation, and advice-giving.[22] But even this document failed to explain the differences between statutory and voluntary contributions.

This volume is not equipped to discuss the roles of voluntary organisations in general but it can say something about their distinctive role in prevention and child care. But before doing so, two points must be made. One is that only statutory bodies have the resources and coverage to provide preventative services for the country as a whole. Prevention is a statutory duty and voluntary bodies should not allow statutory bodies to play down their responsibilities. The other is that the statutory and voluntary sectors are not two unconnected systems in regard to prevention. Staff from both sectors may co-operate in order to help the same families. Both will acknowledge certain standards and values, such as treating consumers with respect and compassion. Sometimes local authorities will fund voluntary bodies to undertake forms of prevention. The systems are related.

So the question remains, what is the particular strength of the voluntaries in regard to prevention in child care? Where local authority SSDs have not decentralised into patch teams, the voluntary agencies can provide a localised service. In her study, of children coming into care in an inner city area, Christine Stair says: 'The main office is located several miles away from the district itself and as there is a notable absence of convenient bus services clients cannot easily drop-in or attend meetings'.[23] Her comment could be applied to many other SSDs. Many people in need lack access to nearby services. Sometimes voluntary projects can fill this gap. Again, where SSDs do not provide family centres, voluntary societies may have a role in running the client-focused centres which offer intensive services to a small number of referred clients.

But patch teams or not, local authority family centres or not, the voluntary projects still have distinct inputs to make to prevention. They spring from the strengths of the neighbourhood and community-development approaches which distinguish their projects from most patch teams and SSD family centres. Their particular contributions can be summarised as follows.

Firstly, the voluntary projects are *adept at utilising local resources*. It is not claimed that local-authority social workers ignore the informal networks of neighbourhoods. The argument is rather that the projects examined in this study showed a greater capacity to do so than their statutory counterparts. The smallness of the areas they covered enabled them to know and be known. Their modest buildings, informal styles and varied activities drew in large numbers of ordinary residents. The outcome was that project staff knew which informal help was available, were able to develop the capacities of local helpers, were able to devise opportunities for residents to become volunteers and full-time workers and, in short, were able to stimulate local individuals, families and organisations to act in preventative ways.

Secondly, the voluntary projects were able to provide *help without stigma*. Again and again studies demonstrate that when social services convey to recipients feelings of shame, inadequacy and stigma, then their problems may be reinforced rather than alleviated. To cite one final investigation, Stair noted how parents, undermined by the compulsory removal of their children into care, could 'respond by becoming either hostile and aggressive or depressed and apathetic'.[24] Local-authority services can and should take steps to reduce the stigma associated with their child-care services. But, at the end of the day, they must, and should, carry the power to investigate, protect and remove children, and the result is that some parents will view them as a threat and some parents will be marked out as failures. But voluntary community projects have proved that they can work with similar kinds of families without conveying stigma. Their neighbourhood orientation allowed residents to come to them by choice and to define their own problems and solutions. The emphasis on local participation meant that the distinction between expert professional and recipient client was reduced. The client image was broken and residents' strengths rather than their failings given prominence. The evidence suggested that this approach helped families to cope. The voluntary bodies were able to convey service without stigma.

Thirdly, the voluntary projects were well placed *to promote prevention*. Much SSD work concerns reactions to crises and the maintenance of statutory caseloads. Even their family centres tended to concentrate on families referred because their problems were deemed by social workers to be at an advanced stage. SSDs therefore found it difficult to give priority to services which so improved the quality of family life that some families were able to avoid reaching those advanced stages. This kind of outreach can be termed promoting prevention and has at least three elements, all of which were contained within the voluntary neighbourhood projects. There are activities which relieve stress without treating them as crises. The drop-in nature and the sheltering aspect of the community projects contributed to this end. Next come services which can improve families' coping skills without imposing a sense of failure. The many groups for parents and children, the after-school clubs, the play schemes and so on not only provided a resource which the families would not otherwise have enjoyed, but they also stimulated the development of parenting skills along with the social growth of the children. Lastly, there were indicators that the projects could be the base for some collective action by residents in order to reach improvements in their own life-styles so that, in the long run, there would be a reduction in their levels of social deprivation – the deprivation which impaired their incomes, their happiness and even the stability of their family units. True, the examples of collective action were modest but the potential for this aspect of promoting prevention was far more evident than in the statutory sector.

The projects' capacities to recruit local resources, to provide help without stigma and to initiate a promotional approach were the strengths of the voluntary sector. In addition, they frequently became allies of people who had already been drawn into the statutory system. As Gardener found in her survey, some clients could not accept the caring and controlling dualism of SSD social workers and yet were reluctant on their own to challenge official decisions.[25] The voluntary projects were prepared to back such clients. One mother, with one son in care and another attending the Roundhill Project, asked a project member whether she could visit her son in care and whether she could appeal against the care order. No doubt the SSD social worker had explained the meaning of care but the trauma of care proceedings and her hostility towards the social worker made her unable to take it in. She could listen to the project member because he possessed the child-care knowledge but had not been party to the removal of her son. Going further, some families enlisted the help of project staff in actively siding against authority. The staff spoke in court against the imposition of care orders which officials were recommending and aided parents to gain access to their children where social workers thought this undesirable. It is much to the credit of the SSDs that they did not allow the differences of opinion to sour their relationship with the voluntary bodies.

Particular groupings

Undoubtedly the neighbourhood approach enabled projects to attract a wide variety of users. Yet within this cross-section they appeared to have much to offer to four particular groupings, all of whom were vulnerable to social deprivations, to distress and even to splits in their family units.

Project participants made frequent reference to the socially isolated. Such observations confirm, what other studies indicate, that loneliness and isolation are a major problem on some council estates and inner-city areas.[26] Lone parents, young mothers who lacked confidence, families rehoused to localities where they had no relatives or friends, were isolated residents who profited from the accessibility, openness and friendliness of the projects.

Unemployed and disaffected teenagers also seemed to find certain of the projects a homely base to which they could turn. They often criticised the lack of equipment, yet the stability and the unofficial status of the centres did make them acceptable to youngsters who felt out of place elsewhere.

Young children from homes where fathers were absent or intermittent were also prone to turn to the projects. The staff's long service and readiness to give time probably encouraged youngsters to trust them. Thus staff members often took on the role of stable life anchors for some children whose own lives were subject to instability and change.

Parents experiencing intense stresses were also a feature of the neighbourhoods. The pressures were associated with low incomes and poor housing conditions, with young parents finding it difficult to cope with small children without the support of relatives, and sometimes with parents being subject to local condemnation because they were known to be visited by 'the cruelty man' or social workers. Such families were often prepared to use the projects because they were approachable, because help was offered without imposing 'the badge of shame', and because staff found ways of raising the parents' confidence by enabling them to contribute to the life of the centres.

Significantly these four groupings may be liable to admission into public care. Lone parents, in particular, may experience the social isolation which pushes them towards public care at times of crises.[27] Teenagers subject to unemployment and boredom are at risk of becoming what Packman calls the 'villains' whose behaviour brings them to court.[28] Next Marsh and his colleagues noticed that the absence of a father or the presence of a new step-father could create, for some children, difficulties sufficient to disrupt the whole family.[29] Lastly, there is evidence that families enduring intense environmental stresses may react with behaviour that threatens their children. Within the topic of child abuse there is much debate as to whether causation rests with the parents' own personality defects – which stemmed from their own disturbed childhoods – or with the effects on behaviour of crushing poverty, isolation and social stress.[30] Probably both explanations have some validity.[31] If so, then it could be that the controlling powers of statutory social workers and the therapeutic skills of their client-focused family centres will be appropriate for abusers with severe personality defects. The strengthening facilities of the voluntary projects seem to be the best form of preventative help for those facing great environmental strains. Notably Goldberg and Sinclair came to this conclusion in their review of services which offer support to families.[32]

This chapter has established that community projects run by a voluntary child-care society can deal with a wide range of prevention. The essential framework of these projects was identified as the springboard from which prevention could be facilitated in a number of directions and by the use of varying tactics. Some of these features were held in common with the efforts of statutory social workers in patch teams and local-authority family centres. But some – notably the facility for using local resources, the capacity to provide help in an acceptable manner and the potential for a promotional rather than a reactive approach – were areas where the voluntary projects were stronger than their SSD counterparts. In turn, these features enabled the projects to be of use to certain groupings which were particularly likely to enter public care or to endure standards of life below that of the majority of the population. In developing community projects based on the neighbourhood or community-development models the voluntary agency has found a way of attracting those in need of help without rejecting the local residents who do not require such help, it has established a means of conveying aid without reinforcing problems, and it has shown that the neighbourhood can be the focus of a preventative approach.

The voluntary societies have changed almost beyond recognition from the Victorian era, when they sometimes displayed hostility towards natural parents who wanted the return of their children. They have come a long way from the post-war period, when their resources were devoted mainly to residential care. Today the voluntary child-care agencies make prevention one of their priorities. But, in contrast with Victorian or even pre-war days, the voluntaries can no longer compare with statutory bodies as the major providers of child-welfare services. If prevention is to advance, then the voluntary role must form part of a wider national strategy. It is this topic which the final chapter must now consider.

7. The Pursuit of Prevention

This volume has attempted to trace the development of prevention in child care, to outline its progress and problems, to discuss how its meaning has expanded and to identify the present contribution of the statutory and voluntary sectors. The final chapter will contain two sections. One will restate the case for prevention while the other will consider a strategy to make it more effective.

The Case for Prevention

Research and family separations

The arguments for prevention draw largely upon studies which reveal the harmful effects upon children of removing them from their natural families. The harm may be due to the children missing the influence of their biological parents and siblings, to the actual trauma of being removed, or to the adverse experiences which the children sometimes undergo in their new surroundings. In Chapter 2 reference was made to some of the pioneer studies which influenced the child-care officers and led many of them to conclude that much damage would be avoided if only the children could be prevented from leaving their own homes.

Subsequent studies have added more sophistication to the research methods employed and a number of qualifications to the findings, but the essential themes remain the same. Firstly, prolonged separations from their natural parents are likely to impair the development of children. Separations are not inevitably disastrous, although they are frequently accompanied by distress, protest and despair. Much depends upon the age of the child at removal, the nature of previous parenting and the way in which the parting is handled. Again, the adverse effects of separation are

197

not necessarily irreversible and much depends on the quality of the new substitute home or establishment. But the quality of the latter cannot be guaranteed and, to say the least, separating children from their parents does introduce another uncertainty into their lives and places them at further risk of suffering emotional and intellectual setbacks.[1]

Secondly, to cite the summary made by Fuller and Stevenson, 'research on older children in residential care confirms that children in care are more likely to exhibit behavioural disorders and emotional disturbance than children in their own homes'.[2] Children who have experienced sustained periods in residential care do seem to meet educational difficulties and trouble in making friendships at a later stage.[3] Bowen makes the telling point that children admitted into public care because of poor school attendance did not receive an improvement in their education once in the hands of the public authorities. He commented: 'They thought nothing of education before the care orders, and they think nothing of it today'.[4] Residential care does not seem a good preparation for adulthood. Thus research by Dowdney suggests that girls raised in children's homes meet difficulties when they become mothers not because they do not love their children but because they have not learned parenting skills.[5] No doubt residential care is the best option for a few children but the general conclusion is that most children are best left in their own homes even if they face difficulties there.

Thirdly, residential care still seems to offer little benefit to youngsters removed from home because of their delinquency. As Fuller and Stevenson conclude their review of the research, 'the overall picture presented by research into the effectiveness of residential treatment as a means of preventing future delinquency is bleak'.[6] There can be little doubt that programmes which contain offenders within their own community are not only cheaper than institutional care but, more important, prevent them from having their delinquent tendencies reinforced by mixing only with other delinquents in custodial establishments.

Fourthly, care placements appear remarkably unstable. The summary of the most recent child care research made for the DHSS concluded: 'Children in care are likely to experience many changes of placement. The instability of "in care" placements is hammered home to the reader of these research studies by the depressing similarity of their findings'.[7] It went on to cite the study by Packman and her colleagues, which revealed that four out of five admitted children had moved at least twice and a quarter at least four times in the space of a few months, and that by Millham and his colleagues, which found that over a 2-year period 56 per cent of the children investigated had three or more placements and 14 per cent more than four moves. In addition, the latter study considered that of 170 children in public care after 2 years, 63 were unsuitably placed.[8] Such findings are particularly serious, as earlier research has established that multiple moves have adverse effects on children's development. Packman and her team also followed up a group of children who were not admitted to care but who possessed similar characteristics to those who were. They wrote: 'In contrast, the not-admitted group were subjected to far fewer moves (almost two thirds had not moved at all) and most of their moves were within the informal system of kin and neighbour-hood networks, leading to less school and day care disruption'.[9]

Fifthly, as Professor Anthony Maluccio puts it, 'in research as in practice, there is evidence of the negative impact of separation on parents as well as children'.[10] To have a natural child removed is a damaging psychological and emotional blow to parents, one which condemns them in their own eyes as well as that of their neigh-bours. Some apparently react by conceiving another child to replace the lost one. Others may feel so rejected and condemned that their own parenting capacities are undermined still further.

The research evidence concurs that separating children from their biological parents introduces another risk factor into their lives. If placed in residential establishments, they lack the emotional benefits of normal family life. Placements with foster parents are likely to have more favourable outcomes, but these too are vulner-able to many break-downs and changes which, in turn, inflict more harm on the children. It is on the grounds of these studies that the preventative school argues that a policy of keeping children with their own families will prevent the trauma of separation and the dangers of residential care, will minimise the chances of multiple placements, and will eliminate the pain inflicted on natural parents by removals. Given the necessary support, parents seem the persons most likely to provide stable and satisfying experiences for their offspring.

The above findings must also cast some doubts on the recent calls for 'positive care'. Official documents, such as the *Review of Child Care Law*, and such prominent writers as Bill Jordan have argued that the creation of a more positive image of public care would make parents more willing to share their children with the local authorities in the kind of public care which would benefit all participants.[11] Such sentiments are to be applauded and everyone associated with child care will concur with the wish to raise standards of care. The doubts arise not over the desirability but over the feasibility of attaining positive care. At a minimum, such care requires a system which parents and children can use without any sense of stigma and which is stable in its continuity. Yet public care is deeply entrenched with feelings of condemnation and shame. As the Barclay Report made clear, 'Children and young people in foster-care or residential homes are at very serious risk of being seen by relatives, teachers and friends as "different" from other children', while children in care themselves observed that neighbours expected they would be worse behaved than children living with their own families and that the authorities were more likely to suspect them of vandalism and delinquency.[12] Perhaps such expectations will disappear. But in a society where living at home with natural parents is the norm stigma against those who do otherwise is very deeply entrenched. The wisest move should thus be to prevent children having to be exposed at all to the stigma of being in care.

Just as it will be a daunting if not impossible task to dispel the sense of shame about being in care, so will it be to provide a form of care which is stable. All studies of child care placements in foster homes or residential settings from the days of the children's departments to the present have come up with the finding that children in public care are likely to experience the trauma and insecurity of frequent changes. The recent research by Bullock and his colleagues stated, 'our study confirmed that stable care situations are difficult to provide: 39 per cent of the children still in care after two years experienced at least one placement breakdown . . . while only 46 per cent had the same social worker throughout this period'.[13] The child-care experts have failed to devise a system which ensures stability for children in their care. Lastly, even short-term care may have adverse effects. One SSD director observed: 'I am concerned about the part that short-term care might be playing in loosening parental bonds that may be fragile already . . . we may actually achieve the opposite of what we are setting out to do'.[14] The prospect for the future still seems to be that children entering public care will be liable to changes which both reinforce their handicaps and also fix them more firmly into a career within the child-care system.

To sum up, there seems no way to guarantee that care will be positive. Yes, let positive public care be an objective. Let it be seen as a resource which parents can call upon. If children do enter care, let every effort be made to reduce their isolation from their families. Let it be gratefully admitted that some children do need and do receive excellent substitute care. But the risks and uncertainties are such that the safest course is to promote measures which prevent children from having to undergo any form of public care at all. As Fuller and Stevenson conclude their review of the evidence,

> There can therefore be no substitute for greater sophistication in supportive work to prevent children coming into care. This is not to suggest that substitute care may not on occasion be inevitable and preferable. But it must be second best . . . given the uncertainties inherent in substitute care, policies to sustain and support natural parents may, in a variety of ways, be more socially and economically effective than those which seek to promote alternative forms of care.[15]

David Fanshel puts it succinctly when he says biological 'parents are by far the most likely source of permanency for children'.[16]

The family in society

The case for prevention rests not just on academic findings about what happens when children are taken into public care, but also depends on certain values held about the families from whom they were removed. It depends on the place which is awarded to the family unit in our society.

The family is conventionally regarded as a man and wife joined together by marriage and the children of their union. More recently the emphasis has been placed on the joining by a relationship of love as much as through the legal contract of a marriage. Further, it has been recognised that families do not always have two parents – indeed, one-parent families have become a feature of our time. Nonetheless the meaning of family is still that of parent(s) and dependent children, born to one or both partners, living together as one household. As such, this family unit is a major institution in society and one which is held in high esteem. Of course the family is not without its critics. In his well known Reith lectures of 1967 Edmund Leach attacked the stresses and insularity of family life and stated: 'Far from being the basis of the good society, the family with its narrow privacy and tawdry secrets is the source of all our discontents'.[17] Indeed, attempts have been made to abolish the family in the USSR and China in this century.

But the family has survived in those countries and shows no signs of vanishing in Britain. The feminist writer Lynne Segal observes that 'Those utopian dreamers of the 1960s with their intrepid search for new life-styles are much less vocal and visible today, while the scholarly writers from those times, like R. D. Laing, who once exposed conflict, tension and alienation in family life, have recently revised their views'.[18] Mary Farmer concluded her study of the family by stating: 'This supposedly moribund institution is proving extremely resilient and the consensus of opinion among sociologists of the last decade or so has been that, not only is the family alive, but that it is continuing to perform important functions strenuously and effectively'.[19] Michael Young and Peter Willmott have studied family life in the East End of London for over a quarter of a century and they reported that 'kinship remains an important force in most people's lives and is in particular still overwhelmingly the main source of informal care and support'.[20] This is not to say that family life is wholly successful, for rising divorce rates tell another story. But even these tend to be followed by remarriages and the formation of other family units. The family survives and, within our society, is seen as the proper means for caring for children.

The family, as Mary Farmer shows, is central because it 'carries out functions which are essential for the maintenance of society'.[21] It enables children to handle personal relationships and group dynamics in such a way as to meet their own and others' emotional needs. It undertakes the socialisation of children so that they acquire the rudimentary skills and knowledge to live later as adults. It teaches the acceptable ideas of right and wrong, so that they know the limits of tolerated behaviour. Not least, the family 'provides the individual with an identity in the wider society'.[22] By relating to their biological parents, children learn who they are and hence accept that they belong to a family and to a wider society.

The family carries out these functions for its children because the fact of birth appears to constitute a powerful and special bond which makes parents want to perform them both on the grounds of duty and love.

It can be concluded that the natural or biological family unit is an accepted part of our society, while the evidence suggests that children generally develop best within it. If children are taken from their families, they are being deprived of what is considered the normal and rightful lot of most children. The prevention school therefore argues that to stop children being split from their families saves them from losing a form of living which is highly regarded within our culture.

Occasionally it is asserted that the word prevention establishes 'a negative attitude of mind' and should be replaced by 'the more positive concept of promotion'.[23] This is strange reasoning. In other disciplines the prevention of illness or accidents is never regarded as negative. In Chapter 4 the word 'defensive' was used to distinguish a form of prevention which reacts to an impending family break-down from the 'positive' form which entails action to forestall crises arriving. But the word was not used in a condemnatory or belittling sense. On the contrary, to prevent an immediate admission into public care is as worthy of praise as the kind of prevention which allows families to profit from resources and environments in such a way that parents and children flourish without recourse to the SSDs. Both kinds of prevention should be valued, because they have the same objective, namely to enable children to remain with their own parents and siblings.

So a strong case can be made for preventing children having to be removed from their own families. But this account has described how the concept of prevention has widened to embrace preventing children experiencing abuse, poor parenting and social disadvantages within their own homes and communities. What is the justification for this stand? One reason is that children from these circumstances may be the very ones most likely to enter care at a later stage. The point has been underlined yet again in a recent study for the DHSS by St Claire and Osborne about the ability and behaviour of children in care. Like others before them, they explain that it is not sufficient to help children once they are in public care but rather that 'concrete policies directed at alleviating social disadvantages of families whose children are placed in care, would be the first and most probably the most effective step in helping them'.[24]

The case for preventing social disadvantage in the homes of children therefore can be made on the grounds that it is one way of averting eventual removals and problems in care. But some children who endure depriving circumstances do not face the threat of removal. The justification in these cases rests less on research findings, more on political, religious or philosophical arguments. It is the belief that all children are of such intrinsic value that they deserve as many of the good things of life as any other children, and that no children should face adverse treatment or experiences which are far removed from what happens to the majority of others in society. In short, the case for the broader kinds of prevention rest on notions of social justice. In turn, our ideas of justice spring from our own personal experiences and values and it is thus appropriate at this juncture to make clear those which I hold.

Personal experiences

As a child evacuee during the last war I endured some of the distress of family separations. Simultaneously I remained part of a close-knit, nuclear family whose members placed great emphasis on visiting and supporting each other. Thus, as a child, I learned to value the family unit while having faced a little of the hardship when it was not maintained.[25]

Probably this background contributed to my later desire to become a child-care officer. I joined a local-authority children's department in time to support the campaign for the preventative duty which was legally placed on local authorities in 1963. Subsequently I spent some years as the leader of one of the Church of England Children's Society's first community projects. These working experiences have taught or reinforced in me these lessons.

Firstly, *the family is the basic unit of our society*. I have witnessed families battling to survive under pressures of poverty, illness, mental break-downs and tensions of all kinds. I have known family members who have supported, loved and put up with each other when everything seemed stacked against them. I believe it is the biological bonds which tie members together and make the natural family unique and worth preserving.

Secondly, *children and families may relate closely to their neigh-*

bourhoods. The longer families stay in one community, so their children form ties of affection and identification with it whatever its apparent defects. I therefore believe that the case for prevention rests on children's right to stay not only in their family but also in their wider social environment.

Thirdly, *families rarely wish to be broken up.* Over the years I have known several families whose children have either been admitted to public care or who were at risk of so doing. In almost all cases such removals are against their wishes. Occasionally the behaviour of parent or child is so extreme that removal comes as a relief, but this is exceptional. If the wishes of parents and children to remain together are to count for anything, then society should award priority to its preventative services.

Fourthly, being in *public care produces complications and sufferings.* I have seen parents whose guilt and remorse at losing their children were so great that they found it difficult to express love for their children when contact was renewed. I have seen the agony of parents whose parental rights have been taken away. I have seen children who have blamed themselves for the break-up of their families. I believe in prevention because it can be the means of avoiding deep human grief and pain.

Fifthly, I discovered that some *admissions to public care and custody could have been avoided.* I think of two teenagers who lived next door but one to each other. Both were alienated from schools, both committed a whole string of criminal offences. One was as eruptive as a volcano, the other withdrawn and isolated. I worked closely with the former, let him use my home, got him to school and headed off further court appearances. He straightened himself out and settled down. I neglected the other boy, who drifted from community school to detention centre to prison. He is now back home, one of the long-term unemployed. The failure was partially mine. But I know that, given the time and resources, prevention could have worked with him as well. Writ large, this means that the social services probably fail many youngsters whose removal from home could have been averted. Thus from these experiences I have become convinced that it is highly desirable to allow youngsters to stay within their own families and neighbourhoods. I am spurred on by the conviction that more effective approaches to prevention could achieve this goal for many of those who at present are removed.

These experiences arise from and are interpreted through the beliefs or philosophies which guide my life. Of these, the foremost is Christianity. When Jesus Christ entered this world as a human, He chose to be born into a family unit. Later He upheld Jewish teachings about marriage but then extended truth by stressing the worth of children. He insisted that mothers be allowed to bring their young to Him with those loveliest of words, 'Let the children come to me and do not stop them because the Kingdom of heaven belongs to such as these'.[26] He never spoke of the care of children outside the context of the natural family and after healing sick children He always handed them back or 'restored' them to their parents no matter how poor they were. It is as a Christian therefore that I place a high value on the worth and happiness of children and it is as a Christian that I regard their rightful place to be with the parents to whom they were born.

I am also a socialist. It is a socialism which flows from Christianity, for, although I acknowledge that the two are by no means identical, I do regard socialism as the political system most likely to build a society which is in accord with Christian principles and which is most likely to facilitate the life-style of the early followers of Jesus. My socialism has been particularly influenced by the writings of the Christian socialist Richard Tawney. He saw fellowship as a crucial element. Indeed, his biographer, Ross Terrill, entitles his book *R. H. Tawney and his Times: Socialism as Fellowship*.[27] Fellowship concerns the quality of interaction between people. It implies feelings of mutual affection and mutual respect and is expressed in an acceptance of responsibility for each other and a readiness to share goods and possessions. Fellowship wants the best for each individual, for each individual is regarded as a valuable member of the whole. It follows that socialism should want all children to experience and enjoy family life because the family is the unit best able to provide love, security and preparation for adult life. In turn, socialism favours the kind of social services which enable parents to reach these objectives, and which prevent children having to leave their homes. In contemporary society the social deprivations which result from the maldistribution of resources often mean that some families are at a severe disadvantage when trying to provide their offspring with satisfactory upbringings. Socialists are committed to a more equal society, for greater equality would reduce social disadvantages and so create an environment which encourages the capacities and better elements in all parents. Thus the socialist concept of fellowship sets the objective of harmonious family and community life for children while progress towards a more equal society should reduce the numbers who miss out on it by virtue of their families' poverty and social deprivations.

Social action

I have outlined why I favour prevention and, indeed, why I possess such an enthusiastic commitment towards it. In visits to a large number of voluntary and statutory agencies I have met members who are equally enthusiastic. The resurgence of pressure groups and the recommendations of official reports during the 1980s is evidence of a growing demand for prevention both from within social-work bodies and from outside. The views of the advocates do not always spring from the same belief systems as mine but the common grounds are a conviction that all children have the right to homes and neighbourhoods which meet their emotional, physical and social needs and which include incomes and environments which do not put them at a great disadvantage when compared with most other children; that children's interests are usually best served within the context of their biological families; and that admission to public care should be avoided if at all possible, but, where it does occur, should entail care of the highest possible quality linked with efforts to rehabilitate them.

The next question is the fundamental one of whether it is the state's responsibility to provide preventative services. Ferdinand Mount believes in the value of the family unit but just as firmly criticises assistance given to it by statutory services. He says that 'education officers, children's officers . . . welfare workers' and all forms of state welfare actually threaten the family by removing its privacy and sense of self-responsibility. He even condemns the visits of a health visitor because she is 'intruding into private space'. His deduction is that if families lived in a pure free-market economy with state help cut to a bare minimum, then families would grow strong by having to learn to survive by their own efforts.[28]

Mount's views are best discounted by referring back to Victorian times, when unrestricted capitalism did hold sway. The result, as explained in the first chapter, was inequalities and deprivations on such a scale that some families were never equipped to survive by their own efforts, suffered enormous degradations, certainly had no privacy, were forced into lives of begging and stealing, and had their children removed as punishment for their failures. If further evidence is required, then recourse should be made to Professor Smout's recent *A Century of the Scottish People, 1830–1950*, which shows how in urban Scotland families were smashed, their health ruined and lives shortened by the free-enterprise system and that improvements had to wait upon the emergence of large-scale state intervention.[29] Even today the forces of unemployment and poverty, which are beyond the control of individuals, can imperil family relationships and shatter some homes. Significantly, as this study has demonstrated, it was the advent of collective welfare services which made prevention possible by equipping some families with the basic resources on which to build family life. Admittedly some forms of welfare can be counter-productive, can impose stigma, and can fail to help. The modern challenge is thus how to provide services which do not degrade people and, indeed, in which they regard themselves as participants and not just as recipients. Nonetheless, if the state values family life, the state has to accept responsibility for creating an environment which aims to preserve it for all families and not just for those lucky enough to be born into advantageous positions. The final question thus becomes, what are the strategies which will best promote prevention?

A Strategy for Prevention

Prevention in child care as a policy hardly existed before the Second World War. Since then much progress has been made. A local-authority duty to undertake prevention has been written into legislation, and social conditions have improved. New statutory agencies and traditional voluntary ones have developed their preventative practices. Yet the number of children still in public care or custody is a testimony that much more remains to be achieved.

The concept of prevention now extends beyond averting immediate receptions into the care of local authorities. It now also concerns preventing the social deprivations which make it difficult if not impossible for parents to provide the kind of stable family life and childhood development which is enjoyed by many other children. The implications for society are threefold. Firstly, the policies and programmes needed to tackle this kind of prevention would add substantially to the expenditure of the social services. Secondly, it implies a more equal kind of society. If successful prevention entails lessening the gaps between the advantaged and the disadvantaged, then the social differences between different groupings of families will be lessened. Moreover, as the cost of public services are largely raised through central and local government taxation, it is likely that the more affluent sections of society would find their own disposable income somewhat reduced. Thirdly, the acceptance of the wide definition of prevention implies a shift in prevailing values towards family life.

Of course it can be argued – rightly – that our society does place a high premium on the family unit. The same could have been said for Victorian Britain, where cosy novels and sugary songs extolled the virtues of strong fathers, devoted wives and obedient children. But the hymns of family praise were sung while thousands of families were split asunder by grinding poverty. The value placed on the family was not strong enough to move the nation to take measures to apply it to the submerged tenth. A modified but similar dualism exists today. Family life is valued and, indeed, many consumer goods are advertised and sold on the basis that families deserve the best. Yet the increasing affluence of those families able to enjoy these goods is allowed to occur in a decade when the number of families dependent upon social security has risen by hundreds of thousands. It follows from these three points that any major preventative programme would have to be accompanied by an increase in public expenditure on the social services, an acceptance of greater equality, and a shift in values on the side of the belief that the 'good' family life should be extended to all families, even to those at present considered to be at the bottom of the social scale.

The argument is not that no progress can be made without such fundamental changes. Helpful programmes and practices can achieve piecemeal gains. It is rather that the successful attainment of all the seven forms of prevention will require the widespread backing of society. The changing of societal attitudes and values is not the sole or major task of people engaged in welfare work. Greater opportunities and responsibilities fall to those employed in politics, the church and the media. But those who believe in prevention must accept some obligation both to publicise their case and also to work for the kind of society which makes prevention possible. If the task appears too daunting, then comfort can be drawn from the lesson of history. In Victorian times a shift did occur in public attitudes in that both the state and voluntary bodies were moved to accept that they should provide humane residential care for children living apart from their parents. During this present century the state has gradually extended its commitment towards the well-being of socially deprived families and, indeed, the welfare state was brought into existence. This book has recorded the progress made in developing preventative practices. Change is possible.

If the case for prevention has been made and if support can be won, how is it to be fully achieved? The Short Report complained that the DHSS had issued no guidance on prevention and that professional social-work bodies spoke only in general terms without furnishing constructive ideas. It continued: 'There is not really a clear understanding of where preventative efforts should be concentrated or how . . . there is as yet regrettably little indication of any concerted strategy which could translate pious thoughts into action'.[30] Since the Short Report, the government has published its *Review of Child Care Law*, whose proposals, if enacted, would both clarify the law regarding prevention and enlarge the duties of local authorities.[31] But the review deliberately avoided discussing the reduction of social deprivation as one way to promote prevention and said little about the role of voluntary bodies. Thus it can hardly be said to have presented a concerted strategy. In closing, this volume will attempt to outline an approach to embrace central government, local authorities and the child-care voluntary societies.

Primary prevention

Prevention is a duty laid upon local authorities. Yet it is decisions made by central government which play the major part in determining how resources are distributed throughout society – particularly through systems of taxation – and it is services run by central government departments which can do much to improve the quality of life for families. The post-war welfare reforms which abolished the last vestiges of the Poor Law, established national assistance and created the National Health Service were at the initiation of central government. Even the simultaneous housing drive by local authorities depended greatly on subsidies provided by the central exchequer. These centralist reforms were not undertaken with child-care prevention in mind but their outcome was to create a social environment which made it possible for more families to stay together. Whatever the intention, the effect was to bolster primary prevention.

Today social deprivations are still closely associated with children having to leave their parents and with them suffering severe disadvantages within their homes. There can be little doubt that government policies directed at reducing poverty, improving the health of lower-income groups, and the provision of adequate housing for all would do much to prevent children having to endure either of these outcomes. Of course social deprivations should be tackled simply because a humane society should not want any of its members to endure them. But the link with prevention becomes another reason for a government to choose policies directed at this end. Therefore the proposal put forward here is that central government should write its commitment towards prevention into social legislation. Statutes dealing with income maintenance, health and housing should be prefaced by a declaration that one of their objectives is to provide all families with the amenities which allow and encourage them to maintain their children in the manner considered customary in our society. Such an outright statement by central government would establish prevention as a leading social goal within our nation, a goal to be pursued by government itself as well as by local authorities and voluntary agencies.

Local authorities

The duty to 'promote the welfare of children by diminishing the need to receive children into or keep them in care . . . or to bring children before a juvenile court', as enacted in the Children and Young Persons Act 1963 and repeated in the act of 1980, is laid upon local authorities as a whole. It has two weaknesses. One is that it conveys a limited notion of prevention – it talks just of avoiding care and custody. It needs amending to extend the duty

to promote the welfare of children by preventing them from
suffering social disadvantages within their families and community. The Short Report commended the wording of the Social
Work (Scotland) Act 1968 which made it a duty 'to promote social
welfare by making available advice, guidance and assistance on
such a scale as may be appropriate for their area'.[32] The other
failing is that, although the duty should apply to the local authority
as a whole, in practice it is executed just through the SSD. This
concentration on just one department has weakened the impact of
local-authority preventative work. For a start other departments,
such as housing and education, which, as previous chapters have
shown, could play a significant role in prevention, have not
awarded it priority in their provision and planning. Indeed, departments which deal with recreation and leisure rarely consider
that their facilities have any connection with prevention. The
Short Report observed: 'It is still apparent that Social Services
Departments still feel that the other major local authority departments . . . are not pulling in the same direction as them . . . At
broad strategic policy level, there still seems to be little collaboration'.[33] Further, the practice of letting prevention be executed
just through SSDs has meant that local authorities have not
considered seriously how prevention could be co-ordinated throughout all their departments and across all their territory. Rarely, if
ever, does a local authority draw up a plan or policy for prevention
which applies to all their services. Prevention is left to the SSDs
and regarded as applicable only to people who have already been
marked as their clients.

A comprehensive strategy must therefore aim to persuade local
government that prevention is a duty to be exercised by local
authorities as a whole. Present legislation would allow for such an
approach but recent proposals have been made to ensure a more
strict adherence. The Children's Society has proposed that local
authorities be given a statutory duty 'to compile and publish at
regular intervals a detailed strategy in respect of the level and
methods of preventive work within their authority'.[34] The *Review
of Child Care Law* argued that the wording of the preventative
duty be widened to ensure that local authorities did not restrict
their obligations to a specific child but rather that they would have
to ensure that 'provisions be on a scale appropriate to the needs of
the area'.[35]

The advantages of a wholesale local-authority commitment to prevention, sharpened by the obligations just outlined, would be twofold. Firstly, departments other than the SSD would have a responsibility to run their services with prevention in mind. If housing departments accepted that prevention in child care was a prime consideration in the provision and allocation of housing, then many children might avoid the fate of the more than 1,000 at present in care because of homelessness, and countless others would be spared the sub-standard existence of bed and breakfast accommodation. Likewise, education departments could link nursery education provision more closely with the needs of families that are vulnerable to losing their children. Secondly, the whole range of a local-authority's expertise and resources, instead of one department's, could be applied to preventative work. Not only would this give a much higher profile to the place of prevention within local government, it would mean also that prevention would be seen as something applicable to whole areas and not just to individuals, to a variety of people and not just to clients, and thus any stigmatising connotations would be reduced. The causes of admission to public care and of unsatisfactory home lives are complex, and a single local-authority department cannot be expected to supply all the solutions. A comprehensive approach to prevention requires that local authorities as a whole accept the duty and that they enlist every relevant department in order to fulfil it.

Social services departments

Within a local-authority approach to prevention, SSDs will still be in a key position. Many families in difficulties will turn to social workers and it is they who play a major part in deciding whether or not children be received into public care. In tracing the development of prevention this volume has shown that the priority awarded to it by the personal social services has fluctuated over the last 40 years. In the days of the children's departments the attention awarded to prevention gathered pace as a number of child-care officers, children's officers and elected members of children's committees perceived its significance. By contrast it suffered something of an eclipse during the 1970s, when the new SSDs gave more prominence to a philosophy and practice which emphasised the rescue and removal of children from their natural parents. The obvious deduction is that if prevention is to flourish, then it must hold some priority in the aims and in the resource allocation of SSDs. One way of establishing such a priority would be to build responsibility for prevention into the senior-management structures of departments. The Family Rights Group has suggested that there 'should be one officer with a clear managerial responsibility' and it specifies that the officer would supervise the provision of alternatives to care and custody, act as a gatekeeper to ensure that no children were unnecessarily received into care, be responsible for the use of section one money, and would liaise with other local authority departments in order to co-ordinate preventative policies.[36] It could be added that the manager also be made responsible for the rehabilitation of children to their own parents.

No doubt the appointment at senior level of a manager with specific responsibilities for prevention would do much to ensure that it wins a position in the forefront of social-work thinking and practice. The analysis of prevention within this book then leads to the suggestions that practice could be strengthened in three directions. Firstly, the approach of SSDs – in conjunction with other departments – to prevention needs to be more promotional or proactive in encouraging adequate care and less reactive to inadequate care. Too often the nature of social-work interventions at a time of family crisis seems to reinforce feelings of inadequacy and mark out parents and children as failures and deviants. No doubt drastic interventions are necessary at times for the protection of some children. But the frequency of such reactive responses would be minimised if families previously had access to the kind of child-care resources which enabled them to cope.

This family-resource model, as it can be called, envisages a whole range of provision, including day care, family aides, home-helps and financial support. A key element would be that many of its resources, particularly day care, would be available in such quantity that the community looked upon them as a service to the public at large rather than as one reserved for special and stigmatised exceptions. With more limited services, such as family aides, section one money or even short-term care itself, the attempt should be made to convey them not as the last resort or as a threat that permanent removal is round the corner, but rather as a means of ensuring that families can maintain or regain the care of their children. The move to a family resource model or proactive approach might require changed attitudes within some departments. It would certainly require the assessment of local needs, the expansion of existing facilities, and therefore much increased expenditure. Some critics will retort that any expansion is impossible in times of economic stringency. While appreciating the immediate shortages of local authorities, which are facing cuts enforced by central government, the response must still be that resources are not lacking within our society. What is lacking, as I have argued elsewhere, is the political will to redistribute society's existing resources.[37]

In Chapter 4 this review identified the role of social workers as one of the key factors in prevention. Their part is crucial when families undergoing severe difficulties approach or are directed to the SSDs. At this point social work involvement can make or break prevention. It follows, secondly, that SSDs will require social workers who possess both a belief in prevention and the skills to execute it. Belief entails not just the acknowledgement that children's best interests are usually served by remaining with their own parents, not just a holding of the value that socially deprived parents have as much right to retain their offspring as more privileged parents. It also entails believing that prevention and rehabilitation are possible. Research summarised in *Social Work Decisions in Child Care* revealed that children often remained in care 'by default', i.e. because social workers had not made a decision to rehabilitate them. In other words they had not been sufficiently convinced that it could happen.[38]

Given that social workers are prepared to attempt prevention, then they require the skills for the job. Some already possess them and it is from their experiences that it is possible to say that the skills include the capacity to communicate with parents and children who are frightened and threatened without increasing their feelings of failure and condemnation, the ability to bring family members into the decision-making while recognising that sometimes social workers make decisions that will displease them, and the readiness to offer resources and social-work expertise in an acceptable way in order to enable families to stay together. Similarly, the rehabilitation of children can be a complex matter, with social workers having to deal with the families' feelings of guilt and loss, perhaps arranging for children to move back into family units whose membership has changed by the arrival of new children or even a new spouse, and often helping the parents to understand and cope with the children's behavioural reactions once they do return home.

An attempt to provide a comprehensive list of social-work skills is not being made. The point is that prevention and rehabilitation will require social workers of quality as well as belief. Yet even these two virtues will need to be allied with persistence and dedication. Studies indicate that, at times, social work with families may have to be extremely time-consuming.[39] So what can be done to ensure that SSDs have such resourceful and committed social workers?

The responsibility does not just rest with SSDs. The beliefs and practice levels of social workers are partly a reflection of the training courses they attend. The course contents and book lists of a number of courses show that until recently both qualifying and post-qualifying social-work courses have given far more attention to the removal of children and the finding of substitute homes than to the skills of prevention.[40] But there are signs that courses are strengthening their preventative input as a response to the revival of the case for prevention. SSDs do seem marked by a growing number of social workers who want to give priority to enabling families to cope with their own children. It then becomes the responsibility of their departments to provide them with the supervision, support and resources to do so. BASW's Special Interest Group in Prevention and Rehabilitation in Child Care has recommended that SSDs should issue a Code of Practice for Prevention, just as they issue codes for investigating child abuse and finding substitute homes. The code would inform social workers of the department's definition of and objectives for prevention; outline the range of skills expected of practitioners; detail the procedures to be followed when carrying out the various kinds of prevention; provide a list of and access to preventative resources both within and without the department; highlight certain key features to be implemented when admission into care is being considered, such as explaining to and giving families written notification of their rights and also showing them where outside help is available to support them in contesting decisions; and stress the social-worker's role, if children are brought into public care, of pursuing rehabilitation by facilitating frequent contact between parents and children and by involving them fully in decision-making and planning for the future. Such a code of preventative practice should ensure some uniformity of action within departments but not necessarily between departments. The Family Rights Group therefore has suggested that the DHSS should issue preventative procedures to be recommended to all SSDs in the same way that it has published procedures for child-abuse cases.

Thirdly, preventative social work within SSDs will be strengthened as it develops its neighbourhood settings. The siting of social workers in patch teams is not the solution to all social work's problems. It is not even applicable to localities characterised by sparse and widely spread populations. Nonetheless it does have a particular relevance for neighbourhoods of high social need. Studies have shown that the greater accessibility of and the increased local knowledge held by the social workers enables them both to head off impending crises and to act quickly when any crises do erupt. Patch-based teams also appear to benefit internally from high morale and increased job satisfaction.

A promotional approach, a substantial body of social workers skilled in and committed to prevention and the increased development of patch settings will be essential to all SSDs as they seek to be more effective in their prevention. SSDs will be the preventative pace-setters within local authorities and it is local government which will have a major influence on prevention in the future. Certainly central government must lay the foundations of primary prevention, while voluntary bodies can make an important contribution. But local authorities tend, through their field-workers, to be much closer to families than central officials, while their coverage and resources are far more extensive than those of voluntary organisations. The range, nature and success of prevention in the forthcoming years will depend much on how seriously local government accepts that it is one of their major tasks.

The voluntary child-care agencies

In discussing the part played by voluntary bodies this book has concentrated on the national child-care societies. Little mention has been made of the hundreds of other yet smaller agencies which also contribute to prevention. Almost nothing has been said of the independent, locally run day-care centres, welfare-rights projects, and community associations which operate on slender resources and amidst great difficulties. My own experience with and assessment of such organisations is that they are of the utmost significance. More than most bodies they tend to be set up by and run by residents of the inner-city and council estates. They have some overlap with the community projects maintained by the child-care societies in that they allow such residents to define their own needs and, within the limits of their resources, to seek their own solutions. Unlike the community projects they lack the outside funding of a major society but even here there is some interconnection as the community projects attempt to channel funds towards local and independent groups.

The review of the work of the national child-care societies has shown that prevention has become increasingly central to their operations. Indeed, they have progressed from the philosophy of their Victorian era, when they favoured the cutting of ties between children and destitute parents, to their present view of prevention as one of their leading objectives. Reference has been made to their development of Intermediate Treatment, their initiatives in respite care and their provision of accommodation for the young homeless. Turning more specifically towards their community projects, it has been shown that they engage in a large range of preventative work and that there are some indications that their work achieves a measure of success. In many regards the efforts of the voluntary bodies are similar to or overlap with those of statutory bodies. The voluntary contribution then becomes either to provide services where local authorities leave gaps – for instance, the provision of client-focused family centres where SSDs have failed to do so – or to pressurise the local authorities to extend their facilities. But, in addition, the comparison of the voluntary projects with local-authority ones led to the conclusion that in three ways the former have a particular contribution to render. In terms of strategy, the suggestion put forward here is that they should increasingly devote their resources to the kind of neighbourhood/community-development type centres which are the marked strength of the child-care societies in regard to prevention.

Most of the voluntary projects were rooted in local neighbourhoods. Their informality and friendliness encouraged residents to call in for no other reason than that they liked being there. The projects were not seen as places 'for baby bashers', but as places for teenagers, for mothers with young children, for people who wanted some advice, for kids who wanted a club. Their premises were regarded as being available to local groups and associations. Certainly they were not viewed as official settings dominated by professional experts. The helpers, the volunteers, the part-time workers at the projects were nearly all inhabitants of the surrounding streets. Increasingly such residents were also becoming the full-time staff. Needy neighbourhoods were thus able to supply their own internal agents of help because an outside body – the child-care agency – had injected funds and a limited number of workers into their midst.

These features of the projects enabled them to develop three outstanding characteristics: they were adept at utilising local resources, conveying help without stigma and promoting broadly based prevention. Their contribution was important because the local resources – be they neighbours, friends or project workers – became valuable means of support to families in times of trouble, because the lack of stigma meant that parents at the end of their tether or teenagers on the verge of removal were prepared to seek preventative help, and because the wide-ranging activities allowed preventative work to be operational at an early stage and through very ordinary channels. The work prospered because the projects lacked any statutory powers to investigate and control, carried no official threats about removing children and were not restricted by statutory caseloads. Of course some forms of prevention do require statutory backing. But some families need help outside the statutory sector; they are more amenable to the neighbourhood approach. Through their community projects, the child-care societies have formed a way of providing it.

In terms of preventative strategy it makes sense if the child-care societies concentrate much of their efforts in neighbourhood projects of this kind. Through them they have found a means of strengthening the functioning of some vulnerable families while simultaneously stimulating local residents to run activities which enhance the well-being of the community as a whole.

While writing these final pages, I received a visit from the foreman of the local glazing company. While away at a camp, our home was burgled and he now came round to replace the windows which had been forced. 'Terrible what kids will get up to, nowadays', he commented. We laughed. The laughter was because years before he too had nicked a large sum of money from our home. Indeed, he had committed a string of offences, made a number of court appearances and refused to attend school. He seemed destined for custody. He lived a few doors from our family and at this juncture became interested in the project where I worked. He related closely to the project staff, who found opportunities for him to gain local status by running the youth club café. The school agreed that he could undertake work experience with the project on condition that he spent the rest of the week at school. It worked and after various ups and downs he managed to steer clear of the court and eventually found a job. Various factors helped him, not least being his forming a steady relationship with a girl-friend. But today he claims that the influence of the project stopped him embarking on a life of crime. Whether this be so or not, he was helped by the voluntary, neighbourhood nature of the project. Strongly opposed to any form of authority, he was prepared to relate to the voluntary staff. Bored and aimless, he appreciated the closeness of a project, which offered time and company when he was at his lowest ebb. The chance meeting with this now confident and stable young married man serves as an illustration of the part that voluntary projects can play in prevention.

It may be recalled from Chapter 4 that a review of preventative studies led to the conclusion that if prevention was to be tackled seriously, then attention had to be directed at five key factors, namely that priority had to be given to making prevention a main objective of policy and practice, that poverty had to be combated, that social workers were in key positions, that services had to be localised and that users of services had to have their status enhanced rather than demeaned. The strategy outlined here incorporates these factors. Legislation is suggested to ensure that prevention is given a major focus within central government and within local authorities as a whole. The role of primary prevention in reducing poverty is underlined. The case is made for SSDs to employ social workers skilled in and committed to prevention. Both local authorities and voluntary bodies are recommended to concentrate on neighbourhood work, i.e. on the localisation of services. Not least, attention is drawn to the contribution of voluntary projects in emphasising the strengths rather than the deficiencies of users. Thus a concerted and comprehensive strategy for prevention run by central, local-authority and voluntary bodies is possible. If implemented, even this would not eliminate all admissions to care and custody, would not prevent all children from suffering abuse and neglect, and would not ensure that all received good parenting along with socially advantageous lives in their homes and communities. But speaking as one who has studied prevention from an academic viewpoint, worked for a local authority and run a project for a voluntary society, I am convinced that such a strategy would achieve a substantial reduction in the numbers of children admitted to public care and would prevent many more from missing out on harmonious and healthy family lives. What more can be asked of a strategy than that it should contribute to both defensive and positive prevention?

The Preventative Neighbourhood

The story of prevention in child care has been traced from Victorian times to the present. In so doing increasing reference has been made to the notions of community and neighbourhood. Community is usually regarded as locations of numbers of people held together by common interests, and neighbourhood as small geographical units whose boundaries are locally recognised. In this volume I have tended to use neighbourhood to comprise both a small physical entity and the system of relationships which exists between its residents. I now wish to end by arguing that neighbourhood can be the basis for promising preventative action.

Some writers believe that neighbourhood is dead and now is seen only in the unreal worlds of *Coronation Street* and the *East Enders*. Large-scale slum-clearance programmes, the decline of small shops and their replacement by distant supermarkets, the closure of local post offices, the creation of enormous local-authority units of administration, and the increasing centralisation of government have all made more difficult the maintenance of links of mutual dependence and interaction between people residing in the same areas. Unfortunately these trends have been taking place at the very time when the socially deprived are having to spend more time on their council estates or inner-city locations. The unemployed, many of the elderly, low-income parents with several children, and lone parents often cannot afford to travel far from where they live. What goes on in their neighbourhood is their life.

The personal social services have been slow to recognise the links between neighbourhood and family life. From the days of the children's departments onwards most departments – with some exceptions – tended to regard families as individual units to be treated by an individual caseworker. In recent years, however, the SSDs and the voluntary child-care agencies have perceived that neighbourhoods can both harm families – as when a family is ostracized or scapegoated by the residents of the street – and yet also be a vital means of support. Consequently the advent of patch teams, family centres and community projects has witnessed the effort to compensate for neighbourhood deficiencies and to utilise its strengths. This localisation of services has made them more accessible to users; the presence of their clubs and groups has reduced the isolation of some families; project workers have drawn out the abilities of relatives, friends and neighbours to run activities, to give encouragement in times of family upheaval and sometimes to provide temporary homes for children; and the unfolding life of the centres has also given rise to some collective action whose emphasis has been on improving facilities for the neighbourhood as a whole. In short, neighbourhoods have functioned in a preventative fashion for they have operated to provide better facilities for many families and, where necessary, have offered more specialised aid to families in danger of breaking up.

I am not claiming that the personal social services are the only agents which bring forth the preventative capacities of neighbourhoods. Obviously much mutual and informal help is conveyed without any contact with social agencies. I am not saying that all projects are successful in stimulating neighbourhood work. I am not pretending that even the successful projects bring forth masses of altruistic volunteers. But I am optimistic enough to argue that numbers of residents, even in the so-called deprived areas, can act in such a way as to earn the title 'a preventative neighbourhood'. My optimism is based partly on what I have seen and heard when staying in a variety of neighbourhoods. More personally it is also based on 10 years of working in and living alongside a council estate. The experience has taught me not only that neighbourhoods already do undertake many caring relationships, not only that further local resources can be galvanised into helping activities, but also that even those residents sometimes written off as deviant or delinquent have the capacity to change and to become neighbourhood strengths.

The SSDs and the child-care voluntary societies are already perceiving that neighbourhoods are or can be preventative agents. Their efforts require to be backed by other services. The use of local-authority sports and leisure complexes, youth clubs and swimming pools would be maximised if they were designed to be smaller and more numerous and placed more frequently in the midst of council estates and inner-ring areas rather than in the middle of city centres. State schools could be regarded as neighbourhood resources rather than as academic institutions to which teachers commuted from outlying suburbs each day. The use of health services would be improved if general practitioners chose to live in the neighbourhoods where they practised and if hospitals were, at least, made accessible by cheaper and more direct transport systems. Such a neighbourhood approach could do much to make life more bearable for sections of the community who are so often the victims rather than the beneficiaries of social and economic policy. The services would be contributing to a preventative neighbourhood.

Needless to say, neighbourhood action is not a panacea. Certainly it should not be used as an excuse for avoiding the large structural reforms needed in society. But the two are interwoven. On the one hand it is only as central action to abolish poverty and to reduce inequality proceeds that the residents of poorer neighbourhoods will be fully equipped to share in and to contribute to the well-being of their localities. On the other hand the same residents have a part to play in building the social and political momentum that will make such reforms a reality.

The preventative neighbourhood is as much a vision as a concept. It is based on the hope of a continuing move to eliminate social deprivations in our society. Against this background I envisage neighbourhoods composed of residents who take upon themselves the responsibilities and powers to promote a locality which cares for its own. I see them helped by statutory services which exist for the sake of residents rather than residents existing for the sake of organisations and professional workers. I see voluntary bodies offering their resources to local inhabitants to run community projects. But something else has to be said. What of the writer and readers of this book? Building a preventative neighbourhood is not just something to be written or read about. It is something to be practised. If we exhort the residents of the decayed inner cities and the isolated council estates to act preventatively, then let us join them to do likewise. If our incomes, wealth, talents, families and selves can contribute to the preventative neighbourhood, then let them be offered. The vision might then end in the reality of a society where far fewer children have to leave their homes and neighbourhoods, where few are subject to neglect and abuse, where all families are prevented from suffering gross social disadvantages, and where all parents are enabled to develop their parenting capacities to the fullest. These ends are worth the sacrifices we might make in pursuing them.

References

1. The Victorian Legacy

1. J. Heywood, *Children in Care*, Routledge & Kegan Paul, 1959.
2. W. Booth, *In Darkest England and the Way Out*, Salvation Army, 1890.
3. C. Booth, *Life and Labour of the People in London*, Macmillan, 1889.
4. A. Calman, *Life and Labours of John Ashworth*, Tubbs & Brook, 1875, p. 117.
5. P. Golding and S. Middleton, *Images of Welfare*, Blackwell & Robertson, 1982, p. 17.
6. J. Heywood, *Children in Care*, p. 90.
7. Cited in Mrs Barnardo and J. Marchant, *Memoirs of the Late Dr Barnardo*, Hodder and Stoughton, 1907, pp. 242–3.
8. Cited in W. Bradfield, *The Life of Thomas Bowman Stephenson*, Kelly, 1913, p. 78.
9. W. Bradfield, *Stephenson*, p. 206.
10. J. Stroud, *Thirteen Penny Stamps*, Hodder & Stoughton, 1971, p. 52.
11. Mrs Barnardo and J. Marchant, *Memoirs*, p. 381.
12. A. Pierson, *George Muller of Bristol*, Pickering and Inglis, 1899.
13. A. Calman, *Ashworth*, p. 102.
14. Cited in T. Ainsworth, *Sydney Black*, Book and Tract Depot, 1911, pp. 82, 98.
15. Cited in J. Heywood, *Children in Care*, p. 53.
16. Cited in Mrs Barnardo and J. Marchant, *Memoirs*, p. 148.
17. W. Bradfield, *Stephenson*, p. 85.
18. J. Heywood, *Children in Care*, p. 35.
19. Mrs Barnardo and J. Marchant, *Memoirs*, p. 183.
20. Cited in Mrs Barnardo and J. Marchant, *Memoirs*, p. 377.
21. Mrs Barnardo and J. Marchant, *Memoirs*, p. 158.
22. Cited in W. Bradfield, *Stephenson*, p. 239.
23. Cited in Mrs Barnardo and J. Marchant, *Memoirs*, pp. 192–4.
24. Cited in G. Kelly 'Natural parent contact – a theory in search of practice', in *Permanent Substitute Families: Security or Severance?*, Family Rights Group, 1984, p. 11.
25. J. Heywood, *Children in Care*, p. 82.
26. J. Hitchman, *Lord of the Barbareens*, Penguin, 1966.
27. D. Haynes, *Haste Ye Back*, Jarrolds, 1973.
28. Mrs Barnardo and J. Marchant, *Memoirs*, appendix 1, p. 381.

29. Cited in G. Kelly, 'Natural parent contact', p. 12.
30. A. Calman, *Ashworth*, p. 168.
31. Mrs Barnardo and J. Marchant, *Memoirs*, appendix G, p. 375.
32. *Waifs and Strays Magazine*, March, 1901.
33. N. Middleton, *When Family Failed*, Gollancz, 1971, p. 57.
34. J. Carpenter, *The Life and Work of Mary Carpenter*, Macmillan, 1881, p. 144–5.
35. Cited in T. Ainsworth, *Sydney Black*, p. 101.
36. Mrs Barnardo and J. Marchant, *Memoirs*, Chapter 10.
37. J. Heywood, *Children in Care*, p. 65.
38. J. Heywood, *Children in Care*, p. 107.
39. L. Stride, *Memoirs of a Street Urchin*, University of Bath Press, 1984, p. 13.
40. G. Lansbury, *My England*, Selwyn and Blount, 1934, p. 99.
41. N. Middleton, *When Family Failed*, p. 83.
42. *Report of the Care of Children Committee*, Cmnd 6922, HMSO, 1946, paras 135–56.
43. Cited in N. Middleton, *When Family Failed*, p. 113.
44. N. Middleton, *When Family Failed*, pp. 119–24.
45. C. Chaplin, *My Autobiography*, Bodley Head, 1964, Chapter 1.
46. L. Sinclair, *The Bridgeburn Days*, Gollancz, 1956, pp. 47–9.
47. Cited in N. Middleton, *When Family Failed*, p. 193.
48. N. Middleton, *When Family Failed*, p. 174.
49. H. Redwood, *God In The Slums*, Hodder and Stoughton, c.1929, p. 24.
50. P. Golding and S. Middleton, *Images of Welfare*, pp. 42–5.
51. N. Middleton, *When Family Failed*, p. 194.
52. P. Self, 'Voluntary organisations in Bethnal Green', in A. Bourdillon (ed.), *Voluntary Social Services*, Methuen, 1945.
53. C. Davey, *Home From Home*, Epworth Press, 1976, p. 14.
54. W. Lax, *Lax His Book*, Epworth Press, 1937.
55. R. Wrong, 'Some voluntary organisations for the welfare of children', in A. Bourdillon, *Voluntary Social Services*.
56. D. Haynes, *Haste Ye Back*.
57. J. Stroud, *Thirteen Penny Stamps*, p. 175.
58. G. Barbour, *Katherine Scott*, Blackwood, 1929, pp. 47–8.
59. R. Wrong, 'Some voluntary organisations'.
60. R. Wrong, 'Some voluntary organisations'.
61. Cited in J. Heywood, *Children in Care*, p. 132.
62. T. O'Neill, *A Place Called Hope*, Blackwell, 1981, p. 22.
63. V. MacLeod, *Whose Child?*, Study Commission on the Family, 1982, p. 17.
64. N. Middleton, *When Family Failed*, p. 309.

2. The Children's Departments and Prevention

1. Cited by P. Thane, *The Foundations of the Welfare State*, Longman, 1982, p. 223.
2. J. Beveridge, *Beveridge and His Plan*, Hodder & Stoughton, 1954, p. 106.
3. *Report on Social Insurance and Allied Services*, HMSO, Cmd 6404, 1942.
4. P. Thane, *Welfare State*, p. 253.
5. A. Marwick, *The Home Front*, Thames & Hudson, 1976, p. 75.
6. The Women's Group on Public Welfare, *Our Towns: A Close Up*, Oxford University Press, 1943.
7. D. Burlingham and A. Freud, *Young Children in War Time*, Allen & Unwin, 1942.
8. R. Parker, 'The gestation of reform: the Children Act 1948', in P. Bean and S. MacPherson (eds), *Approaches to Welfare*, Routledge & Kegan Paul, 1983.
9. M. Allen, *Memoirs of an Uneducated Lady*, Thames & Hudson, 1975.
10. *Report by Sir Walter Monckton, on the circumstances which led to the boarding out of Denis and Terence O'Neill at Bank Farm, Minsterley, and the steps taken to supervise their welfare*, Cmd 6636, HMSO, 1945, para. 52.
11. T. O'Neill, *A Place Called Hope*, Blackwells, 1981, p. 68.
12. *Report of the Committee on Homeless Children* (Clyde Report), Cmd 6911, HMSO, 1946, para. 45.
13. Clyde Report, para. 43.
14. *Report of the Care of Children Committee*, (Curtis Report), Cmd 6922, HMSO, 1946, para. 202.
15. Curtis Report, para. 3.
16. Curtis Report, para. 447.
17. Children Act 1948, Sections 39 and 41.
18. Children Act 1948, Section I (1).
19. Children Act 1948, Section 13 (1).
20. Children Act 1948, Sections 43–4.
21. D. Fraser, *The Evolution of the British Welfare State*, Macmillan, 1973, p. 217.
22. P. Thane, *Welfare State*, p. 261.
23. National Assistance Act 1948, Section I.
24. Children Act 1948, Section 12 (1).
25. Children Act 1948, Sections 29, 31, 33.
26. R. Parker, 'The gestation of reform', p. 212.
27. Curtis Report, para. 425.
28. Children Act 1948, Section 2.
29. Children Act 1948, Section 1 (3).
30. J. Beveridge, *Beveridge and His Plan*, p. 220.
31. J. Stroud, *The Shorn Lamb*, Longmans, 1960, pp. 8–9.

32. Home Office, *The Seventh Report on the Work of the Children's Departments, Nov. 1955, HMSO*, 1955, p. 1.
33. P. Boss, *Exploration into Child Care*, Routledge & Kegan Paul, 1971, p. 38.
34. P. Boss, *Exploration into Child Care*, p. 38.
35. Cited in J. Heywood, *Children in Care*, Routledge & Kegan Paul, 1959, pp. 165–6.
36. G. Trasler, *In Place of Parents*, Routledge & Kegan Paul, 1960, p. 2.
37. J. Heywood, *Children in Care*, Routledge & Kegan Paul, 1959, p. 65.
38. J. Bowlby, *Maternal Care and Mental Health*, World Health Organisation, 1952.
39. J. Bowlby, *Maternal Care*, p. 151.
40. J. Bowlby, *Maternal Care*, p. 151.
41. S. Watson, 'The Children's Department and the 1963 Act', in J. Stroud (ed.), *Services For Children and Their Families*, Pergamon Press, 1973, pp. 46–7.
42. D. Donnison, V. Chapman *et alia, Social Policy and Administration*, Allen & Unwin, 1965, pp. 102–3.
43. Conference reported in *Child Care*, vol. XVI, no. 1, January, 1962.
44. Home Office, *Seventh Report*, p. 23.
45. D. Donnison, *The Neglected Child and the Social Services*, Manchester University Press, 1954.
46. S. Hastings, 'Since the Curtis Report', *Child Care*, vol. 11, no. 4, October, 1957.
47. D. Watkins, letter published in *Child Care*, vol. 16, no. 2, April, 1962.
48. Joint Circular from the Home Office (no. 157/50), the Ministry of Health (no. 78/50) and the Ministry of Education (no. 225/50), 31 July 1950.
49. J. Packman, *The Child's Generation*, Blackwell & Robertson, 1975, p. 62.
50. J. Packman, *The Child's Generation*.
51. *Report on the Working Party on Social Workers in Local Authority Health and Welfare Services* (Younghusband Report), HMSO, 1959, Chapter 12.
52. D. Donnison, V. Chapman, *Social Policy*, p. 106.
53. See J. Packman, *The Child's Generation*, p. 112.
54. See H. Prins, 'Family influences and juvenile delinquency', *Child Care*, vol. xvi, no. 3, July, 1962.
55. Cited in J. Packman, *The Child's Generation*, p. 64.
56. *Child Care*, vol. 15, no. 1, January, 1961.
57. *Report of the Committee on Children and Young Persons* (Ingleby Report), Cmnd 1191, HMSO, 1960, recommendation 6.
58. P. Boss, *Exploration into Child Care*, p. 71.
59. *Ingleby Report*, para. 44.
60. *Ingleby Report*, para. 7
61. *Ingleby Report*, recommendation 1.

62. *Ingleby Report*, recommendations 7 and 8.
63. *Ingleby Report*, recommendation 59.
64. *Ingleby Report*, recommendation 4.
65. Children and Young Persons Act 1963, Section 1.
66. V. MacLeod, *Whose Child?*, Study Commission on the Family, 1982, p. 36.
67. S. Watson, in J. Stroud, (ed) *Services for Children and Their Families*, p. 47.
68. Children and Young Persons Act 1969, Section 1 (2).
69. Children and Young Persons Act 1969, Section 5 (2).
70. Children and Young Persons Act 1969, Sections 11–19.
71. J. Packman, *The Child's Generation*, p. 121.
72. See M. Berlins and G. Wansell, *Caught in the Act*, Pelican Books, 1974.
73. N. Timms *Casework in the Child Care Service*, Butterworths, 2nd edition, 1969, p. 3.
74. N. Timms, Casework, pp. 143–54.
75. A. Brown, *Groupwork*, Heinemann/Community Care, 1979, Chapter 1.
76. B. Davies, 'Groups in Social Work', *New Society*, 14 November 1968.
77. A. Leissner, K. Herdman and E. Davies, *Advice, Guidance and Assistance*, Longman, 1971, p. 1.
78. S. Watson, in J. Stroud, (ed), *Services for Children and Their Families*, pp. 50 and 57.
79. J. Packman, *The Child's Generation*, p. 123.
80. V. MacLeod, *Whose Child?*, p. 37.
81. J. Handler, *The Coercive Social Worker*, Markham, 1973, p. 83.
82. J. Heywood and B. Allen, *Financial Help in Social Work*, Manchester University Press, 1971.
83. S. Watson, in J. Stroud, (ed), *Services for Children and Their Families*, pp. 51–2.
84. S. Watson, in J. Stroud, (ed), *Services for Children and Their Families*, pp. 48–9.
85. Report in *Child Care*, vol. 1, March, 1947.
86. M. Curtis, 'Child care in the voluntary homes', *Child Care*, vol. 1, no. 1, March, 1947.
87. Home Office, *Seventh Report*, p. 15.
88. J. Stroud, *Thirteen Penny Stamps*, Hodder & Stoughton, 1971, p. 230.
89. Home Office, *Seventh Report*, p. 26.
90. *Child Care*, vol. II, no. 4, September, 1948.
91. Home Office, Seventh Report, p. 25.
92. *Child Care*, vol. 15, no. 1, 1961.
93. B. Bagwell, 'Some auxiliary schemes of Dr Barnardo's Homes', *Child Care*, vol. x, no. 3, July, 1956.
94. Report in *Child Care*, vol. xix, no. 2, April, 1965.

95. Report in *Child Care*, vol. 10, no. 2, April, 1956.
96. E. Younghusband, *Social Work in Britain 1950–1970*, Allen & Unwin, 1978, p. 258.
97. *Child Care*, vol. xvii, no. 3, July, 1963.
98. M. Cole, *Beatrice Webb*, Longmans Green, 1945, p. 109.
99. P. Boss, *Exploration into Child Care*, p. 42.
100. J. Packman, The Child's Generation, p. 58.
101. Ingleby Report, para. 10.

3. Problems for Prevention

1. For example, *Crime: a Challenge to us All*, Labour Party, 1964; Scottish Advisory Council on Child Care, *Prevention of Neglect in Children*, Cmnd 1966, HMSO, 1963; Scottish Home and Health Department and the Scottish Education Department, *Children and Young Persons in Scotland*, Cmnd 2306, HMSO, 1964; *The Child, the Family and the Young Offender*, Cmnd 2742, HMSO, 1965.
2. P. Hall, *Reforming the Welfare*, Heinemann, 1976, pp. 7–11.
3. *Report of the Committee on Local Authority and Allied Personal Social Services*, (Seebohm Report) Cmnd 3703, HMSO, 1968, para. 516.
4. *Seebohm Report*, para. 427.
5. *Seebohm Report*, para. 476.
6. *Seebohm Report*, para. 590.
7. *Seebohm Report*, para. 454.
8. *Seebohm Report*, para. 474.
9. P. Hall, *Reforming the Welfare*, pp. 84–5.
10. P. Hall, *Reforming the Welfare*, pp. 82 and 116.
11. DHSS figures cited by R. Hadley and M. McGrath, *Going Local*, Bedford Square Press, 1980, p. 6.
12. R. Parker (ed.), *Caring for Separated Children*, Macmillan, 1980, p. 5.
13. J. Tunstill, chairperson's report to BASW Special Interest Group, unpublished, October, 1984.
14. R. Parker, *Caring for Separated Children*, p. 29.
15. R. Parker, *Caring for Separated Children*, pp. 30–1.
16. R. Parker, *Caring for Separated Children*, p. 36.
17. National Institute for Social Work, *Social Workers: Their Role and Tasks* (Barclay Report), Bedford Square Press, 1982, para. 6.3.
18. R. Parker, *Caring for Separated Children*, p. 135.
19. P. Hall, *Reforming the Welfare*, p. 128.
20. Sir Keith Joseph, speech to the Pre-School Playgroups Association, 29 June 1972.
21. Sir Keith Joseph, speech.
22. Sir Keith Joseph, speech.
23. The former Labour politician Roy Jenkins put forward a similar thesis in R. Jenkins, *What Matters Now*, Fontana, 1972, pp. 47–57.

24. B. Jordan, *Poor Parents*, Routledge & Kegan Paul, 1974, p. 9.
25. R. Fuller and O. Stevenson, *Policies, Programmes and Disadvantage*, Heinemann, 1983, p. 9.
26. B. Jordan, *Poor Parents*, pp. 5–6.
27. A. Paterson, *The Inter-Generational Cycle of Deprivation*, University of Edinburgh Press, 1975, p. 3; and M. Brown and N. Madge, *Despite the Welfare State*, Heinemann, 1982, p. 143.
28. R. Holman, *Poverty: Explanations of Social Deprivation*, Martin Robertson, 1978, Chapters 2 and 3.
29. B. Jordan, *Poor Parents*, p. 48.
30. B. Jordan, *Poor Parents*, p. 48.
31. J. Packman, *Child Care: Needs and Numbers*, Allen & Unwin, 1969, p. 51.
32. See H. Eysenck, *The Inequality of Man*, Temple Smith, 1973, Chapter 5.
33. See B. Spinley, *The Deprived and the Privileged*, Routledge & Kegan Paul, 1953.
34. See A. Cohen, *Delinquent Boys: the Culture of the Gang*, Routledge & Kegan Paul, 1956.
35. D. Forrester, *Christianity and the Future of Welfare*, Epworth, 1985, p. 23.
36. First of all by B. Abel-Smith and P. Townsend, *The Poor and the Poorest*, Bell, 1965.
37. P. Townsend, *Poverty in the United Kingdom*, Penguin, 1979.
38. I have reviewed the poverty studies in R. Holman, *Poverty: Explanations of Social Deprivation*, Martin Robertson, 1978, Chapter 1.
39. P. Townsend, *Poverty in the UK*, p. 915.
40. R. Holman, *Poverty*, p. 22.
41. R. Holman, *Poverty*, p. 26.
42. See R. Berthoud, *The Disadvantages of Inequality*, Macdonald & Jane's, 1976.
43. R. Holman, *Poverty*, Chapter 5.
44. R. Tawney, *Equality*, Allen & Unwin, 1964.
45. DHSS, *Children in Care in England and Wales, March, 1978*, Cmnd 542, HMSO, 1978, Table A.6.
46. R. Thorpe, 'Mum and Mrs So and So', *Social Work Today*, vol. 4, no. 22, 7 February 1974.
47. R. Holman, *Trading in Children*, Routledge & Kegan Paul, 1973, Chapter 8.
48. DHSS, *Children in Care*, Table A.3.
49. J. Tunnard, 'Why Homelessness Still Means Children in Care', unpublished talk to Shelter Conference, 28 July 1984.
50. H. Wilson and G. Herbert, *Parents and Children in the Inner City*, Routledge & Kegan Paul, 1978; and H. Wilson, 'Parents Can Cut the Crime Rate', *New Society*, 4 December 1980.
51. R. Fuller and O. Stevenson, *Policies, Programmes and Disadvantage*, p. 51.
52. National Institute for Social Work, *Social Workers*, para. 7.21.

53. B. Jordan, *Poor Parents*, p. 132.
54. B. Jordan, *Poor Parents*, p. 181.
55. R. Holman, *Poverty*, pp. 276–92.
56. M. Brown and N. Madge, *Despite the Welfare State*, p. 332.
57. DHSS, *Report of the Committee of Inquiry into the Care and Supervision Provided in Relation to Maria Colwell*, HMSO, 1974.
58. For example, see the *Evening News*, 5 September 1974, and *Guardian*, 5 September 1974.
59. J. Howells, *Remember Maria*, Butterworths, 1974, pp. 11 and 63.
60. *Guardian*, 10 November 1973 and 12 June 1975.
61. J. Rowe and L. Lambert, *Children Who Wait*, Association of British Adoption and Fostering Agencies, 1973, Appendix B.
62. J. Goldstein, A. Freud and A. Solnit, *Beyond the Best Interests of the Child*, Free Press, 1973.
63. J. Goldstein *et alia*, *Before the Best Interests of the Child*, Free Press, 1979.
64. N. Parton, *The Politics of Child Abuse*, Macmillan, 1985.
65. N. Parton, *The Politics of Child Abuse*, pp. 74–7.
66. L. Fox, 'Two Value Positions in Recent Child Care Law and Practice', *British Journal of Social Work*, vol. 12, no. 3, 1982.
67. Private communication, Jane Rowe to author, 2 February 1986.
68. *Report of the Departmental Committee on the Adoption of Children*, Cmnd 5107, HMSO, 1972.
69. N. Parton, *The Politics of Child Abuse*, p. 116.
70. L. Fox, 'Two value positions'.
71. V. Macleod, *Whose Child?*, Study Commission on the Family, 1982, p. 59; and J. Tunstill, 'Laying the Poor Law to Rest', *Community Care*, no. 568, 20 June 1985.
72. N. Parton, *The Politics of Child Abuse*, p. 100.
73. DHSS, *Non-Accidental Injury to Children*, LA SSL (74) (13), 22 April 1974.
74. R. Fuller and O. Stevenson, *Politics, Programmes and Disadvantage*, p. 46.
75. N. Parton, *The Politics of Child Abuse*, p. 121.
76. Compare the *Report of the Care of Children Committee*, Cmnd 6922, HMSO, 1946, para. 29.
77. See M. Adcock and R. White, *Terminating Parental Contact*, ABAFA, 1980.
78. N. Parton, *The Politics of Child Abuse*, p. 174.
79. J. Goldstein, A. Freud and A. Solnit, *Beyond the Best Interests*, pp. 4–12, 24–6, 33–45.
80. N. Parton, *The Politics of Child Abuse*, p. 132.
81. R. Fuller and O. Stevenson, *Politics, Programmes and Disadvantage*, p. 65.
82. N. Parton, *The Politics of Child Abuse*, pp. 137, 145–6.
83. Cited in N. Parton, *The Politics of Child Abuse*, p. 120.
84. R. Fuller and O. Stevenson, *Politics, Programmes and Disadvantage*, p. 122.

85. V. MacCleod, *Whose Child?*, p. 57.
86. Cited in R. Fuller and O. Stevenson, *Politics, Programmes and Disadvantage*, pp. 119–20.
87. Reported in the *Guardian*, 23 January 1976.
88. 'A Comprehensive Service', *Child Care*, vol. xxii, no. 4, October, 1968; and 'The Social Seventies', *Child Care*, vol. xxiv, no. 3, July, 1971.
89. See R. Parker, *Caring for Separated Children*, Table 2.6, p. 22.
90. E. Younghusband, *Social Work in Britain, 1950–75*, Allen & Unwin, 1978, p. 258.
91. See J. Cooper, *Patterns of Family Placement*, National Children's Bureau, 1978, Table 6, p. 115.
92. J. Packman, *The Child's Generation*, Blackwell Robertson, 1975, p. 85.
93. Letter to the *Guardian*, 10 October 1979.
94. E. Younghusband, *Social Work*, p. 258.
95. DHSS, *Report of the Committee on One-Parent Families*, vol. 1, Cmnd 5629, HMSO, 1974, recommendation 197.
96. P. Chance, *Simply A Beginning*, Church of England Children's Society, 1976.
97. S. Massey and M. Peacy, *Social Work with the Families of Children away from Home*, Barnardo Social Work Papers, no. 17, 1983.
98. See J. Cunningham, 'Centres to Help Stress Families', *Guardian*, 30 July 1975.
99. *Gateway Magazine*, Summer, 1985.
100. R. Fuller and O. Stevenson, *Politics, Programmes and Disadvantage*, p. 47.
101. Church of England Children's Society, *Annual Report*, 1981.
102. For accounts of the Urban Programme and the Community Development Projects see J. Edwards and R. Batley, *The Politics of Positive Discrimination*, Tavistock Publications, 1978; and R. Fuller and O. Stevenson, *Politics, Programmes and Disadvantage*, p. 174.
103. I. Sparks, *Working with a Community. The Blackhill Project 1972–1977*, Barnardo Social Work Papers, no. 5, 1978, p. 18.
104. I. Sparks, *Working with a Community*, p. 34.
105. M. Brown and N. Madge, *Despite the Welfare State*, p. 3.
106. See the DHSS document cited by R. Parker, *Caring for Separated Children*, p. 44.
107. R. Parker, *Caring for Separated Children*, p. 45.
108. R. Parker, *Caring for Separated Children*, p. 55.
109. R. Parker, *Caring for Separated Children*, p. 45.
110. A. Leissner *et al.*, *Intermediate Treatment Project: An Action Research Report*, National Children's Bureau, 1977, p. 16.
111. J. Turner, 'The Social Services at IT in Norfolk', *New Society*, 2 October 1980.
112. See J. Packman, *Child's Generation*, pp. 127–8.
113. R. Parker, *Caring for Separated Children*, p. 45.
114. R. Thorpe, 'Mum and Mrs So and So'. See also R. Pinder and

M. Shaw, *Coloured Children in Long Term Care*, unpublished, 1974; and R. Holman *Trading in Children*, Routledge & Kegan Paul, 1973, Chapter 10.

115. J. Thoburn, *Captive Clients*, Routledge & Kegan Paul, 1980; D. Shapiro, 'Agency investment in foster care: a study', *Social Work* (USA), vol. 17, no. 4, 1972; D. Shapiro, 'Agency investment in foster care: a follow-up', *Social Work* (USA), vol. 18, no. 6, 1973; D. Fanshel, 'The exit of children from foster care', *Child Welfare*, 50, 1971; D. Fanshel, 'Parental visiting of children in foster care: key to discharge?', *Social Service Review*, vol. 49, no. 4, 1975.

116. *Social Trends 9*, HMSO, 1979, Table 3.7, p. 61.

117. R. Parker, *Caring for Separated Children*, p. 12.

118. *Social Trends 9*, Table 9, p. 205.

4. Prevention at Present

1. *Against Natural Justice*, One Parent Families, 1982.

2. *Permanent Substitute Families: Security or Severance?*, Family Rights Group, 1984, p. 27.

3. H. Geach, 'What safety in numbers?', *Guardian*, 7 December 1983.

4. A. Whitehouse, 'The anguish of the parent', *Community Care*, 6 February 1986; and J. Hodgkin, 'Parents Against Injustice', *New Society*, 16 May 1986.

5. See T. Flynn, 'A lot of dirt being swept under a lot of carpet', *Community Care*, 5 September 1985.

6. See C. Reeves, 'Foster care – a possible choice', paper given to a Family Rights Group conference on 14 May 1985.

7. See J. Laurence, 'Captive families: when families lose their children', *New Society*, 27 May 1982.

8. London Borough of Barnet, 'The Estimated Opportunity Costs of Preventive Social Work with Children and Families', 1981.

9. J. Tunstill, 'Laying the Poor Law to Rest', *Community Care*, 20 June 1985.

10. J. Tunstill, 'Laying the Poor Law to Rest'.

11. Chairperson's Report, annual meeting of the Special Interest Group in Prevention and Rehabilitation, 6 October 1984.

12. Chairperson's Report, Special Interest Group.

13. National Institute for Social Work (NISW), *Social Workers: Their Role and Tasks*, Bedford Square Press, 1982.

14. NISW, *Social Workers*, para. 23.

15. NISW, *Social Workers*, paras 13.25, 3.30.

16. NISW, *Social Workers*, Appendix A, pp. 227 and 232.

17. NISW, *Social Workers*, para. 3.40.

18. House of Commons, *Second Report from the Social Services Committee. Session 1983–84, Children in Care*, HMSO, 1984, para. 13.

19. House of Commons, *Children in Care*, para. 30.

20. House of Commons, *Children in Care*, para. 30.

21. House of Commons, *Children in Care*, para. 31.
22. House of Commons, *Children in Care*, para. 32.
23. House of Commons, *Children in Care*, paras 54–7.
24. House of Commons, *Children in Care*, paras 157 and 161.
25. House of Commons, *Children in Care*, paras 23 and 40.
26. House of Commons, *Children in Care*, para. 192.
27. House of Commons, *Children in Care*, para. 198.
28. DHSS, *Review of Child Care Law*, HMSO, 1985.
29. DHSS, *Review*, recommendation 2.
30. DHSS, *Review*, para. 2.1 and rec. 11.35.
31. DHSS, *Review*, para. 3–26.
32. DHSS, *Review*, para. 21.14 and para. 3.50.
33. DHSS, *Review*, paras. 15.27 and 3.35 and recs. 86–103.
34. DHSS, *Review*, recs. 58 and 177.
35. M. Hawker, 'Child Care Law Review. On the brink', *Community Care*, 2 January 1986.
36. See J. Levin, 'Family Courts – developments since Finer', in *Care Cases: Proposals for Legal Reform*, FRG, 1985.
37. Department of Employment figures cited in the *Daily Telegraph*, 6 December 1985.
38. Statement in House of Commons, 26 July 1986.
39. See *Municipal Review*, no. 653, vol. 55, 1985.
40. N. Murray, 'ADSS Survey', *Insight*, 22–9 March 1986.
41. Cited in the *Guardian*, 3 June 1983.
42. J. Packman, J. Randall and N. Jacques, *Into the Net? Child Care Admissions*, private publication, 1984, p. 23.
43. S. Balloch, C. Hume, B. Jones and P. Westland, *Caring For Unemployed People*, Bedford Square Press, 1985, p. 105.
44. J. Packman, J. Randall and N. Jacques, *Into the Net?*, pp. 4–5.
45. J. Tunstill, 'Laying the Poor Law to Rest'.
46. See M.Stone, *Ethnic Minority Children In Care*, University of Surrey, 1983.
47. House of Commons, *Children in Care*, para. 32.
48. NISW, *Social Workers*, Appendix B, p. 244.
49. NISW, *Social Workers*, pp. 261–2.
50. NISW, *Social Workers*, p. 237.
51. NISW, *Social Workers*, p. 259.
52. NISW, *Social Workers*, p. 254.
53. NISW, *Social Workers*, p. 255.
54. NISW, *Social Workers*, p. 256.
55. NISW, *Social Workers*, p. 237.
56. NISW, *Social Workers*, p. 241.
57. B. Jordan, 'Social work: back to the Poor Law', *New Society*, 6 May 1982.
58. D. Billis, *Welfare Bureaucracies*, Heinemann, 1984, pp. 66 and 78.
59. D. Billis, *Welfare Bureaucracies*, p. 70.
60. D. Billis, *Welfare Bureaucracies*, pp. 71–2.
61. D. Billis, *Welfare Bureaucracies*, p. 66.

62. R. Dingwall, J. Eekelaar and T. Murray, *The Protection of Children*, Blackwell, 1983.
63. N. Parton, *The Politics of Child Abuse*, Macmillan, 1985, p. 184.
64. S. Weir, 'What do people think about social workers?', *New Society*, 7 May 1981.
65. See J. Packman, J. Randall and N. Jacques, *Into the Net?*, p. 30.
66. NISW, *Social Workers*, pp. 11–13.
67. J. MacVeigh, *Gaskin*, Jonathan Cape, 1982.
68. *Pauline. Families of Courage*, ATD, Fourth World, 1984.
69. B. Jordan, 'Prevention is better than crisis – but it's expensive', *Guardian*, 26 August 1981.
70. C. Satyamurti, 'Clients aren't people', *New Society*, 25 June 1981.
71. R. Allen, *Can We De-Stigmatise Social Work?*, Social Work Today/ University of East Anglia, 1983, p. 16.
72. R. Pinker, *Social Theory and Social Policy*, Heinemann, 1971, p. 175.
73. A. Whitehouse, 'The anguish of the parent'.
74. DHSS, *Social Work Decisions in Child Care*, HMSO, 1985, p. 16.
75. D. Berridge, *Children's Homes*, Blackwell, 1985.
76. S. Loveday, *Reflections On Care*, The Children's Society, 1985, pp. 134–5.
77. *Home or Away. Residential Child Care Strategy for the Eighties*, Strathclyde Regional Council, 1984, p. 5.
78. J. Rowe, H. Cain, M. Hundlebay and A. Keane, *Long-Term Foster Care*, Batsford, 1984, Chapter 11 and p. 226.
79. S. Theze, 'Fostering: a responsible profession', *Community Care*, 31 January 1985.
80. R. Fuller and O. Stevenson, *Policies, Programmes and Disadvantage*, Heinemann, 1983, p. 126.
81. B. Jordan, 'Social work'.
82. B. Jordan, 'Why is prevention neglected?', paper given to the FRG, 18 November 1985.
83. See, for instance, R. Bullock, S. Millham, K. Hosie and M. Haak, 'Absent but not forgotten', *Community Care*, 24 April 1986.
84. J. Aldgate, 'Making Or Breaking Families', Barnett House, University of Oxford, 1984.
85. See S. Jenkins and E. Norman, *Beyond Placement: Mothers View Foster Care*, Columbia University Press, 1975; and M. Jones, R. Neuman and A. Shyne, *A Second Chance for Families*, Child Welfare League of America, 1976.
86. DHSS, *Child Abuse. Central Register Systems*, 1980.
87. *The Management of Child Abuse*, BASW, 1985.
88. J. Laurance, 'Captive families: when parents lose their children', *New Society*, 27 May 1982.
89. See E. Roberts and A. Sutton, 'An Experiment in Day Care 1973–1981', in *The Link Between Prevention and Care*, Family Rights Group, 1985, pp. 26–31.
90. J. Tunstill, 'Aiming to prevent misunderstanding', *Social Work Today*, 17 June 1985.

91. See G. Bowpit, *Secularisation and the Origins of Professional Social Work in Britain*, PhD thesis, University of Wales, 1985, pp. 242–52.
92. See *Our Neighbourhood*, National Council of Social Services, 1950.
93. D. Thomas, *The Making of Community Work*, Allen & Unwin, 1983.
94. For a discussion of community, see P. Willmott with D. Thomas, *Community in Social Policy*, Policy Studies Institute, 1984.
95. R. Hadley and M. McGrath, *Going Local*, NCVO, 1980, p. 3; and R. Hadley and S. Hatch, *Social Welfare and the Failure of the State*, Allen & Unwin, 1981, Chapter 2.
96. D. Challis and E. Ferlie, 'All change – but which way?', *Community Care*, 13 February 1986.
97. R. Hadley and M. McGrath, *When Social Services Are Local. The Normanton Experience*, Allen & Unwin, 1984.
98. K. Young, 'The East Sussex Approach', in S. Hatch (ed.), *Decentralisation and Care in the Community*, Policy Studies Institute, 1985, p. 7.
99. I. Sinclair and D. Thomas (eds), *Perspectives on Patch*, National Institute for Social Work, 1983; M. Bayley and A. Tennant, 'Straight across – service collaboration in Dinnington', in S. Hatch (ed.), *Decentralisation and Care*; and R. Hadley, P. Dale and P. Sills, *Decentralising Social Services*, Bedford Square Press, 1984.
100. See J. Speed, 'Co-operation and Integration', in I. Sinclair and D. Thomas, *Perspectives on Patch*, p. 25.
101. N. Murray, 'View from the ground', *Community Care*, 18 April 1985.
102. P. Willmott and D. Thomas, *Community in Social Policy*, p. 28.
103. R. Hadley and M. McGrath, *When Social Services Are Local*, p. 254.
104. Cited in *Community Care*, 18 April 1985.
105. B. Bennett, 'The sub-office: a team approach to local authority fieldwork practice', in M. Brake and R. Bailey (eds), *Radical Social Work and Practice*, Edward Arnold, 1980.
106. M. Cooper, 'Community Social Work', in B. Jordan and N. Parton (eds), *The Political Dimensions of Social Work*, Blackwell, 1983, p. 159.
107. D. Thomas and H. Shaftoe, 'Some Issues in Patch', in I. Sinclair and D. Thomas (eds), *Perspectives on Patch*, p. 33.
108. For a discussion of the Act, see N. Tutt and H. Giller, 'Doing justice to great expectations', *Community Care*, 17 January 1985.
109. D. West, *Delinquency: Its Roots, Careers and Prospects*, Heinemann, 1982, pp. 147 and 158.
110. For a summary of the relevant findings, see N. Tutt, 'Short, sharp but ineffective', *Observer*, 7 October 1984.
111. P. Cavadino, 'Government stays harsh over tougher sentencing', *Community Care*, 2 February 1985.
112. D. Thorpe, D. Green and D. Smith, *Out of Care: The Community Support of Juvenile Offenders*, Allen & Unwin, 1980.
113. N. Tutt and H. Giller, 'Doing justice to great expectations'.

114. See 'Juvenile Crime', NACRO, 1985, p. 15.
115. J. Crook, 'Northampton Juvenile Liaison Bureau One Year On', *Community Care*, 11 July 1985.
116. N. Tutt, 'Short, sharp but ineffective'.
117. J. Jillings, 'Academics on trial', *Community Care*, 11 July 1985.
118. J. Rowe, H. Cain, M. Hundleby and A. Keane, *Long-Term Foster Care*, Batsford, 1984, pp. 95, 99.
119. P. Marsh, D. Phillips, E. Sainsbury and M. Fisher, *In and Out of Care*, University of Sheffield, 1985, Chapter 5, p. 18.
120. J. Vernon, 'Preventing long-term care', *Concern*, no. 5, Autumn, 1985.
121. This research is in the process of being published. The figures are taken from a lecture by Spencer Millham, which I attended, and in R. Bullock, S. Millham, K. Hosie and M. Haak, 'Absent but not forgotten'.
122. P. Marsh, D. Phillips, E. Sainsbury and M. Fisher, *In and Out of Care*, Chapter 5, p. 16.
123. J. Vernon, 'Preventing long-term care'.
124. 'A Child Care Policy for Islington', Islington SSD, 1984, pp. 3, 8 and 18.
125. See J. Rogers, B. Thompson and A. Brennan, 'Helping parents solve their children's problems', *Community Care*, 30 January 1986.
126. J. Rowe, H. Cain, M. Hundleby and A. Keane, *Long-Term Foster Care*, p. 106.
127. G. Kelly, 'Family Contact: a study in Northern Ireland', *Adoption and Fostering*, vol. 9, no. 4, 1985.
128. DHSS, *Social Work Decisions in Child Care*, p. 28.
129. Reported in *Social Work Today*, 12 November 1984.
130. *A Child in Trust*, London Borough of Brent, 1985.
131. See J. Laurance, 'Learning the Lessons', *New Society*, 6 December 1985, and letters from directors to the *Guardian* and *The Times* on 6 December and 11 December 1985.
132. *New Society*, 6 May 1982.
133. *Children's Care in England and Wales, March 1983*, DHSS, 1984, Tables 1A and 1B; and *Social Services for Children in England and Wales 1982–84*, HMSO, 1985, Tables 3.1 and 3.2 pp. 20–21.
134. Avon CC, *Avon Report*, 13 May 1985.
135. This example of Bradford cited in Family Rights Group, 'Family and Child Care Policy (a suggested model)', draft, 1986, p. 24.
136. Family Rights Group, 'Family and Child Care Policy'.
137. Child Care Act 1980, 87 (1).
138. National Council of Voluntary Child Care Organisations, 'Child Care Policy', 1985, paras 3 and 6.
139. NISW, *Social Workers*, para. 5.31.
140. See J. Adamson and C. Warren, *Welcome to St. Gabriel's Family Centre*, Children's Society, 1983.
141. See Aberlour Child Care Trust, *'A Parent and Children's Centre in Langlees, Falkirk'*, undated.

142. J. Phelan, *Family Centres*, The Children's Society, 1983, pp. ix–x, and p. 41.
143. E. De'Ath, *Self Help and Family Centres*, National Children's Bureau, 1985.
144. E. De'Ath, *Self Help*, pp. 7–8.
145. N. McKechnie, 'Family Centres: Partnership with Parents and Children in the Community', forthcoming article.
146. P. Willmott and S. Mayne, *Families at the Centre*, Occasional Papers in Social Administration, no. 72, Bedford Square Press and NCVO, 1983.
147. 'Family Centres', National Children's Home, January, 1985.
148. J. Phelan, *Family Centres*, p. ix.
149. See DHSS, *Review*, para. 11.10.
150. DHSS, *Review*, rec. 116.
151. Personal communication from Mr R. Newby to the author, 3 October 1985.
152. See D. Billis, 'At Risk of Prevention', *Journal of Social Policy*, vol. 10, no. 3, 1981.
153. Family Rights Group, *A Community Care Policy for Children and Families*, draft, 1985.
154. L. Geismer, *Preventive Intervention in Social Work*, Scarecrow Press, 1969, pp. 14–15.
155. *Report on the Committee on Local Authority and Allied Personal Social Services*, Cmnd, 3703, HMSO, 1968, para. 454.
156. R. Parker (ed.), *Caring for Separated Children*, Macmillan, 1980, p. 59.
157. DHSS, *Social Work Decisions in Child Care*, p. 6.
158. *Report on the Committee on Local Authority and Allied Personal Social Services*, para. 2.
159. Cited in R. Fuller and O. Stevenson, *Policies Programmes and Disadvantage*, p. 55.
160. P. Sinanoglu, 'The Reunification Project', in J. Tunstill (ed.), *Working With Natural Parents*, University of Surrey, 1985, p. 40.

5. The Voluntary Projects

1. Letter from Ruth Hall to *Community Care*, 19 June 1986.

6. The Voluntary Contribution

1. See B. Holman, *Kids At The Door*, Blackwell, 1981, Chapter 9; and Gerard Avenue Project, *Half Yearly Report*, Children's Society, 1984.
2. J. Chant, 'The Local Authority Perspective', in *The Link Between Prevention and Care*, Family Rights Group, 1985, p. 23.
3. See G. Coffin and P. Dobson, 'Finding our hidden strengths', *Social*

Work Today, 12 November 1984; M. Simmons, 'Becoming part of the network', *Community Care*, 8 August 1985; and C. Stair, *A One Year Survey of Children Entering and Leaving Care in an Inner City Area*, Personal Social Services Fellowship, University of Bristol, 1985, p. 108.

4. J. Boucherat, *The Southdown Project Survey*, Children's Society, 1984.
5. B. Knight, 'I've got the shopping bag, you've got the brief case', *Community Care*, 3 September 1981.
6. A. Delbecq and S. Kaplan, *The Myth of the Indigenous Community Leader*, University of Wisconsin, 1968.
7. B. Holman, *Resourceful Friends*, Children's Society, 1983.
8. See R. Holman, *Poverty: Explanations of Social Deprivation*, Martin Robertson, 1978, pp. 228–38.
9. For an interesting example, see S. Scrutton, 'Control your children – or else', *Community Care*, 11 October 1984.
10. C. Cannan, 'Family Centres. Sanctuary or Stigma?', *Community Care*, 22 May 1986.
11. DHSS, *Social Work Decisions in Child Care*, HMSO, 1985, p. 8.
12. DHSS, *Social Work Decisions in Child Care*, p. 7.
13. P. Marsh, D. Phillips, E. Sainsbury and M. Fisher, *In and Out of Care*, University of Sheffield, 1985, Chapter 4, pp. 12, 16 and 20.
14. See National Institute for Social Work (NISW), *Social Workers. Their Role and Tasks*, Bedford Square Press, 1982, pp. 244–5; and G. Allan, 'Informal Networks of Care. Issues Raised By Barclay', *British Journal of Social Work*, 13, 1983.
15. F. Gardener, 'Power Failure', *Social Work Today*, 18 October 1983.
16. D. Heptinstall, 'There Must be Trust', *Community Care*, 18 April 1985.
17. R. Hadley and M. McGrath, *When Services Go Local*, Allen & Unwin, 1984, p. 201.
18. S. Croft and P. Beresford, 'Trying to find the right way through the bad patches', *Guardian*, 25 June 1986; and *Whose Welfare*, Lewis Cohen Urban Studies Centre, 1986.
19. A report by Strathclyde also noted this reaction to statutory centres. See Strathclyde Regional Council, *Members/Officers Group on the Under-Fives. Final Report*, 1985, paras 3–18.
20. M. Brenton, *The Voluntary Sector in British Social Services*, Longman, 1985, p. 93.
21. M. Brenton, *The Voluntary Sector*, p. 89.
22. Voluntary Organisations Personal Social Services Group, *The Future of Social Services*, 1986, p. 24.
23. C. Stair, *A One Year Survey*.
24. C. Stair, *A One Year Survey*, p. 49.
25. See, F. Gardener, 'Power Failure'.
26. See, P. Willmott and S. Mayne, *Families At The Centre*, Bedford Square Press, 1983, p. 143; A. Wolinski, *Osmondthorpe, The Area that Time Forgot*, Dr Barnardo's, 1984, pp. 33–6; and M. Brown and N. Madge, *Despite the Welfare State*, Heinemann, 1982, p. 331.

27. J. Packman, J. Randall and N. Jacques, *Into The Net? Child Care Admissions*, private publication, 1984, p. 4.
28. J. Packman, J. Randall and N. Jacques, *Into the Net?*, p. 11.
29. P. Marsh, D. Phillips, E. Sainsbury and M. Fisher, *In and Out of Care*, Chapter 4, p. 5.
30. The personality explanation is given by J. Charles, 'Assessing the Parents of Children Who Are Abused', *Social Work Today*, 24 February 1986; the stress explanation is put by N. Parton, *The Politics of Child Abuse*, Macmillan, 1985, pp. 133–9.
31. See B. Corby, 'After The Beckford Inquiry', *Community Care*, 16 January 1986; and J. Ives, 'How To Halt the Battering', *New Society*, 22 November 1985.
32. T. Goldberg and I. Sinclair, *Family Support Exercise*, National Institute for Social Work, 1986, p. 42.

7. The Pursuit of Prevention

1. See, M. Rutter, *Maternal Deprivation Reassessed*, Penguin, 1972, for an authoritative review of the literature which followed the pioneer studies of John Bowlby.
2. R. Fuller and O. Stevenson, *Policies, Programmes and Disadvantage*, Heinemann, 1985, pp. 114–15.
3. S. Loveday, *Reflections On Care*, Children's Society, 1985, pp. 125, 177, 181 and 186.
4. D. Bowen, *Education – Whose Care?*, M. Phil., University of Bristol, 1985.
5. Cited in *New Society*, 26 July 1985, p. 140.
6. R. Fuller and O. Stevenson, *Politics, Programmes and Disadvantage*, p. 117.
7. DHSS, *Social Work Decisions in Child Care*, HMSO, 1985, p. 10.
8. DHSS, *Social Work Decisions in Child Care*.
9. J. Packman, J. Randall and N. Jacques, *Into The Net?*, *Child Care Admissions*, private publication, 1984, p. 15.
10. A. Maluccio, 'Parents as Partners in Permanency Planning', in J. Tunstill (ed.), *Working with Natural Parents: Implications for Social Work Practice*, University of Surrey, 1985, p. 12.
11. DHSS, *Review of Child Care Law*, HMSO, 1985, para. 2.3; and B. Jordan, 'Prevention is better than crisis – but it's expensive', *Guardian*, 26 August 1981.
12. National Institute for Social Work, *Social Workers: Their Roles and Tasks*, Bedford Square Press, 1982, para. 4.14.
13. R. Bullock, S. Millham, K. Hosie and M. Haak, 'Absent but not forgotten', *Community Care*, 24 April 1984.
14. J. Chant, 'The Local Authority Perspective', in *The Links Between Prevention and Care*, Family Rights Group, 1985, p. 25.
15. R. Fuller and O. Stevenson, *Politics, Programmes and Disadvantage*, pp. 71 and 109.
16. Cited by A. Maluccio, 'Parents as Partners', p. 12.

17. Cited by M. Farmer, *The Family*, Longmans, 1970, p. 2.
18. L. Segal (ed.), *What Is To Be Done About The Family?*, Penguin, 1983.
19. M. Farmer, *The Family*, p. 1.
20. M. Young and P. Willmott, 'The Old East End', *New Society*, 18 April 1986.
21. M. Farmer, *The Family*, p. 14.
22. M. Farmer, *The Family*, p. 17.
23. See letters to *Community Care*, 19 June 1986.
24. L. St Claire and A. Osborne, *The Ability and Behaviour of Children Who Have Been in Care or Separated from Their Parents*, Dept. of Child Health, University of Bristol, 1985, p. 196.
25. B. Holman, 'Children of the Blitz', *Community Care*, 23 May 1985.
26. Matthew, Chapter 19, verse 14, Today's English Version.
27. R. Terrill, *R. H. Tawney and his Times: Socialism as Fellowship*, Andre Deutsch, 1974.
28. F. Mount, *The Subversive Family*, Counterpoint, 1983, pp. 173–4.
29. T. Smout, *A Century of the Scottish People, 1830–1950*, Collins, 1986.
30. House of Commons, *Second Report from the Social Services Committee, Session 1983–1984, Children in Care*, vol. 1, HMSO, 1984, paras 34 and 30.
31. DHSS, *Review of Child Care Law*, HMSO, 1985.
32. House of Commons, *Children in Care*, para. 40.
33. House of Commons, *Children in Care*, para. 27.
34. Children's Society, *Response to Review of Child Care Law*, 1986, para. 2.4.
35. DHSS, *Review*, para. 5.18.
36. Family Rights Group, *Family and Child Care Policy*, draft, 1986, p. 37.
37. See, R. Holman, *Poverty. Explanations of Social Deprivation*, Robertson, 1978.
38. DHSS, *Social Work Decisions in Child Care*, p. 10.
39. See P. Sinanoglu, 'The Reunification Project: New Haven, Connecticut', in J. Tunstill (ed.), *Working With Natural Parents. Implications For Social Work Practice*, University of Surrey, 1985.
40. The Special Interest Group in Prevention and Rehabilitation in Child Care has undertaken a survey of the child-care contents of training courses.

Index